W9-AZY-395

PARTITIONED LIVES

PARTITIONED LIVES

Migrants, Refugees, Citizens in
India and Pakistan,1947–1965

Haimanti Roy

OXFORD
UNIVERSITY PRESS

OXFORD
UNIVERSITY PRESS

Oxford University Press is a department of the University
of Oxford. It furthers the University's objective of excellence in research,
scholarship, and education by publishing worldwide. Oxford
is a registered trademark of Oxford University Press in the
UK and in certain other countries

Published in India by
Oxford University Press
YMCA Library Building, 1 Jai Singh Road, New Delhi 110 001, India

© Oxford University Press 2012

The moral rights of the author have been asserted

First published in 2012

This volume only contains maps of historical significance and does not
cover all the geographical locations. The international boundaries, coastlines,
denominations, and other information shown on any map in this work do not
imply judgement on the part of Oxford University Press concerning the legal
status of any territory or the endorsement or acceptance of such information. For
present boundaries and other details, please refer to maps authenticated by the
Survey of India.

ISBN 13: 978-0-19-808177-7
ISBN 10: 0-19-808177-4

Typeset in ITC Giovanni 9.5/13.2
by MAP Systems, Bengaluru 560 082, India
Printed in India at De Unique, New Delhi 110 018

CONTENTS

Figures and Tables

Figures

Tables

Acknowledgements

One of the many pleasures of writing a book is the opportunity to be able to thank those who have provided generous support through its many avatars. I am grateful to Barbara Ramusack, mentor and friend, whose meticulous reading, challenging questions, and unfaltering support have made my academic journey worthwhile. I am indebted to Maura O' Connor, whose unbridled enthusiasm for my different projects at the University of Cincinnati has been a constant source of inspiration. I am grateful to Ann Twinam, Kwan Man Bun, Willard Sunderland, and Laura Jenkins for their support during my years at the University of Cincinnati.

I owe many intellectual debts to individuals in multiple locations and different stages of the research and writing process. In India, Rajat K. Ray significantly shaped my intellectual trajectory early on. I owe special thanks to my teachers at Jawaharlal Nehru University, Neeladri Bhattacharya, Sabyasachi Bhattacharya, Indivar Kamtekar, Rajat Datta, and Susan Viswanathan for challenging my ideas about India and its histories, and for teaching me to evaluate and question different narratives. In Bangladesh, Shaukat Ali, Sonia Amin, Anisuzzaman, Ratanlal Chakrabarty, Meghna Guhathakurta, Ahmed Kamal, Ameena Mohsin, and Badruddin Umar opened their hearts and homes to me, provided me access to their collections, and shared their ideas and thoughts on Bangladesh, past and present.

At Massachusetts Institute of Technology (MIT), Harriet Ritvo, a colleague *par excellence*, offered unstinting support, read and offered critical advice on my manuscript and has been always ready to share her thoughts on anything ranging from the two-headed calf in Idaho to the fate of the Red Sox. Jeff Ravel, the purveyor of delicious home-cooked meals and timely words of encouragement, has been an extraordinary friend. Emma Teng offered advice at a critical stage of the writing process that has helped rethink certain paradigms within the global context. Patricia Flaherty proofread an earlier version of the manuscript and helped me improve the text. Beyond MIT, I have been lucky to have the support of Doug Haynes, whose extensive and thoughtful comments on the manuscript have enriched the final version. Karthika Sasikumar provided much needed fellowship, exotic food, and kept me appraised on some of the contemporary implications of my historical project. Special thanks to the anonymous reviewers for the book and the team at Oxford University Press, for turning the manuscript into a book and patiently guiding me through each step.

Institutional support for my project has come from various sources. A pre-dissertation research grant from the Bangladesh Program of the Social Science Research Council and another from the Cincinnati Chapter of the English Speaking Union supported my initial forays to the archives libraries in Britain, India, and Bangladesh. The University of Cincinnati has been especially generous in awarding me a Distinguished Dissertation Fellowship and a Charles Phelps Taft Memorial Graduate Fellowship, both of which allowed uninterrupted research and writing over two years in the archives and libraries located in London, New Delhi, Dhaka, and Calcutta (Kolkata for those who are historically challenged). The School of Humanities and Social Sciences at MIT provided another fellowship that enabled further time at the Delhi and Calcutta archives and the transition of my dissertation into this book.

Research support provided by the librarians at the Oriental and India Office Collections, London, the Nehru Memorial and Museum Library, National Archives of India, Central Secretariat Library in New Delhi, West Bengal State Archives, Government of West Bengal Police Archives, SB and IB Branches, National Library in Calcutta, Dhaka University Library, Bangla Academy and the Bangladesh National Archives, libraries at Harvard, MIT, University of Denver and University of Cincinnati, and the Center for Research Libraries are most appreciated. I am indebted to Md Hashanuzzaman Hydari (Bangladesh National Archives), Jaya Ravindran (National Archives of India), Saktidas Roy (ABP Group), Ananda Bhattacharya (West Bengal State Archives), Mikaila Corday (University of Cincinnati), Raymond Lum (Widener Library, Harvard), and Michelle Ballidon (MIT) all of who went beyond the call of duty to find me materials in their respective institutions.

Many have shared their ideas, unpublished works, and comments during the last decade. I have presented parts of this book at different academic fora such as the American Historical Association (AHA), Association for Asian Studies (AAS), South Asia Conference at Madison, Wisconsin, Royal Holloway, Wellesley College, University of Wyoming, Cornell University, and MIT. Many thanks to Itty Abraham, Sara Ansari, Gautam Bhadra, Joya Chatterji, Prachi Deshpande, Geraldine Forbes, the late Anjan Ghosh, Gautam Ghosh, David Gilmartin, the late Omar Khalidi, Barbara Metcalf, Ian Petrie, Uditi Sen, Wendy Singer, Ornit Shani, Ajantha Subramanian, Vazira Zamindar, for their critiques and suggestions which have enriched the book. I would also like to thank Mabel Chin and Margo Collett for their support in ensuring that my time at MIT went as smoothly as possible and to Bob Booth who graciously agreed to recreate the maps for the book.

Irfat (Bithe) Ara extended comradeship during the long hours at the Bangladesh National Archives. The Daula family and Anupam Ray were generous and gracious hosts during my stays in Dhaka and introduced me to different aspects of Bangladeshi politics and Indian diplomacy. In Delhi, Balakrishnan Nair provided a home away from home and regaled me with his versions of the Indian present and patiently listened to mine. In Calcutta, Sumona Roy provided me with much needed 'quiet time' away from the demands of family to put the finishing touches to the book.

Friends have been an important part of my life and this project by creating space for diversions, volatile and non-volatile discussions and camaraderie through the rigours of research, writing, and teaching. Varuni Bhatia and Sayata Ghose have been, in different ways, unflagging champions, and have always been there to listen, offer advice, and solidarity. I am thankful for the camaraderie provided by Anuradha Agarwal, Sandy Alexandre, Tuli Banerjee, Cristelle Baskins, Sharmadip Basu, Meriam Belli, Subhra Bhattacharjee, Nilanjana Bhattacharjya,

William Broadhead, Prasanta Chakravarty, David Ciarlo, Sabyasachi Dasgupta, Partho Datta, Sharatee Ghosh, Subrata Ghoshroy, Mahesh Gopalan, Iftekhar Iqbal, Indivar Kamtekar, Jodie Krieder, Nandini Manjrekar, Anne McCants, Aaron Moore, Madhubanti Mukherjee, Neeti Nair, Alita Nandi, Raisur Rahman, Pritam Roy, Wajid Hasan Shah, Sunil Sharma, Meeta Sinha, Priyanka Srivastava, Abha Sur, Aparna Vaidik, Saleema Waraich, and Bonnie Zare.

This book would not have been possible without the love and patience of my parents Haripada and Gouri Roy, and my sisters, Anindita and Priyadarshini. I have greatly benefited from my father's knowledge of the intricacies of the Indian bureaucracy. My family in the U.S., the Nairs, Anupama, Rajiv, Puja, and Vivek, have ensured I get all the love and comforts of home away from home. My parents-in-law, the late K.N. Syamasundaran Nair and P.A. Sarojini, encouraged me to keep on writing even if it meant less visits with them.

Karna arrived as I began the last stages of revisions. He has been a constant source of joy, amazement, and necessary diversions. He has patiently shared his mother with a monograph he will not read for another twenty years. Finally, I owe the most to Rahul Nair, who has uncomplainingly read many versions of the book, provided critical commentary, and most importantly, taken care of Karna while I wrote, even when he had his own manuscript to finish. He has managed to remain surprisingly calm in the face of adversity, even as he continues to challenge some of my paradigms about traditions, histories, and life in general.

Abbreviations

AICC	All India Congress Committee
AIML	All India Muslim League
BNA	Bangladesh National Archives
BPCC	Bengal Provincial Congress Committee
BPHM	Bengal Provincial Hindu Mahasabha
BPML	Bengal Provincial Muslim League
BSF	Border Security Force
CAI	Constituent Assembly of India
CAP	Constituent Assembly of Pakistan
CID	Criminal Investigation Department
CPI	Communist Party of India
DM	District Magistrate
DUL	Dhaka University Library
EBLA	East Bengal Legislative Assembly
FIR	First Information Report
FR	Fortnightly Report
GoEB	Government of East Bengal
GoEP	Government of East Pakistan
GoI	Government of India
GoWB	Government of West Bengal
HM	Hindu Mahasabha
HS	*Hindustan Standard*
IB	Intelligence Branch
ICS	Indian Civil Service
IG	Inspector General

INA	Indian National Army
INC	Indian National Congress
KPP	Krishak Praja Party
MEA	Ministry of External Affairs
ML	Muslim League
MLA	Member of Legislative Assembly
NAI	National Archives of India
NMML	Nehru Memorial Museum and Library
NWFP	North West Frontier Province
OIOC	Oriental and India Office Collections
RCPI	Revolutionary Communist Party of India
RCRC	Refugee Central Rehabilitation Council
SDO	Subdivision Officer
SP	Superintendent of Police
SPM Papers	Shyama Prasad Mukherjee Papers
UCRC	United Central Refugee Council
WBPSB	West Bengal Police, Special Branch
WBSA	West Bengal State Archive

Note on Terminology

East Bengal formally changed its name to East Pakistan in 1956. It became Bangladesh in 1971 severing all ties with West Pakistan. The official records and newspaper reports use both East Bengal and East Pakistan alternatively between 1947 and 1965. I have used each term as historically appropriate but they refer to the same region. I have tried to be specific when it comes to the policies of the Government of India and those of Government of West Bengal but also use the term 'Indian State' to encompass them together. Records at the Bangladesh archives, at times, do not indicate whether the policies of the East Pakistan government formulated at Dhaka were independent of inputs from the Government of Pakistan at Karachi. Unless indicated otherwise, I use Government of Pakistan to also mean the Government of East Pakistan.

I use the old English name 'Dacca' as they appear in contemporary documents; it refers to the city of Dhaka and the district of Dhaka as appropriate. I use Calcutta to depict the city of Kolkata which recently underwent a name change.

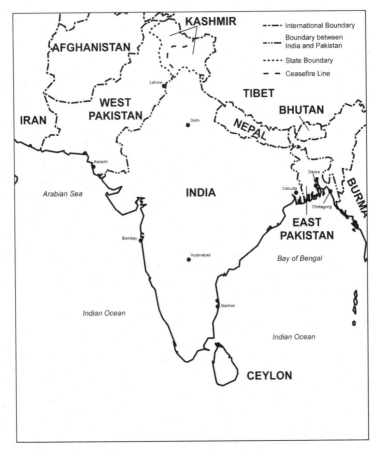

Figure 1: India Pakistan Overview 1947

Introduction
Partitioned Histories, Divided Identities

I n the summer of 1951, Laila Ahmed returned to Calcutta, the city of her birth. Before the Partition of India in 1947, she had married Lt Hyat Rizvi, a naval officer in the Royal Indian Navy, and like any dutiful wife had followed her husband to Karachi when he decided to opt for service in Pakistan.[1] However, domestic difficulties and marital discord forced her to return home and she filed for divorce in August 1951 at the Calcutta High Court. Laila's story should have ended with the dissolution of her marriage. Instead, it became entangled in the processes of establishing the new nations of India and Pakistan in the aftermath of the Partition. Her move from one country to another and her subsequent return raised questions about her rightful domicile, national identity, and citizenship.

In the absence of any rules and regulations that defined Indian citizenship legally, Laila's status within India was guided by the Succession Act of 1925[2] which dictated that the domicile of the wife followed that of her husband. Indian officials in Calcutta thus determined that Laila Ahmed had Pakistani domicile until the last date of her marriage and had, by virtue of living with her husband until that date, become a Pakistani citizen. However, they argued that with the dissolution of her marriage, she did not automatically regain her Indian citizenship. She had to re-acquire this nationality. The matter was further complicated by the fact that until the Indian Citizenship Act was passed in 1955, the official policy in India dictated: 'no one can acquire Indian nationality except by birth or marriage'.[3] Laila was thus in identity limbo, one of a growing number of people without nations who were unsure whether they were citizens of India or

Pakistan, because of the ambiguities associated with what determined such citizenship.

The processes of establishing new national orders in the aftermath of the Partition entailed that minorities—Hindus in Pakistan and Muslims in India—had to renegotiate their identities as rightful citizens. This book focuses on minorities such as Laila and examines issues of territoriality, identity, migration, citizenship, and the subsequent reordering of national identities in India and East Pakistan (present-day Bangladesh). The narrative begins in 1947 with the Partition, and ends with the second Indo-Pakistan war in 1965, by which time citizens of each country had to make their permanent domicile in one or the other country.

There were three partitions in 1947—of British India and of the provinces of Bengal and Punjab—that created the new nation-states of India and a spatially fragmented West and East Pakistan. It engendered the largest recorded population transfer in history amidst horrific mass violence. Between 1946 and 1965, nearly 9 million Hindus and Sikhs moved into India and approximately 5 million Muslims moved to both parts of Pakistan.[4] Partition as the twin facet of freedom remains an apocalyptic event within the South Asian popular imagination, reinforced by family and personal memories of violence, exile, movement, and resettlement.

Bengal's Partition, which is the focus of this book, entailed that approximately two-thirds of its area was carved out to create East Pakistan. It produced the longest international border between two countries in South Asia and millions of new citizens who were marked as majorities and minorities based on religious demography. Unlike the Punjab division, with its large-scale horrific violence and swift exchange of minority populations, the Bengal Partition witnessed protracted migration of Hindu and Muslim minorities engendered partly by routine small-scale violence and partly by the new states' attempts to decide the fate of their respective minority populations. It meant that it took almost two decades after the Partition of India and Pakistan to map and delineate their territories, determine who could and could not be their citizens, and implement laws which would constitute the national identities of their respective citizens. A focus on the *longue duree* of Partition's impact not only allows us to better realize the imperfect and unfinished nature of post-Partition initiatives by the new States of India and Pakistan, but also to put in historical context, the actions of ordinary men and women living during these extraordinary times.

Rather than framing 1947 as the 'break' between colonial and post-colonial histories of South Asia, or as the year that marked the 'moment of arrival',[5] this book joins new histories of the Partition,[6] which sees it as a process rather than a single event, thereby unsettling time and region-bound nationalized histories. Partition continued to influence and modify State policies and people's lives beyond 1947. Further, the book uses a cross border analysis to show that rather than dissociating from each other after 1947, both India and East Pakistan were intricately linked in their projects to establish respective post-Partition national orders.

Two specific understandings about their new citizens in divided Bengal informed most official policies of the Indian and East Pakistani states. First, they continued to operate within colonial understandings of community identity as primarily a function of religion. Thus, state policies ossified religious affiliation and viewed their citizenry as either a member of the majority and minority communities. Second, both states perceived of a specific paradigm of Partition violence, which viewed the large-scale and cataclysmic riots in Punjab of 1947–8 as standard, informed, and influenced policies with regard to both minority nationals and refugees. Since the small-scale and chronic nature of violence in post-Partition Bengal remained outside this paradigm, the Bengal Partition became, in the eyes of the post-colonial states, a site of illegitimate victimhood and unwarranted migration.

In post-Partition Bengal, the discourse over citizenship animated the project of 'nationalizing the nation'.[7] Who were the rightful citizens of the new nations and how could such claims be justified? Did minorities, the Hindus in East Pakistan and the Muslims in India, by crossing the international border become refugees and have automatic rights to demand citizenship? I argue that the new nation states or their minorities did not *assume* such identities and issues of citizenship. Rather, they were *produced* categories, debated within the hallowed halls of officialdom in Delhi, Calcutta, and Dacca, and given legal sanction through ordinances and laws debated and passed by parliamentary and state legislations.

Defining categories of identity such as evacuees, refugees, displaced persons, aliens, and infiltrators was a major element of the process of establishing post-Partition national orders and turning colonial subjects into national citizens. Further, these identities were produced discursively, mediated through the actions of officials located at the periphery of the nation, especially at the borders and diplomatic missions. Refugee documents, border slips, and passports became the means through which the Indian State sought to differentiate between refugees, migrants, aliens, and citizens. Legislations surrounding the rights to own and transfer property became intrinsic within the renegotiations of nationality in East Pakistan. Implicit within these redefinitions were the attempts of each state to establish a minority citizen's loyalty to the state. The determination of such loyalty was susceptible to contingent political, social, and economic contexts and was predicated on successful negotiations between minorities and the nation states.

While Indian and East Pakistani state policies contributed substantially in constituting new identities in divided Bengal, minority citizens were by no means passive bystanders to such top-down processes. Rather, as the book shows, minority citizens—Hindus in East Pakistan and Muslims in West Bengal—repeatedly contested official attempts to define national territory and identity through their persistent movement across the border, protests against requisition of houses, rallies to demand rehabilitation, and continuation of family ties across the border. Moreover, it was the everyday interactions between majority and minority communities, now predicated on new ideas of belonging and nationality, that produced a protracted state of uncertainty and fear amongst the latter, and continued to influence contingent decisions to move from one's home and to become evacuees or refugees in another country.

PARTITION AND ITS PRE-HISTORIES

The extensive scholarship on the Partition is problematic in several crucial aspects. The Partition serves as a template for the reinvention of national histories within India and Pakistan. In these national narratives, Partition is represented as the momentous culmination of an anti-colonial national struggle that acceded to the division for the sake of a larger Indian unity, or as a unilinear movement towards national self-representations of distinct communities. Paradoxically, while Partition persists as the defining moment for those engaged in reinterpreting cultural and national identities in contemporary South Asia, Partition historiography remains trapped within a teleological and chronological barrier of 1947. This axiomatic end date for historical enquiry has led to the creation of 'pre-histories' of the Partition[8]—to an obsessive focus on the high politics that preceded the event in an attempt to explain *why* it happened[9] and to assign 'responsibility'[10] either to the negotiations between the British and the major Indian political parties—the Indian National Congress and the Muslim League—or to the actions of leading political figures such as Lord Mountbatten, Jawaharlal Nehru, Mohammed Ali Jinnah, and Sardar Vallabhbhai Patel.[11] The contradictions inherent within anti-colonial nationalism, between nation, religion, and group identity, were sought to be resolved through the construction of Muslim separatism or 'communalism' as the evil doppelganger of 'secular' nationalism.

In the late 1980s, historical enquiry on the Partition shifted its focus from the national to the provincial arena.[12] However, the historiographical focus remained firmly directed at the level of provincial high politics. In the case of Bengal, such enquiry involved a reassessment of provincial identity politics in the 1940s vis-à-vis national politics. The political dissensions between the all-India platforms of the Congress and the League and their provincial counterparts are now well documented[13] as scholars focused on different points within Bengali politics that marked the decisive turn away from anti-colonial nationalism towards the path to separatism or communalism.[14]

One of the paradigmatic problems that has haunted the historiography of the Partition is this communal–national binary that seeks to explain communalism as the causal force that, at the expense of nationalism, marked the inevitable path towards Partition.[15] In the case of Bengal, one of the main proponents of the communalism–nationalism binary is Joya Chatterji, who explains the Bengal Partition as an event that Hindu communalism engendered. She argues that the public demands for a separate 'homeland for Bengali Hindus' on the eve of Partition reflected the end result of a decisive shift 'from nationalism to communalism' that had marked

Bengal politics and identity from the 1930s.[16] Chatterji attributes a
central role to elite Bengali Hindus in spearheading the campaign that
led to the fateful division of the province in 1947. Having identified
the main actors in the promotion of Hindu communalism, she then
makes the problematic leap to make the case for all Bengali Hindus
who, in her view, were not 'passive bystanders'.[17] Chatterji's larger
argument provides a convenient historical trajectory to this colonial
representation and seeks to explain the religious demographic
calculations behind the Partition as a process that reflected inherent
divisions within the Indian socio-political milieu. Partition, thus, was
inevitable not only because Indian leaders such as Nehru, Patel, and
Jinnah forced the British hand but also because of the intrinsic and
age-old communal fault lines. Such arguments not only tend to deflect
the role of British politics in India, but they also provide no space
for the examination of alternatives to the nationalism–communalism
binary.[18]

That provincial politics in Bengal saw an increasing presence of elite
Hindu and Muslim communalism cannot be denied. From the 1930s
onwards, Hindu organizations began to mobilize lower-caste groups,
such as the Namasudras in Bengal, within the larger Hindu fold.[19] The
subsequent shifts in class and community relations were critical in
garnering support for the Partition. Organizing the Muslim peasantry
in Bengal along communitarian lines also involved mobilization along
class divisions.[20] These factors do not necessarily indicate that public
discourse and political rhetoric in the 1930s and the 1940s assumed
a Hindu or Muslim identity at the expense of anti-colonial nationalist
agitation. Rather, nationalist leaders had strategically deployed both
Hindu and Muslim religious symbols in their efforts to incorporate
the masses since at least 1905. The anti-colonial nationalism of both
Bengali Hindus and Muslims had always been influenced and informed
by religion and religious symbols.[21] However, a critical distinction
needs to be made between the communitarian struggles of non-elite
social groups in which religion played an important organizational
role and the communal mobilizations within provincial politics
informed by colonial constructions of politically representative
religious groups.[22]

Religion as the raison d'être of the politics of Partition becomes
problematic when the focus shifts to the eastern part of Bengal. The

East Bengal/East Pakistan story is subsumed within a broader schema of Partition historiography that fails to appreciate that for some Muslim Bengalis, the Partition was a way to emerge from Hindu domination and experience cultural autonomy as a Muslim and a Bengali.[23] However, such explanations lead to yet another kind of pre-history that seeks to explain the emergence of Bangladesh in 1971 as a repudiation of arguments in favour of Muslim or Hindu communalism. Unfortunately, the narrative of Bangladeshi nationhood has not only erased the Partition of 1947 from public memory there, but also rewritten the history to locate the birth of the Muslim Bengali 'national self-consciousness' from the first Partition of Bengal in 1905.[24]

In recent years, academic scholarship has shifted away from the *pre-histories* of Partition to its immediate impact, from causality to 'lived experience',[25] in order to render a human and gendered narrative of the Partition and its aftermath.[26] Ethnographic studies focus on the period leading up to the Partition and its immediate repercussions on the experiences of the displaced and on the narratives of the horrific acts of rape, violence, and murder, both between and within communities in the Punjab. These studies have conclusively established the gendered nature of Partition violence as it targeted women as symbols of their community and family honour.[27] The most important contribution of these writings has been to draw attention to the disjuncture between national histories of the Partition and the personal narratives of 1947 and to reveal the multiple ways in which the latter contest and subvert the former. Communities and local traditions reconstituted themselves through the language of Partition violence that privileged a particular reconstruction of the past.[28] Collective and individual memories of violence are also mediated along caste, class, and gendered lines. Scholarly enquiry has thus shifted emphasis from the structural analysis of Partition violence to the analysis of modalities of memory and forgetting of such brutality.

The focus is now on Partition and its impact on subcontinental nations, cities, and their citizens.[29] Partition and its outcomes, as recent research shows, were products of hasty planning within high politics and contingent decisions of millions who attempted to make sense of their new status as citizens of new countries after 1947. Rather than neatly marking the end of colonialism and the beginning of nationhood in India and Pakistan, Partition, within this scholarly shift, appears as unfinished, messy, and protracted, continuing to influence the identities of those who were the most affected by the division.

However, like the earlier binaries of communalism versus nationalism, recent scholarship has tended to examine post-colonial nationhood through yet another binary: secular state versus non-secular, especially in the case of India. The focus has been on examining the Hindu majoritarian underpinnings of Indian secularism and the imperfect implementations of such ideals when it came to its citizens.[30] Zamindar's excellent study of the aftermath of Partition in Karachi and Delhi falls within this category in its examination of official policies designed to control migration after Partition. She captures the uncertain status of those caught on the *wrong* side of the border, as they negotiated the documentary terrain of permits, passports, and evacuee property that were instituted by both India and Pakistan to prevent migration and return of Muslims in Pakistan and India respectively. In the process, she questions both the proclaimed secular identity of the new Indian State as well as the assertions of the Pakistani state that it was the homeland of *all* Muslims.[31]

Zamindar's central thesis of 'governmentality' as primary in engendering national difference sits awkwardly when one shifts focus to the division in the east. In post-Partition Bengal, state legislations were kept to a minimum[32] but efforts to control the chronic and protracted migration produced parallel ideas about nationality. Here, too, as another recent book by Joya Chatterji highlights,[33] Muslim minorities in West Bengal were ghettoized and dispossessed as in Delhi, and minorities, both Hindus and Muslims, had to juggle multiple identities as they crossed the border or attempted to return home. However, even as they became a minority, Chatterji argues, in subsequent years, the Muslims in West Bengal became critical to the political balance within the province as no political party could afford to ignore this significant vote bank. Similarly, Hindu refugees from East Pakistan were active agents who demanded rehabilitation from the Indian State as a matter of human right and became significant in the emergence of Left politics in West Bengal.[34]

This book joins both Zamindar and Chatterji in their examination of the impact of the Partition on those living in the divided regions. However, it differs from such scholarship on two crucial aspects. First, although it examines official policies in India and East Pakistan that were significant in defining and imposing national identities on minorities, this book, additionally, shows that contingent actions and decisions of lower-level functionaries, minorities, and refugees were central to how such new configurations of citizenship and belonging came into being. Rather than being passive victims of state legislations, these ordinary citizens manipulated legal clauses to better able to manage their status, and negotiated, complained, and sometimes ignored official dictates. Their ultimate migration and/ or dispossession in the subsequent decades of the Partition were a result of the combined effects of state policies and individual and group action contingent on the continuation of routine violence in the region. In this respect, this book highlights the role of Partition itself, rather than of regional particularities, in reconstituting national identities for minorities.

Second, this book takes a cross-border perspective in its analysis of both official policies and individual actions. It shows that minorities, be it Hindus in East Pakistan or Muslims in West Bengal, faced similar sets of discriminatory circumstances and questions of national belonging. A cross-border analysis further allows to provide a counter to India and Pakistan's projects of nationalizing their respective citizens by showing that for most ordinary men and women, the border served utilitarian purposes rather than defining the limits of each nation. New citizenships were, for them, functional at best and they retained old ties of wealth, kinship, and local identity even after new nationalities had been imposed on them through the documentary regime of passports and visas.

The aftermath of the Partition in Bengal presents us with several ways to understand the larger impact of the Partition counter to what have become the two *normative* paradigms of the Partition experience in South Asia. First, Partition in these analyses remains regionally confined in their analyses of the Punjab division.[35] Second, they assume that for the most part, the large-scale violence engendered migrations and renegotiations of citizenship and belonging. Although violence was integral to how the Partition affected people's lives, it was not, as new studies have revealed, the only experience.[36]

The low-scale routine violence in divided Bengal fits awkwardly within this effort to represent and rewrite a specific subcontinental partition experience. This is not to suggest that the Partition of Bengal has not received any attention within academic scholarship, but such attention has been primarily focused on the rehabilitation of refugees from East Pakistan into India.

This book argues that such differences in relief and rehabilitation policies stem from the understanding of violence as cataclysmic and physical and the attempt to define refugees as victims of such violence. This understanding of Partition violence, which characterized the Punjab experience but not the small-scale chronic violence in Bengal, influenced refugee rehabilitation policies of the Indian State. The Indian State thus considered the migration of Bengali refugees to be unwarranted, and consequently viewed these individuals as illegitimate candidates for rehabilitation. It viewed these refugees primarily as economic migrants rather than as victims of violence or simply as persecuted Hindu minorities. Thus, the book suggests a different, more complicated understanding of the constitution of secular ideals in the early years of Independence.

The scholarship on refugee rehabilitation itself remains problematic, as researchers view refugees as an undifferentiated mass whose experiences of migration and resettlement are similar. While the socio-economic background of those crossing the borders were influential in their relocation, the timing of their migration, whether after 1947, or after the riots of 1950, or beyond, was critical to how they were viewed by the state and their subsequent rehabilitation. In actuality, the reconstitution of identities depended on a variety of factors, some of which were created in collusion with official policies of the new nation states.[37]

This book counters such normative understandings of the aftermath of the Partition, by examining the impact of open borders, laissez-faire state policies, routine violence, and continuous and protracted migration in the east. It argues that it was migration in the east that forced India and Pakistan to craft legislations such as the passport system that ascribed nationality to their minority citizens. However, the implementation of these legislations continued in a piecemeal fashion, and minorities in the region consistently faced questions of loyalty as they negotiated between their residential and national identity. However, they were often active agents in reshaping their new identities as they contingently moved back and forth across the border but kept open the channels of negotiation with the state for their rights as citizens, evacuees, and refugees. The aftermath of the Partition in Bengal thus offers a better template to understand the protracted processes engendered in 1947. Here, the border remained porous even after 1952, citizenship continued to be contested even after the Citizenship Act of 1955, refugees still continued to come after 1958 when the last refugee camp was shut down, and ownership of property was disputed between the state and who it termed as evacuees until 1965 when the such property became enemy property.

NEW STATES AND THEIR CITIZENS

Establishing 'national' states was the primary task at hand after the Partition for India and Pakistan. Both states deployed a range of symbolic, discursive, and actual methods that produced states as authoritative entities, which controlled the political and social life of each nation. In the Indian context, the 'practice of post-colonial nation-statism' involved visual representations, ritual practices of commemoration such as the Republic Day parades, discourses on science and technology, and urban planning designs as ways of constructing the new nation-state.[38] Although far apart, West and East Pakistan also embarked on the process of nationalizing their identity through the declaration of Urdu as the national language, creating a 'political economy of defence'[39] and weighing the economy in favour of the West at the expense of the east.[40] In East Pakistan the authorities focused on new legislations affecting people and property in the divided provinces, the appointment of new personnel to implement these policies, and the investment in, and construction of, new infrastructure to enable the control and dispersal of state policies at the periphery.

The legislations that directly impacted the partitioned regions aimed both at delineating the nations' boundaries and controlling access to its territories. More importantly, they were instrumental in categorizing citizens—those who belonged and those who did not. Both India and Pakistan instituted the permit system in 1948 and the passport and visa scheme in 1952 that allowed certain groups to refugees to enter and prevented others from returning back home.[41] In addition, evacuee property laws in both states promised guardianship of abandoned properties until the time their owners returned, and requisition laws targeted these very properties as means to rehabilitate refugees from the other side. Migration and property became *nationalized*: the act of moving from one state to another meant the relinquishing of one's property, indicating a sort of declaration of intent, a 'natural' inclination towards the other nation. Interestingly, the Permit system was not put in operation in the eastern sector with both governments preferring to keep that border open until the establishment of the Passports in 1952. Further, the Indian Evacuee Property Legislations did not encompass properties of refugees in the eastern zone. In spite of such differential policies, Hindus in East Pakistan and Muslims in West Bengal and Bihar were prone to be seen as trans-territorial citizens whose loyalty to their respective nations would always be suspect.

While the focus on official policy and different legislations provides a window into the creation of post-Partition nations, it is important to examine the operational aspects of these policies. How did these legislations, enacted in the capital cities of Delhi, Karachi, and Dhaka, translate and affect the people they aimed to categorize? Who were responsible for their implementation? The book focuses on the actions of intermediary officials who were entrusted with the implementation of these laws, which sought to create strong and centralized post-Partition states.[42] These low-level officials, often located at a distance from central and higher authorities, had substantial discretionary power in their districts and towns to interpret the law as they saw fit.[43]

Moreover, they were crucial in determining who could and could not belong to the nation. This is not to argue that these bureaucrats necessarily had little regard for the law and were autocratic in their actions. But in state–society relations, one must recognize the inherent flexibility of human actions. In the case of divided Bengal, the interactions of these low-level officials were often informed by economic and religious imperatives. Thus, even though official policies and legislations were avowedly non-discriminatory on paper, they often followed discriminatory paths when implemented by some of these officials.

State–society relationships are further complicated when one looks at one of the universal and characteristic features of the modern nation state: its citizenship, defined primarily through the group membership of its citizens within a definite territorial unit. Territory and membership are closely related—the modern state is simultaneously a territorial organization and a personal association.[44] Citizenship is not a mere reflex of residence; it is an enduring personal status that is not generated by passing or extended residence alone and does not lapse with temporary or prolonged absence.[45]

In the case of divided Bengal, citizenship followed a different path. Migration from one territorial unit to another, even if temporary, defined one's nationality; it signalled the intent of acquiring a new citizenship and simultaneously giving up the original identity. In the years between the Partition and the enactment of appropriate legislation laying down the regulations and definitions of citizenship in India and Pakistan, individuals who crossed the border had to constantly negotiate the ambiguities surrounding their migration, residence, and putative and 'natural' national identity.

The initial policy of the Government of India had been to allow citizenship rights to those migrants who officially declared their intention to become citizens of India and later acquired the necessary documentation. Getting one's name on the electoral rolls was one of the primary ways to ensure subsequent citizenship rights. Such a policy presented two contradictory dilemmas for Indian authorities. On the one hand, by allowing any migrant to acquire citizenship, it could limit its rehabilitation responsibilities towards the refugees. On the other hand, the government feared that such a policy might encourage Hindu minorities to opt for migration in such large numbers that would not only create an economic strain but also threaten the secular façade of the Indian State. In order to stem the continuing tide of migration, the Indian government fixed a time limit by which a refugee/migrant had to declare his/her intention to stay in India,[46] and in the early 1950s, declared that inclusion within the electoral rolls would not guarantee automatic citizenship rights.

No easy coincidence between citizenship, religious identity, and the territorial limits of the nation existed. The demand for a Muslim homeland that had pervaded the countdown to Partition, and its tangible success embedded within the establishment of Pakistan, meant that there was an implicit understanding that Muslims would 'naturally' identify with Pakistan, while non-Muslims—Hindus, Buddhists, Christians, and others—would automatically become part of India. Consequently, minority Hindus and Muslims who continued living in Pakistan and India after 1947 became what Willem

Van Schendel defines as 'proxy citizens'.[47] Minority Hindus in East Pakistan, though legally citizens of the Pakistan state, were categorized as putative citizens of the Indian State which endeavoured to ensure their rights and security through agreements and the establishment of institutions such as minority boards. Similarly, newspapers in East Pakistan consistently highlighted the plight of the Muslims in India. Such trans-territorial concerns were integral to the project of nation building even as they belied the limits of distinct nationhood and contradicted the project of secular identities.

For each newly independent state, the security of the minorities within India and East Pakistan became the acid test of legitimate nationhood. Minority migration became central to the game of numerical one-upmanship between India and Pakistan, as each accused the other of creating conditions that stimulated the protracted migration on the eastern border. Both countries evolved processes that sought to quantify the human movement across their mutual border. At one level, the direction and magnitude of the migration indicated the successes and failures of India and East Pakistan to establish their national order. In this game, India claimed a moral edge as the Census of 1951 recorded that more Hindus had migrated there from East Pakistan than did Muslim migrants leave India for East Pakistan. India blamed East Pakistan for not guaranteeing minority right and the latter countered by accusing India of creating 'pull factors' for the East Pakistan Hindus, which went counter to its proclaimed secular identity. Implicit within such accusations was the question of legitimacy predicated on each state's ability to guarantee equal citizenship rights to their respective minorities.

For the East Pakistani authorities, migration of its minorities reflected an intricate weave of loyalty and territory that defined citizenship not by birth but by domicile. Thus, any movement across the border was interpreted as inherently disloyal, destabilizing the new state and siphoning its minimal resources. The very real predicament of establishing the infrastructure for the new East Pakistani state was a potent factor within this equation. In 1948, the East Pakistan state legislated the Evacuee Property Act to assure its minorities that authorities would guard their property and hand it back to them if they returned from India. But by the time of Indo-Pakistan war of 1965, the East Pakistan government changed this legislation, pleading wartime exigencies that led to the Enemy Property Act of 1965. As the name suggests, this law usurped the very property that it had, in the earlier decade, claimed to protect. The historical trajectory of this metamorphosis highlights the critical connections between state processes and minority dislocation in post-Partition Bengal.

The chronic and prolonged nature of the migration from the east illustrates that even as minorities in West Bengal and East Pakistan developed into trans-territorial citizens in the eyes of each state, such identities remained negotiable at the individual level. Hindu and Muslim minorities identified with the state of their co-religionists only under extreme circumstances when they perceived that their territorial nation could not guarantee their citizenship rights in the face of threats from extra-state actors. Thus, for East Pakistani Hindus, migration was not always predicated on permanent uprooting but on the belief that they would be able to retain their kinship and social ties with their ancestral homes. They were also following the traditional pattern of urban–rural migration that took place in the region during colonial times. In the past, there had been the possibility of return. However, the requirements of post-Partition states to define their boundaries and identify their loyal citizens made it almost impossible for the continuance of such ties. Similarly, within the communally charged environment of India's relations with the princely states of Kashmir and Hyderabad in 1947–8, the issue of loyalty became controversial for the minority Muslims of West Bengal. As members of a community that had been closely connected with the demand for Pakistan, they easily became the usual suspects in regard to anti-state activities. The Bengal Partition, thus, generated a unique form of trans-territoriality where national citizenship was defined by domicile, but religious community defined proxy citizenship. This duality reinforced the marginality of minorities as loyal citizens of their territorial nation.

THE NATION'S BORDERLANDS

The establishment of international borders was the *sine qua non* of the Partition enterprise. The impossible task of determining a border in six weeks to accommodate religious demography was delegated to Cyril Radcliffe, a British civil servant with little knowledge of the Indian subcontinent. Radcliffe was the chairman of the five-member Boundary Commission which was hampered by unclear and contradictory terms of reference.[48] The conflicting claims of the leading political parties and a restricted schedule of six weeks made their task more difficult.

Although maps are essential tools of knowledge and control, defining not only topography but also the conceptual nation,[49] the new borders and their creation in 1947 have since been peripheral both within political discourses on nation building and, until recently, within scholarly accounts. Ironically, within post-1947 South Asia, accurate maps were largely non-existent because India, Pakistan, and Bangladesh restricted and continue to restrict public access to maps under claims of national security. Such cartographic anxieties, whose underlying fear is that of national disintegration, are clearly a legacy of the Partition. Despite such difficulties, recent studies have managed to elaborate on the uncertainty and confusion that were fundamental to the establishment of the line of division.[50] Expediency rather than accuracy guided British decolonization efforts in 1947. Thus, the accuracy of colonial maps and the basic realities of the ultimate border mattered less than the façade that the Boundary Commission had deliberated and resolved issues along democratic principles.[51] The process of creating the border encompassed both the desire for an honourable withdrawal on the part of the British and the first steps among Indian and Pakistani leaders to map the contours of their respective nations. The final determination thus reflected the political and personal imperatives of those who were intimately connected with its deliberation.[52]

Not surprisingly, the boundary awards, published two days after 15 August 1947, failed to meet most expectations and unsettled the regional societies of Punjab and Bengal. Recent scholarship has begun to trace the impact of the border on the lives of those living in and around the border, and have questioned the claims of 'closed' national boundaries by focusing on the movement of border dwellers which continuously tested the irrevocability of political boundaries. The porosity of borders, especially the one in divided Bengal, meant that there was a gap between the rhetoric of border maintenance, of its absoluteness and success in excluding and including certain groups, and the reality of life at the border. Scholars such as Schendel and Baud have urged for a focus on the borderland as a unit of analysis rather than only the border.[53] An examination of borderlands as a site of interaction and negotiation between people from both sides serves as an important corrective to the unchanging and linear representation of the border on maps. Further, the borderland defined itself as a vibrant site of economic activity even as the new nation states endeavoured to criminalize such activities. In divided Bengal, the border simultaneously evolved as a barrier to work and a site of new employment for state-appointed officials, militias, and armed forces who were called upon to guard the new national frontiers.[54]

Borders generally define both the origin and the territorial limits of imagined national communities. After Partition, identities at the periphery had to simultaneously negotiate the emergence of the South Asian region as a 'unified' entity[55] and the reflexive nationalisms that critically depended on each other for self-definition. In the case of the Bengal border, there was no clear correlation between territory and national identity. Identities were *produced* not so much by the physical location of the border but more due to India and Pakistan's attempt to control the movement of border crossers. This book focuses on the emergence of a document regime of passports, visas, migration certificates, and refugee slips which aimed to count and classify border crossers into different categories of belonging vis-à-vis the new nation states. Thus, border crossers now could be officially classified as temporary or permanent migrants, refugees, infiltrators, aliens, or as citizens depending on what kind of documentation they were able to obtain. Those who crossed without documentation faced the possibility of deportation but that happened rarely in the first few decades after the Partition. While the emergence of documentary identity at the border was similar to processes in Europe after the First World War[56] where such documents were central to the emergence of citizenship, different conditions in Bengal entailed that these documents held a more utilitarian value to the border crossers even as India and Pakistan hoped to equate some of these documents with citizenship.

In Bengal, there was no 'natural' succession of laws to control the border once the line had been drawn on the map. In contrast to the western boundary, Indian authorities in New Delhi and Calcutta did not view an 'open' Bengal border as a threat to India's security. The Bengal border thus evolved primarily as an economic frontier immediately after 1947, and remained legally open until 1952 when the continuous migration of East Bengali Hindu refugees who demanded the 'right' to rehabilitation from India led the Indian government to take action to close the border in the east. The need to control this 'unending trail' ensured that by the mid-1950s, the border assumed territorial sanctity in official discourse and action. This book argues that the processes of delineating the political and territorial jurisdiction of the nation state enabled the emergence of national identity as the principal axis of state control over mobility and citizenship.

SOURCES AND PARAMETERS

'Destroyed by white ants and water'—this was one of the many similar descriptive entries in one of the catalogues at the State Archives in West Bengal.[57] Although only sixty years old, documents relating to the post-Partition period in India and Bangladesh have remained inaccessible partly because some files continue to be restricted to the researchers, partly because records were dispersed to different archives and libraries after 1947, and partly because of the deteriorating conditions in these archives which ensure that termites become responsible for destroying both papers and histories of three nations. Researching for this book took me to numerous archives across four countries in Bangladesh, India, the United Kingdom and the United States. Archival sources in Bangladesh and India are fragmented, erratic, kept in dilapidated archival storage in different cities, and sometimes in different locations of the same city. Representing the fractured beginnings of India and Pakistan, these sources primarily comprise 'official' voices: files containing memos, legislations, official directives of various ministries in India, East Pakistan, and Britain which kept up a healthy interest in its erstwhile Indian empire; local police records which noted movements and activities of 'suspicious elements'; parliamentary debates recording differing opinions of legislators; and private papers of the principal political parties.

But read closely, one finds that these official files contain 'unofficial' voices, of ordinary people who sent in letters, memoranda, and petitions to their official and political representatives demanding amelioration of their particular grievances within the context of becoming new citizens. These hitherto ignored voices reflect and represent the *experience* of Partition as much as government records and high politics dictated its official trajectory. Although both official and unofficial records come with their attendant epistemological problems, I have attempted to read them 'against the grain', to highlight the contingent conditions under which ordinary citizens of India and East Pakistan lived and experienced post-Partition projects of the two nations. In conjunction with personal memoirs and oral narratives that were recorded in the 1960s, such sources provide us with the *mentalite* of the post-Partition period. Further, when read as a dialogue between ordinary citizens and state policies, such sources provide insights into the nature and limits of state–society relations in post-colonial South Asia.

Newspaper reports and police records have been invaluable sources in piecing together the arc of India and Pakistan's official policies and public statements on various issues relating to border disputes, acts of violence, riots, and refugee relief. Further, newspapers also published letters from concerned individuals who used them as a public forum to raise awareness and share opinion on specific issues. Although such sources come with their own set of issues regarding veracity and were sometimes clearly embellished accounts, I have used them not for factual data but as records indicating the multiple possibilities and contingencies that existed within the contemporary public sphere. Given the constraints of the recorded sources, this book draws on the border between West Bengal and East Pakistan as representative of border experiences between 1947 and 1965.[58]

Further, it examines post-Partition legislations that did not always have a parallel correspondence in both India and East Pakistan. For example, the Evacuee Property Act was in operation in East Pakistan but India's Evacuee Property Act did not include areas in Bengal and Assam, primarily because the official expectation at the time of Partition was that there would be very little migration and hence no need for rehabilitation on the eastern side.

Because Partition elicited a divided Pakistan, for the sake of this study, I have used 'East Pakistan' to denote the geographical entity and used Pakistan and the Government of East Pakistan interchangeably to denote its official stature. I have used the term 'East Bengal' to correctly denote the same region up until 1956 when it officially became 'East Pakistan'. The Pakistan central government was located and concerned primarily with legislations and politics in West Pakistan and for most purposes, East Pakistan dealt with its inter dominion relations with India on its own. However, this is not to say that it had much say or influence on how national Pakistani policy was framed.

The book is divided into three thematic sections, each containing two chapters. The first section focuses on the theme of territories—both the delineation of a national border in Bengal and the diverse ways in which India and Pakistan sought to control movement across this border. On 3 June 1947, political leaders in India and Britain informed their citizens that India would gain independence by 1948 and would also be partitioned into two nations, namely, India and Pakistan. Within days of this momentous announcement, the date of independence was brought forward to 14–15 August 1947. The blueprint for decolonization and independence required the setting up of a Boundary Commission to establish a new national border. Chapter 1 examines in detail the deliberations of both the officially constituted Boundary Commission and the public debates surrounding its inception. It contends that even though the logic of the Partition demand was predicated on religious demography, the public and political demands for territory had little to do with communal concerns. The new border drawn at independence failed miserably both at separating Hindus from Muslims and as a distinct marker of national jurisdiction.

Although it was clearly defined on paper by August 1947, the border dividing Bengal took shape over the next two decades. Confusion about its location and its power to demarcate national sovereignty meant border conflicts over territory, livestock, and people; smuggled goods became a common feature of border life almost immediately. Simultaneously, India and Pakistan attempted to control refugee movements by requiring new documents such as passports, visas, and refugee slips as measures to classify and tabulate those who crossed the border. Chapter 2 explores the emergence and constitution of this *document regime* characterized by new forms of marking identity. Pieces of paper were the means of controlling and categorizing persons who legally wanted to cross the new international border. It was thus at the periphery that these nation states began to exercise their newly won sovereign powers, as they sought to decide who could and could not enter their territorial boundaries.

The second section examines the processes of nation building in the aftermath of the Partition which engendered and crafted new forms of citizenship, new ways of belonging to the new nations. The post-Partition period raised critical questions about national belonging: who was an Indian and who was a Pakistani?; and on what basis were these questions to be resolved? Chapter 3 focuses on the Evacuee Property Act of 1951, promulgated in East Pakistan. It examines how the Act framed and complicated the ideas of citizenship amongst those who were primarily affected by its rulings, namely, the minority Hindus. The Act allowed the Pakistan state to requisition the property of those whom it viewed as potential evacuees to India. Further, by placing restrictions on items such as gold, foreign exchange, and even livestock, the Act redefined the very notion of property, and linked the rights of citizenship with property ownership and nationality.

The act of migration, even if temporary, served to define one's nationality. It came to be seen as an indication of one's intent to acquire a new citizenship and to relinquish one's original identity. In this process, the same person could be designated an *evacuee* in one country and a *refugee* in another. Neither term guaranteed citizenship rights. Chapter 4 examines the Citizenship of India Bill, and the official and public debates surrounding it, in order to trace the development of the idea of legal citizenship in India. It argues that continued migration from the east (rather than the west) forced the architects of the Act to confront the modalities of defining a 'citizen' and to formulate rules that would directly impact the refugees from East Pakistan and aid in their transformation to Indians.

The third section addresses the theme of identities, specifically those of minorities and refugees. Minorities in each nation faced questions about their supranational identities and had to justify their decision to remain in their ancestral localities. Religious identity collided with national identity, as minorities in India and Pakistan became trans-territorial citizens who resided in one nation but were alleged to profess loyalty to the other nation, the home of their religious brethren. Essentially, this was manifested through routine, small-scale violence that specifically targeted minorities in each country. Chapter 5 calls for a redefinition of the current paradigmatic view of Partition-generated violence as being large scale and primarily physical. Rather, in the case of divided Bengal, Partition violence was daily, small-scale, and often transmuted through psychological threats, both verbal and written. The routine of violence continued for two decades after 1947 and engendered migration across borders both to and from India.

Partition created another category of people: refugees or the displaced. In the case of Bengal, as Chapter 6 shows, the Indian State operated on the belief that migration from East Pakistan was unwarranted and temporary. Rehabilitation policies thus were ad hoc, limited, and had the expectation that refugees would be able to self-rehabilitate, albeit with the help of Indian State. In the light of policy failure, it was easy for the emergence of a paradoxical entity: the Bengali refugee, who was lazy yet pioneering, shorn of agency yet subversive, and who clung on to his 'refugee' identity yet demanded the rights of citizenship.

The following chapters hope to present an analysis of how India and East Pakistan engaged with their post-Partition predicaments that had to square the needs of building distinctive nations and nationalities with the realities of lack of resources, imperfect and erratic legislations, and continuous movement of people and goods which tested the limits of each nation. Categorization of their people into citizens and foreigners was a necessary part of their nationalizing projects. It also hopes to present the story of how ordinary people on both sides of the Radcliffe line, such as Laila Ahmed, were impacted by such nationalizing projects and how they reacted, adopted, negotiated, and often ignored such classifications. Luckily for Laila, the Indian authorities allowed her to stay on with her parents on 'compassionate grounds'[59] until the Citizenship Act was passed and she could acquire Indian citizenship.

NOTES

1. Indian Citizenship of Foreigners, 1955, No file no., Sl. no. 8, Home (Political) Confidential, West Bengal State Archives (henceforth WBSA), Calcutta.

2. *Ibid.*

3. Internal memo to Chief Secretary, 26 February 1953 (*ibid.*).

4. There are varying assessments on the exact numbers. According to Government of India estimates, 4.5 million Sikhs and Hindus left their homes in West Punjab and migrated to India and 5.5 million Muslims moved from different parts of India to West Pakistan (India [Dominion] Ministry of Information and Broadcasting, 1948, *After Partition*, New Delhi: Publications Division, Government of India, p. 50). In Bengal, the Government of India's Census of 1961 recorded around 3 million displaced non-Muslims from East Pakistan. A million-and-half Muslims left West Bengal for East Pakistan in the

two decades after the Partition. See Joya Chatterji, 2005, 'Of Graveyards and Ghettos: Muslims in Partitioned West Bengal, 1947–67', in Mushirul Hasan and Asim Roy (eds), *Living Together Separately: Cultural India in History and Politics*, New Delhi: Oxford University Press, p. 228.

5. Partha Chatterjee uses this term to describe the Nehruvian project of the nation state which began in the 1930s and found fruition after 1947. See Partha Chatterjee, 1991, *Nationalist Thought and the Colonial World: A Derivative Discourse?*, Minneapolis: University of Minnesota Press.

6. Sarah Ansari, 2005, *Life after Partition: Migration, Community and Strife in Sindh, 1947–1962*, Karachi: Oxford University Press; Joya Chatterji, 2007, *The Spoils of Partition: Bengal and India, 1947–1967*, Cambridge: Cambridge University Press; and Vazira Zamindar, 2007, *The Long Partition and the Making of Modern South Asia: Refugees, Boundaries, Histories*, New York: Columbia University Press.

7. Gyanendra Pandey, 2001, *Remembering Partition: Violence, Nationalism, and History in India*, New York: Cambridge University Press, p. 17.

8. Gyanendra Pandey, 1994, 'The Prose of Otherness', in David Hardiman and David Arnold (eds), *Subaltern Studies, Volume VIII*, New Delhi: Oxford University Press, pp. 188–221.

9. Fuelled by the publication of the N. Mansergh and E.W.R. Lumby (eds), 1977, *Constitutional Relations Between Britain and India: The Transfer of Power, 1942–7, Vol. 1–12*, London: Her Majesty's Stationary Office., historical scholarship on the endgames of empire and the Partition began to emerge from the 1970s. For varied empirical analyses on the causes of Partition, see Ajit Bhattacharjea, 1997, *Countdown to Partition: The Final Days*, New Delhi: HarperCollins; Robin Moore, 1983, *Escape from Empire: The Attlee Government and the Indian Problem*, New Delhi: Oxford University Press; David Page, 1982, *Prelude to Partition: The Indian Muslims and the Imperial System of Control, 1920–1932*, New Delhi and New York: Oxford University Press; Anita Inder Singh, 1987, *The Origins of Partition of India, 1936–1947*, New Delhi and New York: Oxford University Press.

10. Writing on the Partition began as early as 1947 itself, in the form of official inquiries, memoirs, and eyewitness accounts by British and Indian officials. For example, see M.A.K. Azad, 1960, *India Wins Freedom*, New York: Longmans, Green and Co.; A. Campbell-Johnson, 1953, *Mission with Mountbatten*, New York: Dutton; M.L. Darling, 1949, *At Freedom's Door*, London: Oxford University Press; G.D. Khosla, 1949, *Stern Reckoning: A Survey of Events Leading up to and Following the Partition of India*, New Delhi: Oxford University Press; V.P. Menon, 1957, *The Transfer of Power in India*, Bombay: Orient Longman; P. Moon, 1961, *Divide and Quit: An Eyewitness Account of the Partition of India*, London: Oxford University Press; and Sir Francis Tucker, 1950, *While Memory Serves*, London: Cassel. Most of these books received a new lease of

life as reprints became easily available to the public in South Asia in the late 1980s and the 1990s. Their popularity confirms the idea that narratives of the Partition continue to capture and inform the public imagination.

11. See S. Gopal, 1975, *Jawaharlal Nehru: A Biography*, London: J. Cape; Ayesha Jalal, 1985, *The Sole Spokesman: Jinnah, the Muslim League and the Demand for Pakistan*, Cambridge: Cambridge University Press; and B.R. Nanda, 1958, *Mahatma Gandhi: A Biography*, London and Boston: Allen & Unwin and Beacon Press. The Indian government aided the project by the publication of personal writings of Gandhi. See 1958–73, *Collected Works of Mahatma Gandhi*, New Delhi: Publications Division, Government of India; S. Gopal (ed.), 1972, *Selected Works of Jawaharlal Nehru*, New Delhi: Orient Longman; and Z.H. Zaidi (ed.), 1993, *Quaid-i-Azam Mohammad Ali Jinnah Papers*, Islamabad: National Archives of Pakistan.

12. For the broad trends in the Partition historiography, see Tai Yong Tan and Gyanesh Kudaisya, 2000, 'Introduction: The Place of Partition in South Asian Histories', in *The Aftermath of Partition in South Asia*, London and New York: Routledge, pp. 1–28.

13. Jinnah's control over Bengali politicians such as Fazlul Haq and H.S. Suhrawardy was tenuous at best. For differences between the All India Muslim League and the Bengal Provincial Muslim League, see Shila Sen, 1976, *Muslim Politics in Bengal, 1937–1947*, New Delhi: Impex India, and Harun-or-Rashid, 2003, *The Foreshadowing of Bangladesh: Bengali Muslim League and Muslim Politics, 1906–47*, Dhaka: Dhaka University Press.

14. The coalition politics that ensued after the All India Congress failed to capitalize on their win in the provincial elections of 1937 has been seen also as a lost opportunity for Hindu–Muslim unity in Bengal politics. Harun-or-Rashid argues that the failure of a Congress–League coalition after the 1946 elections prepared the ground for increasing communal hostility.

15. For a detailed critique of 'communalism', see Ayesha Jalal, 1997, 'Exploding Communalism: The Politics of Identity in South Asia', in Sugata Bose and Ayesha Jalal (eds), *Nationalism, Democracy, and Development: State and Politics in India*, New Delhi: Oxford University Press, pp. 76–103.

16. Chatterji traces the proliferation of communalism in Bengal thus, 'Nationalism was directed against imperialism and gave top priority to anti-British action. The communalism of the *bhadralok* was directed against their fellow Bengalis. History for the one was the struggle against British liberation from the despotism of Muslims. Its key political objective was to prevent this "despotism" from returning when the British left India, and to deny that Muslims could be Bengalis, and by extension Indians.' See Joya Chatterji, 1994, *Bengal Divided: Hindu Communalism and Partition, 1932–1947*, Cambridge: Cambridge University Press, p. 268.

17. In an attempt to provide agency to the colonized, Chatterji argues, 'Bengalis were not passive bystanders in the partition of their province; nor were they victims of circumstances entirely out of their control, forced reluctantly to accept the division of their "motherland". On the contrary, a large number of Hindus of Bengal, backed up by the provincial branches of the Congress and the Hindu Mahasabha, campaigned intensively in 1947 for the partition of Bengal inside an Indian Union' (*ibid.*, p. 227).

18. Other historians of Bengal have argued for a successful synthesis between elite and popular communalism in the Bengal countryside that found culmination in the 1946 riots, for example, Suranjan Das, 1991, *Communal Riots in Bengal, 1905–1947*, New Delhi: Oxford University Press. Here, too, is an argument for the unilinear path of communalism, this time of Muslim communalism, that makes Partition inevitable.

19. Sekhar Bandyopadhyay, 1997, *Caste, Protest and Identity in Colonial India: The Namasudras of Bengal, 1872–1947*, Richmond, Surrey: Curzon Press.

20. Taj ul-Islam Hashmi, 1992, *Pakistan as a Peasant Utopia: The Communalization of Class Politics in East Bengal, 1920–1947*, Boulder: Westview Press.

21. Sugata Bose, 2001, 'Between Monolith and Fragment: A Note on Historiography of Nationalism in Bengal', in Sekhar Bandyopadhyay (ed.), *Bengal: Rethinking History, Essays in Historiography*, New Delhi: Manohar, p. 288.

22. Sugata Bose, 1993, *The New Cambridge History of India: Peasant Labour and Colonial Capital*, Cambridge: Cambridge University Press, p. 142.

23. M. Anisuzzaman, 1993, *Creativity, Reality, Identity*, Dhaka: International Centre for Bengal Studies, University Press Limited.

24. The erasure of the Partition of 1947 is stark in its omission within the three volumes of Sirajul Islam (ed.), 1992, *History of Bangladesh, 1704–1971, Vols 1–3*, Dhaka: Asiatic Society of Bangladesh. The only essay within the first volume which deals partially with the Partition is by Ahmed Kamal, 'East Bengal at Independence', Sirajul Islam (ed.), *History of Bangladesh, 1704–1941*, Dhaka: Asiatic Society of Bengal, pp. 407–35.

25. E.P. Thompson defines experience as '"the mental and emotional response, whether of a individual, or of a group, to many interrelated events or to many repetitions of the same kind of events'. See E.P. Thompson, 1995, *The Poverty of Theory or an Orrey of Errors*, London: Merlin Press, p. 7.

26. Urvashi Butalia, 2000, *The Other Side of Silence: Voices from the Partition of India*, Durham, NC: Duke University Press; Veena Das, 1990, *Mirrors of Violence: Communities, Riots and Survivors in South Asia*, New Delhi: Oxford University Press, 1990; Mushirul Hasan (ed.), 1993, *India's Partition: Process, Strategy and Mobilization*, New Delhi: Oxford University Press; Suvir Kaul, 2001, *Partitions*

of Memory: The Afterlife of the Division of India, New Delhi: Permanent Black; Ritu Menon and Kamla Bhasin, 1998, *Borders and Boundaries: Women in India's Partition*, New Delhi: Kali; Ian Talbot and Gurharpal Singh (eds), 1999, *Region and Partition: Bengal, Punjab and the Partition of the Subcontinent*, Oxford, NY: Oxford University Press.

27. Butalia, *The Other Side of Silence*; and Menon and Bhasin, *Borders and Boundaries*.

28. Pandey, *Remembering Partition*.

29. See Ansari, *Life after Partition*; Yasmin Khan, 2007, *The Great Partition: The Making of India and Pakistan*, New Haven, CT: Yale University Press; Ian Talbot, 2006, *Divided Cities: Partition and its Aftermath in Lahore and Amritsar, 1947–1957*, Karachi: Oxford University Press.

30. Shabnum Tejani, 2008, *Indian Secularism: A Social and Intellectual History, 1890-1950*, Bloomington, Indiana: Indiana University Press.

31. Zamindar, *The Long Partition*.

32. There was no permit system in Bengal and the evacuee property legislations only operated in East Pakistan.

33. Joya Chatterji, *The Spoils of Partition*, pp. 159–208.

34. *Ibid.*, pp. 105–58.

35. Few academic scholars find it problematic to use the Punjab experience as the quintessential Partition experience. Some have problematized it briefly. See Mushirul Hasan, 1998, 'Memories of a Fragmented Nation: Rewriting the Histories of India's Partition', *Economic and Political Weekly*, vol. 33, no. 41, 10 October, p. 2662–8; Menon and Bhasin, *Borders and Boundaries*, p. 12; and Pandey, *Remembering Partition*, p. 18. Of the most recent works on Partition and its aftermath, the focus remains firmly on the north. Even the recent works which proclaim to focus on the Partition experience in general, exhibit a clear bias towards the western Partition. See Khan, *The Great Partition*; and Ian Talbot and Gurharpal Singh, 2009, *The Partition of India*, Cambridge: Cambridge University Press.

36. In its examination of the Partition experience, recent scholarship has broadened its enquiry to include the processes that went into the making of post-1947 nation states. For example, see Chatterji, *The Spoils of Partition*; Lucy Chester, 2009, *Borders and Conflict in South Asia: The Radcliffe Boundary Commission and the Partition of Punjab*, Manchester: Manchester University Press; and Zamindar, *The Long Partition*.

37. Md. Mahbubar Rahman and Willem Van Schendel, 2003, '"I am Not a Refugee": Rethinking Partition Migration', *Modern Asian Studies*, vol. 37, no. 3, pp. 551–84.

38. See Srirupa Roy, 2007, *Beyond Belief: India and the Politics of Post-Colonial Nationalism*, New Delhi: Permanent Black, pp. 66–104.

39. Ayesha Jalal, 1990, *The State of Martial Rule: The Origins of Pakistan's Political Economy of Defence*, Cambridge: Cambridge University Press, p. 3

40. Willem Van Schendel, 2009, *A History of Bangladesh*, Cambridge: Cambridge University Press, pp. 135–7.

41. Zamindar argues that Muslims who had temporarily migrated from India to Pakistan after 1947 were prevented from returning to their homes due to the implementation of the permit system by India (see Zamindar, *The Long Partition*, pp. 85–96).

42. Here I follow, in modified form, Joel Migdal's argument that people who implement policies at the local level have an important effect on the nature of the state. He notes, 'The indirect impact of politics of survival upon them, their centrality to the implementation of politics, and the calculus of social and political pressures they face have placed them in a critical role to influence whether states can actually accomplish what their leaders purport'. See Joel S. Migdal, 1988, *Strong Societies and Weak States: State–Society Relations and State Capabilities in the Third World*, Princeton: Princeton University Press, p. 238.

43. In another context, Myron Weiner, talking about India's experience with policy implementation notes, 'The system gave a great deal of power to the individuals at the local level who were often able to impede the carrying out of national policies'. See Myron Weiner, 1977, 'Motilal, Jawaharlal, Indira and Sanjay in India's Political Transformation', in Richard J. Samuels (ed.), *Political Generations and Political Development*, Lexington, MA: Lexington Books, p. 72.

44. Rogers Brubaker, 1992, *Citizenship and Nationhood in France and Germany*, Cambridge, MA: Harvard University Press, p. 22.

45. *Ibid.*, p. 21.

46. This date was initially fixed at July 1948, less than a year after the Partition.

47. Willem Van Schendel, 2002, 'Stateless in South Asia: The Making of the India–Bangladesh Enclaves', *The Journal of Asian Studies*, vol. 61, no. 1, February, p. 127.

48. Tai Yong Tan and Gyanesh Kudaisya, 2000, 'The Making of South Asian Borders', in *The Aftermath of Partition in South Asia*, pp. 78–100.

49. Focusing on the British cartographic enterprise in early nineteenth century India, Mathew Edney argues that the colonialists sought to describe an imperial conception of *British* India. 'British India which was otherwise a quite arbitrary entity was naturalized by the British to be a constant timeless "natural" uniform geographical entity, political nation and cultural state.' Mathew Edney, 1997, *Mapping an Empire: The Geographical Construction of British India, 1765–1843*, Chicago: University of Chicago Press, p. 334.

50. See Joya Chatterji, 1999, 'The Fashioning of a Frontier: The Radcliffe Line and Bengal's Border Landscape, 1947–52', *Modern Asian Studies*, vol. 33,

no. 1, pp. 185–242; Chester, *Borders and Conflict in South Asia*; and Willem Van Schendel, 2005, *The Bengal Borderland: Beyond State and Nation in South Asia*, London: Anthem.

51. Chester, *Borders and Conflict in South Asia*.

52. Joya Chatterji, 'The Fashioning of a Frontier', p. 213.

53. Michiel Baud and Willem Van Schendel, 1997, 'Toward a Comparative History of Borderlands', *Journal of World History*, vol. 8, no. 2, p. 220.

54. See Willem Van Schendel, 2001, 'Working through Partition: Making a Living in the Bengal Borderlands', *International Review of Social History*, vol. 46, no. 3, December, pp. 393–421.

55. Ranabir Samaddar, 1997, 'The History that Partition Creates', in Ranabir Samaddar (ed.), *Reflections on Partition in the East*, Calcutta: Vikas, pp. 10–11.

56. John C. Torpey, 2000, *The Invention of the Passport, Surveillance, Citizenship, and the State*, Cambridge: Cambridge University Press.

57. WBSA, Writers' Building, Calcutta, accessed March 2007.

58. The post-Partition experience in Assam has been dealt with in detail in Sanjib Baruah, 1999, *India against Itself: Assam and the Politics of Nationality*, Philadelphia: University of Pennsylvania Press.

59. Indian authorities had a specific category of permits on compassionate grounds which entitled people of 'old age, infirmity, illness, women and minor children who are dependent on Indian citizens' to remain in India on a semi-permanent basis. Such regulations were clearly guided by the patriarchal stance of the Indian State that sought to differentiate between able male petitioners and those that needed its protection.

I

Territories

1

Drafting a New Nation

The boundary will be an international boundary, separating two independent sovereign states. Such boundary marks the limits of the region within which a state can exercise its sovereign authority, and with its location, various matters relating to immigration and restriction on visitors, imposition of custom duties, and prevention of smuggling and contraband trade are bound up. The boundary should undoubtedly be drawn up in such a manner as would obviate chances of friction and clashes in peacetime.[1]

1947 began with a series of high-level political decisions which were going to have significant impacts on the lives of people living within the Indian subcontinent. The British announced in February of 1947 that they would leave by 1948 and hand over the political reigns to appropriate representatives . In Bengal, the largest province of British India, the focus of Bengali political and public discourse almost immediately shifted from the communal riots of 1946 to debates on whether India and Bengal should be partitioned. In an atmosphere of confusion, contingent proclamations supported by multiple claims, the Bengali public remained divided on the potential political fate of their province. Similarly, the leading political entities such as the Bengal Provincial Congress, Bengal Muslim League, or the Bengal Provincial Hindu Mahasabha could not claim complete support either for united India or the formation of Pakistan.[2]

The public endorsement of Governor Louis Mountbatten's Plan of June 3 by both the leaders—Congress and Muslim League leaders—ended the debate on the probability of India's Partition. Mountbatten's Plan brought forward the Independence of India from the earlier date of July 1948 to August 15, 1947. Further it clearly outlined the possibility of Partition: the Muslim-majority provinces of Bengal, Punjab, Sind, the North West Frontier Province (NWFP), and Baluchistan would have the option to either use the existing constitutional assembly to frame their future constitution within a united Indian Union or establish a new and separate constituent assembly. Within two weeks of the announcement of the Plan, the Bengal Legislative Assembly voted in favour of the Partition by a clear majority.[3]

In hindsight, the vote in the provincial legislative assembly proved to be the simplest verdict taken by its members. Having taken the decision to partition, the leaders now had to figure out the logistics of framing a new border, and more importantly, the location of this new line. The first step towards this process was the appointment of a Boundary Commission. The authorities hoped that the Commission would be an impartial judicial arbitrator to lend credence to idea that the decision was fair and democratic, rather than authoritarian.[4] Thus, Mountbatten brought in Cyril Radcliffe, who had been the Director-General of the British Ministry of Information, to be the Chairman of both the Bengal and Punjab Boundary Commissions. Each of these Commissions also had four Indian members; Radcliffe had the deciding vote within each of them.

Both Nehru and Mountbatten were of the opinion that the rudimentary coordinates of the new borders should be in place by the time of independence, which meant that the Commission had less than six weeks to define the two international borders in the eastern and western parts of British India. Any disputes and popular demands could be resolved once India and Pakistan began functioning as new states.[5] Thus time constraints severely limited the deliberations about who would be the appropriate members and the rules and the regulations that would guide such a Commission.

Attempts at rationality were contradicted by the six week time frame and lack of credible material on which to base their deliberations on. Maps and field surveys were outdated and in some cases unavailable. There was no time to bring in or request input from district administrators who had local knowledge of their areas. Given that the Partition was going to be based on religious demography, Census data became critical. However, the Commission based its deliberations on the information from the controversial 1941 census, which the Congress representatives to the Commission argued had been conducted at a time when political power and representation depended on an increase in numbers. They claimed that the Muslims had deliberately skewed the census in their favor, bending administrative boundaries to show more Muslim majority areas. The members who had been nominated by the Muslim League claimed that the 1941 Census was authoritative.

The appointment of Cyril Radcliffe was itself problematic. Radcliffe had neither local knowledge nor any previous association with any kind of boundary-making process. Oddly enough, this made him a suitable candidate in the eyes of British and Indian leaders who argued that Radcliffe's lack of knowledge about India would make him impartial. Recent scholarship suggests that instead of being objective, Radcliffe was biased towards maintaining British interests that impelled him to not only take up the chairmanship but also ensure that the Commission and its verdict have a façade of rational deliberations rather than one taken hurriedly.[6]

To add to the confusion, Radcliffe's mandate for the Bengal Boundary Commission was simple but ambiguous: 'to demarcate the boundaries on the basis of ascertaining the contiguous majority areas of Muslims and non-Muslims, and in doing so take into account also other factors'.[7] Where a clear contiguous majority or minority became difficult to establish, the 'other factors' would assume primacy. What comprised the 'other factors' remained undefined, giving the Boundary Commission considerable room for manoeuvre.[8] Such ambiguity, while favourable to the decision makers, also created the potential for claims and counterclaims for the boundary, all of which could be regarded as valid depending on the interpretation of 'other factors'. The major political parties that were required to submit depositions to the Boundary Commission regarding the location of the border exploited this ambiguity to the maximum. Given the adverse time frame, lack of resources, and vague instructions, the Boundary Commission was fated to fall short but under Radcliffe's direction, went forward to attempt some sort of resolution to an impossible task.

In keeping with the rational judicial façade of the whole process, the members of the Commissions were all well-known judges. The Bengal

Boundary Commission consisted of well-known judges, B.K. Mukherjee, C.C. Biswas, Abu Saleh Muhammed, and S.A. Rahman.[9] The choice of legal experts as potentially impartial and logical members of the Commission found support within the Bengali public as well. Calling it a 'crisis in the life of the nation', Pannalal Bose, a retired judge whose name had become famous in the Bhowal Case in the 1930s, noted that the present situation was 'without precedent in history and there is no experience to guide the judgment of the Commission of those who will assist them ... the judges who will determine the boundary will be persuaded not by threat or fear of riots or propaganda of any sort, but by argument and everything will depend upon its cogency'.[10] For Bose, himself a litigator, the law would thus prevail even in times of chaos. However, the fact that the Congress and the League nominated two each of the Commission members meant that impartiality was going to be the first casualty as the deliberations began.

CLAIMS AND COUNTERCLAIMS

In the summer of 1947, leaders of major political parties in Bengal went about soliciting, organizing and collecting the support of their constituents and framed them as depositions to the Boundary Commission. The Bengal Provincial Congress, Hindu Mahasabha, the Indian Association, and the New Bengal Association formed themselves into a joint Central Boundary Coordination Committee, with barrister Atul Chandra Gupta as Chairman. In addition, each party also set up their own Boundary Committee, or the purposes of garnering local support for their plans. The Bengal Provincial Musim League set up a committee that requested its supporters to provide suggestions on where the boundary should be drawn, while others like the New Bengal Association, distributed questionnaires to collect facts and figures to justify inclusion within India.[11] Local representatives of the Congress in the district of Khulna constituted a Boundary Consultative Committee to collect and present facts and figures before the Central Coordination Committee.[12] This activity provided, however mistakenly, a sense that public opinion on this issue mattered and that political representatives wished to hear from their constituents.[13]

The Muslim League was the only major political party who presented a case for eastern Bengal to the Boundary Commission.[14] According to the terms of reference, the Muslim-majority districts in

Bengal would most likely go to East Bengal. In addition, the League demanded substantially more territory on the basis of two factors. First, they insisted that the unit of partition should be a union or more appropriately, a subdivision,[15] a 'self-contained administrative unit', rather than *thanas* (police stations), which were smaller units defining criminal jurisdictions.[16] Such a method, League representatives claimed, would yield a straighter and less complex boundary between the two states. Although such an argument had its merits, a division based on subdivisions would also give more territory to East Bengal.[17]

Second, the League insisted that the principle of contiguity should be limited to areas within Bengal. This meant that if an area were contiguous to other non-Muslim-majority areas in India but was not contiguous to any such areas within Bengal, then it should automatically be assigned to East Bengal. Using such a definition, the League demanded that the non-Muslim-majority districts of the Chittagong Hill Tracts, Jalpaiguri, and Darjeeling belonged to the future Pakistan. To bolster their claims on Darjeeling and Jalpaiguri, the League pointed out that these districts were the catchment areas of the Tista river system and control of this area was necessary for the 'physical and economic health' of East Bengal.

The League also maintained that the city of Calcutta and its surrounding areas should be taken as one entity, and that the decision to award it to either state should not be based on the fact that the city had an overwhelming non-Muslim population. They argued that Calcutta as the economic and commercial centre of the entire province of Bengal should go to East Bengal to ensure continuity in the linkages between the jute mills in the city and the jute-producing hinterland in East Bengal. Further, assigning Calcutta to East Bengal would not only balance the revenues in proportion to the population but also ensure that East Bengal was self-contained with its own ordinance factories, military installations, and railway networks. Such arguments allowed the League to claim nearly four-fifths of the territory of the Bengal province.[18]

In effect, the League's territorial claim would place around two-third of the Hindu population within the proposed East Bengal. The League members insisted that the aim of partition was not to provide maximum self-representation for each community but rather to determine the line of division to ensure that religious contiguity of territory be maintained.

Although this was contrary to the earlier demands of communal self-representation that had been the central core of the Pakistan demand, it was in line with the political and demographic realities in Bengal. Here, Muslims were a majority at 55 per cent of the population and additionally, the League had won a comfortable victory in the 1946 provincial elections. Thus, the League members assumed that if India was partitioned, they had a good chance at claiming the whole of Bengal for Pakistan rather than only a portion of it.

The territorial dimension of the new West Bengal province proved to be central dividing line between the members of the Central Coordination Committee, and ultimately led to a split. Members belonging to the Congress urged for a compact West Bengal which they argued would be viable, while those belonging to the Hindu Mahasabha, the New Bengal Association, and the Indian Association urged for the maximum possible area. In fact, S.N. Modak, the Chairman of the Boundary Committee of the New Bengal Association, declared, 'I may assure my country men, specially those residing in the border line districts that we are fully conscious of their anxiety and of the responsibility that has been placed on us. We shall leave no stone unturned in our effort to incorporate in the New Bengal province as many areas as we are reasonably entitled to.'[19] To this end, the Bengal Provincial Hindu Mahasabha, the New Bengal Association, and the Indian Association demanded, in addition to the non-Muslim-majority districts of Burdwan, Midnapore, Birbhum, Bankura, Howrah, Hoogly 24 Parganas, Khulna, Darjeeling, and Jalpaiguri, the two Muslim-majority districts of Malda and Murshidabad. They also claimed some thanas in Jessore, Faridpur, and Rajshahi on the grounds that these areas had a numerical majority of Schedule Castes or the Namasudras.[20] Their demand would have included about 57 per cent of the land for 46 per cent of the population in West Bengal.[21]

On the other hand, the Congress decided to put forward two proposals: a 'Scheme' which asked for maximum territory; and a 'Plan' which demanded a more compact state based strictly on contiguous majorities which would give the Hindus a demographic majority of around 70 per cent.[22] In their Scheme, the Congress advocated two cardinal principles. First, the partition must be effected to ensure the inclusion of as many non-Muslims as possible in West Bengal and similarly, as many Muslims in East Bengal.[23] Such a distribution should also ensure that the proportion of Muslims in East Bengal to the total Muslim population of the province should not be unduly lower or higher than the proportion of non-Muslims in West Bengal to the entire non-Muslim population of the province. Notably, none of the demands for territory for either West Bengal or East Bengal reflect any anticipation, on the part of debaters, that there might be a large-scale population movement once the Partition went into effect. Both sides assumed that any mass migration could be prevented if they achieved religious balance between Hindus and Muslim in divided Bengal.

Second, the Coordination Committee advocated the use of the *thana*, the area under the jurisdiction of one police station, as the basic unit of enumeration. The thana was the smallest unit of census enumeration, and such a method would allow the Congress to demand a much larger territory, albeit one with a complex boundary. Although in direct contrast to the League's demand for the *subdivision* to be the unit of enumeration, the Coordination Committee's guiding principle also reflected a claim for maximum territory. In addition to contiguity of non-Muslim areas, the Congress claimed the Muslim-majority district of Murshidabad arguing that awarding the district to East Bengal would not only disrupt the Hoogly river system but also hamper the activities of the Port of Calcutta and hence, the economy of West Bengal. They also insisted on the inclusion of the Sunderbans within West Bengal, claiming that it did not have any resident population. Since it was uninhabited, it should be attached to Khulna, a non-Muslim-majority district that was contiguous to West Bengal. In the case of Murshidabad and the Sunderbans, the Congress concern for land and economic factors took priority over the basic terms of reference.[24]

PUBLIC DEMANDS FOR A BORDER

While political leadership wrangled and negotiated the coordinates of the border that would be most suitable to their constituencies, local civic bodies and socio-political groups entered the debate by forwarding petitions and memoranda to the Boundary Commission expressing their views on how and where the border should be determined. In addition, self-styled Bengali intellectuals offered their opinions in the form of essays and letters sent to the major Bengali and English language newspapers and journals, to their elected local and national political leaders, and sometimes, to the British administrators in Calcutta, Delhi, and London.

In effect, the impending partition and the line that would be its manifestation generated a vibrant debate within the Bengali public sphere. Most scholars have largely ignored this public dimension, viewing the Boundary Commission's work as behind closed doors and insulated from the public.[25] This maybe so because there is no evidence to suggest that either Radcliffe or the four members of the Boundary Commission solicited inputs from anybody other than the major political parties, or that they read the essays in the news media or the public petitions sent to them. But this does not imply that the Bengali public were disinterested in their political future or were passive bystanders to decisions that were being taken far away from them. Rather, they actively wrote to the Boundary Commission, and shared their ideas and suggestions in newspapers and journals too, feeling that it was their duty to aid the members of the Boundary Commission in making the *right* decision. They put forth census data, self-drawn geographical and geological maps, and details about the religious and national significance of their particular areas in support of their petitions for inclusions in either western or eastern Bengal.[26] Several of these petitions came from recently created *samities*, civic organizations comprising prominent, English-educated local Hindus and Muslims, and set up for the sole purpose of submitting these documents to the Commission.[27] Sometimes, local magistrates or union board leaders put forward petitions on behalf of particular sections of the population. Thus, even though the final decision on the boundary was taken by five men, the Bengali public felt that they had a stake in their future and could possibly influence it. These proposals generated from civic organizations and the general public provides us with crucial evidence on the formation of putative national identities that sought inclusion within specific imagined communities that had tangible territorial boundaries.

A critical element of this discourse related to demands for territory and living space for Hindus in western, and Muslims in the eastern, part of the province. How much territory was sufficient for the proposed West Bengal province? On what basis should the territorial coordinates be decided? Before the announcement of the 3 June plan, there were no guidelines for such concerns, except the understanding that any division or demand for inclusion would involve mainly those areas that were unlikely to be part of the proposed Pakistan. Once the plan became public, the terms of reference made it clear that religious demography would be the primary constituting factor in drawing the line. Not surprisingly, for some petitioners, territorial projections of the new states were circumscribed within continuing communal demands.

The primacy of religion was in keeping with the raison d'être of the Partition announcement, which demanded that people identify themselves primarily as Hindus or Muslims. For instance, the non-Muslim population of Gournadi police station in Backerganj district in East Bengal submitted a memorandum to the Lord Mountbatten, which detailed why their area should form a part of the Indian Union. The petition noted that the Gournadi population was 57 per cent Hindu making it a Hindu-majority area according to the requirements of the Boundary Commission. In addition, the memorandum highlighted Gournadi as an important seat of Hindu culture with the largest number of Sanskrit *tols* or village schools and temples in the district. In case such arguments failed to convince the British government, the memorandum also pointed out traditional social and economic ties with Calcutta and the intricate connections to the Gopalganj subdivision by 'ties of marriage'.[28] The demand was not for the entire district of Backerganj, but only for the thana of Gournadi, which, according to the memorandum, was contiguous to the non-Muslim-majority subdivision of Gopalganj.

History, religion, and patriotism often provided the three primary bases for these petitions. A petition from the Hindus of Vikrampur, Mymensingh, stressed its religious identity as a historical site for Buddhist and Hindu culture that, it argued, had provided the basis for success for people born in the region. Further, it established its patriotic credentials by naming several Congress leaders who had been born there. Thus, the petition argued, 'in consideration of the important role played by the sons and daughters of Vikrampur by their suffering and sacrifices in the freedom movement of India and especially in consideration of the fact that the Hindus are a majority by 57 percent this area should be ... included in the Indian Union along with West Bengal.'[29] As regional history became interwoven with the history of the freedom struggle, it emerged reinvented as one in which the participants were only Hindus.

In keeping with the terms of reference of the Boundary Commission, the aim was to find a neighbouring area with a non-Muslim majority and then demonstrate a case for contiguity. An editorial in the nationalist newspaper, the *Hindustan Standard*, appealed for the inclusion of parts of Faridpur and Backerganj even though they did not 'pass the strict test of contiguousness' since in this area, the river Padma would provide a natural boundary between the two Bengals. Further, the editorial urged the need for at least half the territory of Bengal for the new province of West Bengal because 'it seems certain that sooner or later the Hindus of East Bengal will have to be accommodated in West Bengal and provided with honest means of livelihood'.[30]

This claim was echoed at the national level in the constituent assembly. Two members, M.N. Mahalonobis and Pandit Lakshmi Kanta Maitra, jointly published a statement where they demanded that not less than half of the area and population of Bengal be placed within the West Bengal-cum-north Bengal province: 'This demand ... is modest in view of the size of non-Muslim population and the property owned by it. Every effort should also be made to include within the province the most important places of Hindu pilgrimage and the seats of Hindu religion and culture'.[31] Concerns about Hindu culture were one of the key factors in public demands for inclusion within India. For Tinkari Bagchi, the Commissioner of Nabadwip municipality, a centre of the Vaishnava sect, it was imperative that his district of Nadia be awarded to India. He elucidated that: 'Apart from the fact that the two most important subdivisions (in the district) namely the Sadar and Ranaghat being Hindu majority areas, Nabadwip and Santipur are the two famous historic towns which have for several centuries been the seat of Hindu learning and culture'.[32] Like Bagchi, many feared that the continuation of their cultural traditions would be disrupted by the border which 'was not the demarcation between two provincial units under one constituted authority' as had been the case in the Partition of 1905, but 'a clear cut line between two independent sovereign states, viz. the Indian Union and Eastern Pakistan'.[33] Inclusion of their area within India would ensure the preservation of their religion and cultural traditions.

At one level, these demands for inclusion and concern about Hindu culture are indicative and constitutive of a widespread Hindu communal movement demanding territory for a 'Hindu homeland'.[34]

The Hindu Mahasabha was the key mobilizing force demanding division of the province. Such mobilizing efforts were not confined to the middle class but encompassed a substantial portion of the Scheduled Castes in Bengal, who, on the eve of Partition, identified themselves as part of the Hindu minority.[35] Thus, it would seem that the Bengali Hindu demands of inclusion within India on the eve of Partition indicated that religious identity had transcended cultural linguistic boundaries and evolved a broader spatial association.

While the cognitive mapping of the new borders may have been influenced partially by the reality of religious demographics, what needs to be highlighted is the contingency of political negotiations and the dynamic shifts in position within public discourse in 1947. Rather than an affirmation of en masse Hindu identity coming to the fore, the public opinions at this stage of the Partition process reflect a faith that the rules of the game had been laid out by the British government in India and they needed to abide by them for appropriate results. Further, the fact that their political representatives had accepted the fiat of the Boundary Commission also seemed to indicate that public demands needed to be couched within the calculus of religious demography.

The need for 'communal unity' was only one line of reasoning for the demand for territory. The desire to preserve natural frontiers, to guarantee the military strategic unity of the new international border and aid a successful future foreign policy and the political sustenance of the new Indian nation and citizenship within it, and to ensure economic stability and social continuity were some of the other major factors associated with the scramble for territory. Santosh Kumar Mukherji's *Boundary Problem in New Bengal* is a case in point. This booklet, published with a mind to influence both the Boundary Commission as well as Bengali public opinion, outlined in detail what should considered in determining the new boundary. First and foremost, since the boundary would be an international border between two countries, Mukherji argued that its demarcation was not a provincial issue but a *national* issue. While communal demography was an important factor, Mukherji urged that the economic welfare and defence of the new West Bengal province would be better served if one used natural frontiers such as the rivers Atreyi, Tangan, and Mahananda in the north, Ganges–Padma in the east, and Garai–Madhumati–Haringhat in the south-east.[36]

Mukherji was not alone in making the connections between economics and the new territorial outlines. A memorandum from a committee called 'People of the Ranaghat Sub-division, District of Nadia', argued that the districts of Nadia, Murshidabad, and Jessore needed to be excluded from East Bengal for the 'maintenance and protection of the city and Port of Calcutta'.[37] Further, these areas were the catchment areas of the rivers Bhagirathi, Jalangi, and Mathabhanga, and thus were crucial to the commercial and agricultural well-being of western Bengal. They also pointed out that if these areas were excluded, then students from this region would be denied access to the long-established tradition of attending Calcutta University thereby causing disruption to their educational development. In the event that these reasons were not sufficient to sway the Boundary Commission, the memorandum also added that this region was a well-known centre of Hindu culture, and that Ranaghat was the birthplace of Adwaita Mahaprabhu, a Goudiya Vaishnav leader, and Krittibas, the author of the Bengali Ramayana.

Territorial calculations were clearly primary in a memorandum from the Muslim Citizens' Committee of Calcutta when they argued that the unit of division should be the entire province of Bengal rather than districts, unions, or thanas within the province. This would, the petitioners pointed out, produce a much clearly delineated frontier and allow for the existence of Bengal independently and as a part of Pakistan.[38] Another group of Muslim citizens from 24 Parganas urged that the Boundary Commission should fix the frontier along the Bhagirathi for military and strategic reasons. This would provide East Bengal with adequate space to mount a defence against any potential attack from India.[39] Of course, this suggested boundary would also ensure that Calcutta would become part of East Bengal.

The seat of Bengali urban culture for both Muslims and Hindus, Calcutta, was the most sought after territory because of its logistical, industrial, and business infrastructure. The same petition proclaimed that 'East Bengal has created Calcutta, her seamen line thousands of vessels that sail out of her port every year. West Bengal has contributed nothing to Calcutta except a few million tons of coal.'[40] By virtue of providing economic sustenance to the city, the petitioners demanded that Calcutta be part of eastern Bengal after the division. Another detailed petition to Lord Listowel, from S.M. Usam, ex-Mayor of Calcutta, Mr Abdus Sabur

Khan, and Mr Mahisuddin Ahmed, the President of the Bengal Jute Growers' Association, couched their demands for Calcutta in economic terms. The petition began by indicating 'East Bengal is the homeland of Jute and Calcutta is the byproduct of the marriage of Bengal jute with Hoogly River and it is for this reason Calcutta is rightly called the city of jute and port of jute'. Jute, the petitioners reminded, was produced solely by East Bengal Muslim peasants and Scheduled Castes. This organic connection between Calcutta and its eastern hinterlands would be severed if Calcutta was awarded to West Bengal.[41] Thus, the petitioners, as representatives of not only the Muslim farmers but also the port and industrial workers in Bengal, urged the British authorities to rethink and rework their decision to partition Bengal.

Two ideas stand out when reading these petitions. First, there was utmost confusion in the public mind with regard to the 'terms of reference' by which the Boundary Commission was to operate. Some interpreted them in economic and strategic terms, while others stressed cultural and religious continuities. Several petitions began with a methodical outline of different factors such as 'Population', 'Contiguity of that particular area', 'Natural boundary or strategic importance', 'Commercial importance', and 'Holy places of worship' to show the religious significance of the place. Thus, the debate on future location within a particular nation evolved along multiple axes of territory, economics, and religion even though the terms of reference cited communal demography as the primary principle.

Second, 'contiguous territories' became a relative term as petitioners took it to define contiguity only with their surrounding areas. For example, the argument for the inclusion of a region like Backerganj, which was clearly in eastern Bengal and had a Muslim majority according the 1941 census, pointed out that it was contiguous to Khulna, a Hindu-majority district, and thus could justifiably be included within the Indian Union. A ten-page petition from the 'Astagram Pallimangal Samity' in Backerganj argued that although it had been denoted as a Muslim-majority district, parts of it had a non-Muslim majority. Urging a reworking of district boundaries, the petition made the following case for contiguity:

The north-western portion of the district of Backerganj, which is contiguous to portions of Madaripur and the whole of Gopalganj sub-divisions form a compact Non-Muslim majority area. This combined portions again contiguous to some portion of Jessore, which again is linked up with Khulna. This shows that district Khulna which is a Non-Muslim majority district is connected, simultaneously with the district of Backerganj, Faridpur and Jessore. The position being so we can legitimately demand that a new district be made out of the portions of Backerganj, Faridpur, Jessore or Khulna.[42]

The Boundary Commission's terms of reference had made it clear that the western districts of Bengal would join the Indian Union. Consequently, the status of the eastern districts became central to the extension of a potential border and to maximize the territory of the West Bengal province. Khulna, a non-Muslim-majority district contiguous to the proposed western Bengal, was widely believed to be awarded to the Indian Union. Thus, most of the petitions from the eastern districts argued for contiguity with this particular district.

By the first week of August, although the idea that India would be partitioned had begun to be accepted in the public mind, misconceptions remained about how this partition was going to take effect. Thus, the local Muslim League in Malda, which had several Muslim majority thanas, had hoisted the Pakistan flag on 15 August, only to find two days later that most of Malda had, in fact, been awarded to India.[43] Similarly, Hindus in Khulna had hoisted the Indian flag in anticipation of inclusion within India.[44]

THE BOUNDARY AWARD

The Boundary Commission announced its decision on 17 August 1947, two days after the declaration of independence. Although the award was ready by 12 August, Mountbatten, fearing civil strife, had arranged for its publication only after the British had relinquished constitutional control over India. The award assigned 36.36 per cent of land to accommodate 35.14 per cent of population to West Bengal, while East Bengal received 63.6 per cent of land to accommodate 64.85 per cent of the population. The two states had an equal proportion of majority and minority populations in a ratio of approximately 70:30. In effect, this was in line with what the Congress Plan had urged for in their deposition. However, the award was inequitable in its distribution of the minority population within each area, as West Bengal contained 16 per cent of the total Muslim population of Bengal, while East Bengal retained 42 per cent of the total non-Muslims of undivided Bengal.[45]

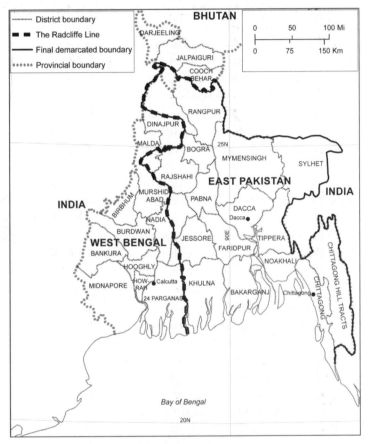

Figure 1.1: The Radcliffe Line

The boundary divided the five districts of Nadia, Jessore, Dinajpur, Jalpaiguri, and Malda. The Boundary Commission acceded to the Congress's argument that Murshidabad was crucial to the survival of the Hoogly river system and assigned it to West Bengal. Khulna, which had provisionally been included in West Bengal, was granted to East Bengal.[46] Similarly, by awarding non-contiguous portions of Darjeeling and Jalpaiguri to West Bengal, the Boundary Commission counterweighed the awarding of the non-Muslim region of Chittagong Hill Tracts to East Pakistan. Calcutta, which had acquired new significance in the debate for a new boundary, went to West Bengal, as per the Congress demand.

To be fair, the task of the Boundary Commission was not easy. In addition to the short time within which they had to operate, the lack of maps and experience, and the vague directives of the terms of reference, the Commission's task was not a simple division of Bengal. It had to decide the fate of not only the province of Bengal but also the areas adjoining it, which included two princely states, Cooch Behar and Tripura. The areas surrounding the sixteen districts of eastern Bengal became part of India. East Pakistan thus had an almost complete international boundary with India on three sides and the Bay of Bengal on the other side. Tripura and Cooch Behar formally became part of India by 1950. However, the Radcliffe award was unable to resolve the case of enclave territories, remnants from Bengal's Mughal past which now acquired national identities. After 1947, India had 130 enclaves within East Pakistan and Pakistan claimed ninety-five enclaves within Indian territory.[47] The inhabitants of these enclaves became 'stateless' people as neither state made efforts to claim them as their own.

The award failed to meet people's expectations and initiated confusion and a sense of betrayal among Hindus and Muslims. Press comments after the announcement characterized it as 'A departing kick of British imperialism' (*Amrita Bazar Patrika*), 'Self Contradictory' (*Hindustan Standard*), and 'Territorial Murder' (*Dawn*).[48] N.C. Chatterjee, a prominent member of the Bengal Provincial Hindu Mahasabha, protested the award, describing it as 'an outrage on the principle of self determination and all canons of political morality' and maintaining that it had ignored the cultural and economic needs of the people of Bengal.[49] The leading English daily in Calcutta, *Hindustan Standard*, explicitly noted in an editorial that the setting up of the

Boundary Commission had a been a 'meaningless formality' and 'It would be misleading to describe it as the impartial decision of the tribunal; for the entire scheme Sir Cyril Radcliffe alone is responsible'.[50] Radcliffe became, almost overnight, the poster boy of the hypocrisy of British authorities.

The initial confusion and anger gave way to the conviction that the award was not set in stone. Bengalis sent telegrams and letters to various political leaders and British officials requesting that the boundary be revised to include their respective areas so that they would then be included on the 'right' side of the border. For instance, Sarat Das, a member of the Khulna District Congress Boundary Committee, sent telegrams to the Clement Atlee, the British Prime Minister, and to Lord Addison, Secretary of Commonwealth Relations, and even to King George VI, declaring that the boundary award was 'unsatisfactory, unreasonable, objectionable, inconsistent, arbitrary, illegal, absurd, ultravires, unconstitutional' and needed immediate rectification.[51] Such petitions sent to British officials as late as October 1948 reflect not only a continuing association with British rule on the part of the senders but also a faith in the 'prayer and petition' methods of the moderate nationalists of earlier decades to redress grievances against colonial rule. Similarly, representative Muslim groups such as the Muslim National Guards of Pabna were upset that the award did not include more of Bengal in Pakistan.[52]

The case of Khulna, a Hindu-majority province awarded to Pakistan, and Murshidabad, a Muslim-majority province awarded to India, demonstrated the betrayal the general population felt by the announcement of the award. Citizens of Khulna declared that they had been sacrificed at the altar of division and been exchanged for Murshidabad. While the Khulna Congress representatives petitioned the Congress high command that their district be included in the Indian Union even if it meant an exchange with Murshidabad, local Hindu leaders of Murshidabad appealed against such a potential exchange and accused the Khulna Hindus of being selfish.[53] The boundary award had divided not only Hindus and Muslims but also members within a single community.

Given the level of confusion about the location of the new border, it is not surprising that demands for boundary readjustment followed soon after the boundary award. English and Bengali newspapers carried pleas from individuals, civic organizations, and political groups requesting authorities to change the fate of their particular region. Some sought recourse by sending letters to political authorities such as Jawaharlal Nehru. The Lalbag Mahakuma Rashtriya Samiti (Lalbag Nationalist Union Association) of Murshidabad requested Nehru to define the boundary demarcations for char[54] Sarandaspur, Bhasgara, and the char lands of Jangipur subdivision, and officially declare them to be part of the Indian Union. Their letter emphasized that they had been actively agitating for inclusion within India and thereby had incurred the displeasure of East Pakistan. Unless and until Nehru took steps to right the wrongs done to them, these inhabitants could not return to their land without fear.[55] In their minds, the letter writers had clearly established their loyalties to one nation and now expected the boundary to readjust and conform to their cognitive national identity.

Demands for boundary readjustment along with concurrent inter-dominion border disputes led to the formation of the Indo–Pakistan Boundary Disputes Tribunal in December 1949. Headed by Algot Bagge, member of the Supreme Court of Sweden, this tribunal adjudicated on the actual location of the boundary where the Ganges acted as the border. The Radcliffe award had stated that 'the line shall then turn south east down the river Ganges along the boundary between the districts of Malda and Murshidabad; Rajshahi and Nadia; to the point in the north western corner of the district of Nadia where the channel of the river Mathabhanga takes off from the river Ganges'.[56] The Pakistani member of the tribunal, Justice M. Shahauddin, judge on the Dacca High Court, interpreted this to mean that the border would be a fluid one, shifting with the course of the river. However, the Indian member, N. Chandrashekhara Aiyer, who was a retired judge of the Madras High Court, pointed out that the Radcliffe award also clearly stated, 'The district boundaries and not the actual course of the river Ganges shall constitute the boundary between East and West Bengal'.[57] Thus, Aiyar maintained that Radcliffe had intended the boundary to be a permanent fixed line.

The decision on the boundary was ultimately left in the hands of the chairman of the tribunal and Justice Bagge agreed with Aiyar; he announced that the boundary should be the fixed along the district boundary line of Murshidabad and Rajshahi. However, the Bagge award was also not the final word on the location of the Bengal border.

Subsequent years witnessed a number of negotiations and transfer of territories across the border between India and Pakistan[58] as border disputes and claims of territory continued to be a regular feature of national life in both countries.

The framing of an international border was central to the Partition process. However, it was neither easy nor infallible, and reflected the contingency of the time. In the weeks in which Radcliffe and the Boundary Commission deliberated privately on the location of the new border, educated Bengalis, both Hindus and Muslims, discussed its fate publicly, expressing a desire not only to be part of the process but claiming a stake in their political futures. The task of creating a border based on religious demography was bound to fail and in the end, pleased no one. As we shall see in the next chapter, Radcliffe's award ended up creating an unyielding conundrum for both the people living on either side of the new border and the two new nations who sought to define their territorial limits.

NOTES

1. Report of Justice Mukherjea and Justice Biswas, File Misc. B-1/1947, Home Political (Secret), *Proceedings before the Boundary Commission*, 1947, West Bengal State Archives (henceforth WBSA), Calcutta, p. 13.

2. See an elaboration of this point in my article, 2009, 'A Partition of Contingency? Public Discourse in Bengal, 1946–47', *Modern Asian Studies*, vol. 43, no. 6, November, pp. 1355–84.

3. For details on the voting blocs, see Joya Chatterji, 1999, 'The Fashioning of a Frontier: The Radcliffe Line and Bengal's Border Landscape, 1947–52', *Modern Asian Studies*, vol. 33, no. 1, pp. 188–190, 213.

4. Lucy Chester details the imperatives in the constitution of the Boundary Commission and Radcliffe's logic in delineating the new borders. Her focus, however, is on the border in divided Punjab that presented different geographical and ecological challenges than Bengal. See Lucy Chester, 2009, *Borders and Conflict in South Asia: The Radcliffe Boundary Commission and the Partition of Punjab*, Manchester: Manchester University Press, chapters 3, 4, and 5.

5. 12 June 1947, Nicholas Mansergh (ed.), 1977, *The Transfer of Power 1942–7, Vol. XI*, London: Her Majesty's Stationary Office, p. 158.

6. Chester, *Borders and Conflict in South Asia*, pp. 40–9.

7. Mansergh, *The Transfer of Power*, Appendix 1, p. 488.

8. Some scholars argue that the Partition Council deliberately desisted from attempting to define specific considerations since there were too many issues

to deliberate upon and they had little time. See Anthony Read and David Fisher, 1998, *The Proudest Day: India's Long Road to Independence*, New York: W.W. Norton & Company, p. 483.

9. The Punjab Commission consisted of Justices Din Mohammad, Muhammad Munir, Mehar Chand Mahajan, and Teja Singh. See India (Dominion) Ministry of Information and Broadcasting, 1948, *After Partition*, New Delhi: Publications Division, Government of India, pp. 22–3.

10. Santosh Kumar Mukherji, 1947, *Boundary Problem of New Bengal*, Calcutta: Hindustan Socialist Party, p. 2.

11. *Hindustan Standard* (henceforth *HS*), 25 June 1947, p. 3.

12. Also see Petitions submitted by Magura Sammilani, Chittagong Hill Tracts People's Association. *HS*, 26 June 1947, 3.

13. Such coordinated efforts to gather public opinion by political organizations were not new. Earlier in the year, the Congress and the Hindu Mahasabha received over 400 petitions, mainly from the western districts of Bengal, which urged in favor of partitioning the province. File: G-54/1947,Part I; CL-14 (A)/ 1946; CL-14 (B)/1946-47, *All India Congress Committee* (henceforth *AICC*) *Papers*, Nehru Memorial and Museum Library (henceforth NMML), New Delhi.

14. At this point, the Bengal Provincial Muslim League was divided into two factions: one led by Nazimuddin, who was close to Jinnah and the All India Muslim League; and the other led by Suhrawardy who, along with Abul Hashim, had floated the United Bengal Plan and was publicly against the partition of Bengal. It was the Nazimuddin faction who presented a case for East Bengal to the Boundary Commission. For more details on the schism within the Bengal Muslim League, see Shila Sen, 1976, *Muslim Politics in Bengal, 1937–1947*, New Delhi: Impex India, pp. 203–45.

15. In the colonial administrative structure, a presidency or province was divided into a number of divisions, each comprising of a number of districts. Each district was again divided into a number of *taluka*s or *tehsil*s. Three to four talukas together constituted a subdivision.

16. Report of Justice Akram and Justice Rahman, *Proceedings before the Bengal Boundary Commission*, 1947, WBSA, Calcutta, pp. 1–26.

17. Report of Justice Mukherjea and Justice Biswas, pp. 1–65. The non-Muslim members of the Boundary Commission pointed out that the census population figures were only available for the thanas and not for unions, thus making it difficult to accede to the League definition.

18. Report of Justice Akram and Justice Rahman, pp. 24–5.

19. *HS*, 25 June 1947, p. 3.

20. The Namasudras were one of two main Scheduled Caste groups in Bengal, the other being the Rajbanshis. Known as *Chandals* of Bengal, they inhabited the mainly the eastern districts of Dacca, Bakrganj, Faridpur, Mymensingh, Jessore,

and Khulna. Sekhar Bandyopadhyay has argued that in the context of Partition politics, 'religion' replaced 'caste' solidarities as the Scheduled Castes joined the Hindu nationalist groups to agitate for a Hindu homeland. For details, see Sekhar Bandyopadhyay, 1997, *Caste, Protest and Identity in Colonial India: The Namasudras of Bengal, 1872–1947*, Richmond, Surrey: Curzon Press.

21. The Hindu Mahasabha and the New Bengal Association submitted a separate memorandum to the Boundary Commission. Joya Chatterji, 2007, *The Spoils of Partition: Bengal and India, 1947–1967*, Cambridge: Cambridge University Press, pp. 32–4.

22. *Ibid.*, p. 41.

23. Report of Justice Mukherjea and Justice Biswas, p. 3.

24. *Ibid.*, pp. 34–5.

25. See, for example, Chatterji, *The Spoils of Partition* and Tai Yong Tan and Gyanesh Kudaisya, 2000, *The Aftermath of Partition in South Asia*, London: Routledge.

26. *Bengal Boundary Commission, Memorandum Submitted by Various Non-Muslim Parties Before the Commission*, 24 (19)-Pak III/55, Part III, Ministry of External Affairs (henceforth MEA), Government of India (henceforth GoI), 1955, National Archives of India (henceforth NAI), Delhi. Also see, *Memoranda Submitted by Various Muslim Organizations and Parties other than the Provincial Muslim League*, 24(18)-PIII/55, Pak III, MEA, 1955, GoI, NAI, Delhi.

27. See, for example, the petitions from Sanatan Dharma Parishad, Calcutta, South-Bikrampur Sammilani, Idilpur Seva Samity, and others, included in *Bengal Boundary Commission, Memorandum Submitted by Various Non-Muslim Parties Before the Commission*.

28. *Ibid.*, p. 7.

29. Petition from Jogendra Lal Nandy on behalf of the Hindus of Vikrampur, Mymensingh, 11 July 1947, in *Bengal Boundary Commission, Memorandum Submitted by Various Non-Muslim Parties Before the Commission*.

30. *HS*, 11 July 1947, p. 4.

31. Statement by Dr P.N. Bannerjee, former leader of the Nationalist Party, Pandit L.K. Maitra, M.N. Mahalonobis, P.R. Thakur, and B.C. Mukherjee, in *HS*, 1947, 'Hindu Bengal: Question of Determining Right Boundary', 7 June, p. 4.

32. Tinkari Bagchi, Letter to the Editor, *HS*, 12 July 1947, p. 4.

33. *Ibid.*

34. Joya Chatterji, 1994, *Bengal Divided: Hindu Communalism and Partition, 1932–1947*, Cambridge: Cambridge University Press.

35. Bandyopadhyay, *Caste, Protest and Identity in Colonial India*.

36. Mukherji, *Boundary Problem of New Bengal*, pp. 20–1.

37. People of the Ranaghat Subdivision, 'Memorandum to the Bengal Boundary Commission', 15 July 1947, in *Bengal Boundary Commission, Memorandum Submitted by Various Non-Muslim Parties Before the Commission*.

38. 'Memorandum on behalf of Muslim Citizens' Committee of Calcutta', in *Memoranda Submitted by Various Muslim Organizations and Parties other than the Provincial Muslim League.*

39. 'Memorandum submitted to the Boundary Commission on behalf of the Muslims of 24 Parganas and Calcutta by The Study Circle' (*ibid.*).

40. *Ibid.*

41. Letter to Lord Listowel from S.M. Usam, ex-Mayor of Calcutta and President Indian National Maritime Union, Mr Abdus Sabur Khan, Member of Legislative Assembly (MLA), and Mr Mahisuddin Ahmed, President and Vice President, Bengal Jute Growers Association, Calcutta, in protest against any scheme of partitioning of Bengal, 22 May 1947 (approx.), in File no. L/P&J/7/12068 6076, January 1947–January 1948, Political Department, Oriental and India Office Collections (OIOC), London.

42. 'Memorandum of Astagram Pallimangal Samity, Backerganj' (*ibid.*).

43. Telegram postmarked 23 August 1947, *Boundary Commissions of Punjab and Bengal: Petitions, Memoranda and Telegrams and Protests,* August 1947–October 1948, IOR: L/P&J/7/12465 9920, Oriental and India Office Library.

44. Telegram postmarked 22 August 1947 (*ibid.*).

45. India (Dominion) Ministry of Information and Broadcasting, *After Partition,* p. 31.

46. Joya Chatterji has argued that the Congress were tacitly willing to exchange Hindu-majority Khulna for Muslim-majority Murshidabad in order to ensure that the Hoogly river system remained within India. Chatterji, *The Spoils of Partition,* p. 59.

47. During the seventeenth century, as the Mughals expanded in Bengal, they failed to occupy parts of Cooch Behar which remained under the control of independent landlords. Conversely, the Mughals were able to acquire pieces of territory within Cooch Behar which were taxed by Mughal landlords. Both such pieces of territory came to known as *chits*. In the nineteenth century and up until 1947, Cooch Behar's status as a friendly princely state meant that it was never under direct colonial rule. The boundary award included only lands which were directly part of the British empire which meant that those chits which had become part of the colonial empire were awarded to East Pakistan. When Cooch Behar opted to join India, its enclaves in East Pakistan became part of India. Meanwhile, pieces of land which had belonged to the British empire and had been awarded to East Pakistan remained within India. For details on the origins and current status of these enclaves, see Willem Van Schendel, 2002, 'Stateless in South Asia: The Making of India–Bangladesh Enclaves', *The Journal of Asian Studies,* vol. 61, no. 1, February, pp. 115–47.

48. Reported in D.F. Ebright, 1954, *Free India: The First Five Years,* Nashville: Parthenon Press, p. 25.

49. Speech by N.C. Chatterjee, a prominent Hindu Mahasabhite, at University Institute Hall (*HS*, 24 August 1947, p. 4).

50. *HS*, 1947, 'The Award', 20 August, p. 4.

51. Telegrams postmarked 18, 23, and 26 August 1947, and 6 October 1948, File no. L/P&J/7/12465 9920, *Boundary Commissions of Punjab and Bengal: Petitions, Memoranda, Telegrams, and Protests*, August 1947–October 1948, OIOC, London.

52. Telegram postmarked 26 August 1947 (*ibid.*). Other Muslim groups like the District Muslim Welfare Society of Noakhali also sent petitions urging a change in the award (*ibid*). Telegram postmarked 26 August 1947.

53. Letter from Ramgopal Banerjea to Acharya Kripalani, 10 September 1947, File no. G 33/1947, *AICC Papers*, NMML, New Delhi.

54. Alluvial plains that existed in the middle of large rivers like the Ganges and the Padma which were sometimes large enough to have villages on them.

55. Letter 15 March 1948 from Jitendranath Roy to J. Nehru, File no. 12-12/48, Pak I, MEA, GoI, 1949, NAI.

56. *Decisions of the Indo-Pakistan Boundary Disputes Tribunal 1949*, 1958, Delhi: Government of India, p. 19.The tribunal also deliberated on boundary disputes between East Bengal and Assam.

57. *Ibid.*

58. The Indo-Pakistan Agreement of 10 September 1958 awarded portions of Beruabari Union to East Pakistan, and came to an agreement on the exchange of the Cooch Behar enclaves. For more details on the enclaves along the India–East Pakistan border, see Schendel, 'Stateless in South Asia'.

2

Limits of the Nation

On 8 May 1952, several men and women were reaping boro paddy along the border between Malda (India) and Rajshahi (East Bengal) as usual when some East Pakistani border policemen, accompanied by one Moulavi Karim Shah of Porsha, Rajshahi, crossed over and kidnapped these peasants. Karim Shah claimed that the land belonged to him and these peasants were trespassing. The Indian government claimed that the land in question belonged to an Indian national by the name of Ramdayal Prasad Bhakat and sent an official letter of protest to the Government of East Bengal which stated in no uncertain terms that:

This government strongly protest against (sic) such repeated infringements of Indian territory by your policemen posted in this area who have been found indulging in most objectionable acts of high-handedness and with impunity. Such incidents are bound to create bitterness and disturb the maintenance of law and order on the border. I am accordingly to request (sic) that if there is no objection, immediate steps maybe taken to release the kidnapped Indian nationals and also to bring the offending policemen to book with a view to stop the recurrence of similar incidents in this particular are (sic).[1]

The above incident and the response it generated between India and East Pakistan is neither singular nor did it generate a 'flashpoint' of international hostility beyond the official protest. In fact, it was generic, like the hundreds of border incidents that were recorded each year in the files of each country. However, each of these routine border incidents was symptomatic of larger processes at work which contributed to the making of new international border. These disputes operated largely due to the fact that although Radcliffe had clearly delineated the border on paper, it could not as easily be demarcated on ground. Up until the 1970s, there were hardly any physical markers of territorial sovereignty to guide and warn the people on the ground when they had mistakenly or deliberately crossed nations. Moreover, as this chapter will show, border disputes became a method through which the new states communicated and practised their newly required skills of diplomatic exchanges.

A NATIONAL FRONTIER

The importance of the Bengal border as a national frontier was not lost on the authorities in Calcutta or Dacca and they quickly proceeded to establish tools to monitor and ensure the integrity of their territorial nations. Border outposts, spaced within a few miles of each other and manned by newly recruited policemen and custom officers, were set up almost immediately after the Partition. By 1949, Pakistan had increased the number of border outposts on the north Bengal border from eighty-five to 162.[2] East Pakistan had to set up a new government from scratch, which meant large-scale recruitment of new manpower and the creation of an army corps, the East Bengal Regiment, and a paramilitary force, the Eastern Pakistan Rifles. For India, the process was relatively easier since it had inherited the colonial centres of power in this region, but it also deployed police and border militias to guard the new frontiers.[3] Along with armed sentinels, the border was also the location for other state personnel from the customs department and after 1952, from the Ministry of External Affairs (MEA) that regulated entry and exit from one nation to the other.

Fear of loss of territory was a constant feature of national anxieties about the international border, accentuated by the ecological shifting of natural boundaries and the theft of manmade pillars marking the limits of the nations.[4] In defining the border, Radcliffe had also used natural features such as rivers as boundaries. However, rivers changed courses over time and this also generated confusion amongst border dwellers and border officials alike. Some of these rivers remained dry except during monsoons when they would flood their banks, obscuring the borderline completely. The Mathabhanga, which formed the border for the north-western part of Nadia, India, illustrates the confusions that arose out of such ecological issues. The dated Bengal Government Press map that Radcliffe had consulted did not chart the current course of the river Mathabhanga that formed an important part of the new border.[5] Consequently, almost 500 square miles of territory inadvertently went to Pakistan instead of India.[6] Organizations such as the New Bengal Association took up this particular issue in their demands for boundary readjustments in the post-Partition period.

Radcliffe's use of rivers as boundary lines created other problems. In April of 1957, the District Magistrate of 24 Parganas reported that Pakistani policemen had seized a country boat loaded with grocery goods and belonging to an Indian national when it was plying along the midstream in the river Ichamati.[7] Although similar to other cases of trespassing into Indian and East Pakistani territory, this incident was of particular significance because only parts of the river Ichamati were in Pakistan territory.[8] The authorities of both dominions decided to prohibit use of the entire width of the navigable river between Sodepur and Bhatchhala by the boatmen of both sides in the interest of border peace and Indo-Pakistani trade.

The new border was ecologically challenged due to chars, alluvial plains that existed in the middle of large rivers like the Ganges and the Padma. The Padma River, which divided Murshidabad, India, from Rajshahi, Pakistan, was dotted with such chars, which at times were large enough to have entire villages built upon them. Immediately after Partition, the alleged East Pakistani 'occupation' of char Sarandaspur, one of the biggest char areas on the Padma, provided the background for the deployment of military forces of India and Pakistan at the border.[9] Inter-dominion talks at the highest official level managed to diffuse the situation, and both countries agreed to treat this area as no-man's land and withdraw their armed forces five miles away from the char.

Such claims to national territory became part of routine border disputes in subsequent years. After the monsoons of 1957, some Pakistani nationals and policemen attempted to take possession of new char lands that had appeared on the other side of the Murshidabad–Rajshahi border, claiming them to be Pakistani territory.[10] The issue was resolved with the agreement that Pakistan would stop sending patrols to the disputed area and the Indian patrol party would not cross the river just below the disputed char.

The disputes over the char lands cropped up not only in terms of boundary demarcation but also in terms of territorial sovereignty and national citizenship as expressed in the right to tax the char inhabitants. In the summer of 1948, news reached the Indian authorities that East Pakistani officials were carrying out unilateral surveys of villages within the boundaries of Murshidabad district and detaining crops grown by Indian cultivators on their own char lands. The Indian authorities saw such action as direct encroachment on their territory and decided to take over the rent collection and *khas mahal* (government-owned land) management of these chars immediately.[11] In addition, the inhabitants were informed by the beat of drums that char lands were part of Murshidabad and India, and that the producers were free to bring back their paddy 'by any means within their power and that if they do not assert their rights we [Indian government] shall not be responsible for their starvation'.[12] Thus, the residents could prove their citizenship to India by resisting East Pakistani authorities. The fact that most of the population in this area was Muslims further complicated and obscured the line between residency and national allegiance.

WHO GETS TO CROSS THE BORDER?

Border disputes, in some ways, were the means to establish each state's sovereignty, and to convey the meaning of a border, as a line that differentiated between domestic and foreign, to the people who lived in the borderland and to those who had hitherto travelled across the region routinely. For the new states, the border was now also the putative line, which would define routine travel and set apart and categorize travellers. Disagreements over the demarcation of territory led to claims of 'trespassing' by livestock and people. Cattle proved to be a nuisance for official intent on preserving the sanctity of the boundary as they grazed wherever they wanted.[13] Local cattle lifting became international disputes as each country reported that nationals of the other country had not only trespassed but had carried away herds of cattle, sometimes including the 'cowboy'.[14]

The trouble with cows became so pervasive that officials of the border districts had to devise a plan to deal with such trespassing and thievery. At the Border Conference in 1953, Indian and Pakistani officials decided that if stray cattle were found on either side of the border, the officer-in-charge of the zonal border outpost would file a report and inform his opposite number immediately. Efforts would be made to find the bona fide owner and hand over the cows once his credibility had been established.[15] Subsequently, both governments also evolved a system of permits that would allow cow herders to graze their cattle away from the border. But such measures failed to prevent either the straying of cows or their theft by nationals of the other country. For example, on 25 January 1964, some Pakistani nationals allegedly entered Indian territory at Tentulia on the Malda–Rajshahi border and 'forcibly lifted 378 head of cattle and 11 sheep belonging to Indian nationals and kidnapped a cowboy'.[16] Indian officials immediately sent telegraphic protests to the Pakistani authorities and claimed that not one but two cowboys had been kidnapped and that one was rumored to have been killed. In his reply, the Deputy Commissioner of Rajshahi declared the allegations of trespass and kidnapping to be 'totally false and baseless'.[17] He claimed that upon enquiry, it was found that a Pakistani patrol party had seized 300 heads of cattle that were found to be damaging public property on the Pakistan side. They had found no claimant for these cattle and had disposed of them as unclaimed property. Thus, the question of returning cattle did not arise. This dispute was later resolved by the recovery of 278 heads of cattle from Pakistan and with the promulgation of new documentary regulations that required cow herders to get permits from block development officials on the Indian side to graze their animals near the border.[18]

The seasonal migration of Muslim labourers from East Pakistan, who crossed the border to work on the paddy and jute fields, or the tea gardens of Darjeeling and Jalpaiguri, also came under the purview of such national anxieties. The West Bengal government's policy with regard to such migration was clear: as long as the border crossers were casual labourers who entered India for work and then returned home to East Pakistan after a certain period of time, the government did not challenge them. However, it became a security issue if these labourers decided to settle on the Indian side. The case of some Pakistani Muslim labourers working in tea gardens owned by Janab (Nawab) Musharraf Hussain illustrates the complexities of such fears. Trouble started when the Deputy Commissioner of Jalpaiguri, a border district where Musharraf Hussain owned four tea gardens, found that the latter was ostensibly 'importing' Pakistani Muslims under the guise of casual labourers and settling them on vacant land in his estates.[19] Although the officials acknowledged that in pre-Partition days, tea garden labourers tended to settle in the areas where they worked, such a practice could not now be 'viewed with complacence'. When Musharraf Hussain protested to higher authorities in Calcutta and Delhi, claiming that such a curb on recruitment would affect the production of tea, the West Bengal government pointed out the easy availability of Indian labourers from Bihar who worked in the tea gardens in high numbers and 'who can be depended upon to be loyal to the state'.[20] The Indian government made it clear that the 'question of security in the area is however vitally involved ... and vastly outweigh the alleged interests of production of a little more tea'.[21]

Such anxieties were also influenced by the perception that minorities in each country were potential fifth columnists. Several high-level officials in India, including Sukumar Sen, the then Chief Secretary of West Bengal, alleged that the East Pakistan government had taken steps 'to eliminate all Hindus from a depth of about 10 miles from the (East Pakistani) border'.[22] In addition, intelligence reports noted that there was a 'deliberate movement to import Pakistani Muslims and settle them in the (Indian) border areas in that the Muslim preponderance here might, later on, be urged as a ground for annexing these areas to Pakistan'.[23] As preventive measures, the West Bengal government often externed those Muslims who, they felt, had deliberately encouraged the immigration of Muslims from East Bengal. Further, in some cases where Muslims had transferred land to Muslim newcomers from the east, the West Bengal government had requisitioned the land for the purposes of resettling Hindu refugees from East Bengal.[24] Demographic homogeneity at the border made a lot of 'sense' to officials both in India and East Pakistan, although it was never a publicly stated policy.[25]

Concern over the migration of Muslim citizens from East Pakistan into West Bengal and Assam continued to influence the Indian government's policies on border issues and the granting of citizenship rights.[26] Even when it became clear that the Muslim migrants, rather than occupying vacant lands and claiming ownership, were more likely to be absorbed within the labour force and existing kinship networks, the Government of India remained suspicious of their intentions.[27] In 1950, the Assam government passed an ordinance to order the removal of any persons deemed to have come to the state from outside of India and 'whose stay in the State is detrimental to the interests of India'.[28] Sure enough, this controversial ordinance aimed to address both the issue of *infiltration* by East Pakistani Muslims and the *migration* of East Pakistani Hindus. Moreover, the timing of the ordinance coincided with language politics within the state that aimed to evict non-Assamese-speaking groups. Policies at the border thus helped to nationalize both territory and the people who inhabited that region and used the border on a regular basis.

AN ECONOMIC FRONTIER

Initially, in Bengal, the border demarcated a political line of division between India and Pakistan. Several agreements between the new states promised free trade and the uninterrupted flow of goods and people across the Bengal border. This was in contradistinction to the border policies set forth in the west, where restrictions on the free flow of goods and people came into being by the middle of 1948. The Standstill Agreement concluded before the Partition emphasized the interdependence of the new nations and the need for open borders.[29] Such a policy of free trade stipulated that the two dominions should not establish any customs barriers or impose prohibitory excise taxes on goods before they agreed on long-term trade policies with each other.

Unlike the western border where both India and Pakistan set up a permit system to control human traffic, the states took a laissez-faire attitude on the eastern front, allowing free movement of people. This was partly influenced by the perception that migration in the east was going to be a temporary phenomenon. Officials hoped that freedom of movement would allay doubts and insecurities in the minds of minorities in the region and encourage return migration. Thus, migrants, both Hindus and Muslims, were allowed to retain titles to their lands on either side of the border. At the Inter-Dominion Conference in Calcutta in April 1948, Jawaharlal Nehru and Liaqat Ali Khan agreed to set up Evacuee Management Boards on both sides of the Bengal border to safeguard evacuee property until the rightful owners returned to claim them.[30] Further, border dwellers who now lived in one country and worked in the other were allowed free movement across the border on a daily basis. In February 1948, representatives of East and West Bengal agreed to 'allow nationals of one state to move the produce of his land lying in another state in the border areas'.[31] Additionally, transit trade—transport of goods from one country going to another part of that country through the territory of the other country—was permitted. This benefited India more than Pakistan as the former had to maintain its connection with states in the north-east by sending goods via rail through East Pakistan. In theory, the new border aimed to disrupt as little as possible the lives of those that it divided. In practice, the Bengal border soon became an economic frontier that began to regulate not only goods but also people.

With the expiration of the Standstill Agreement in February 1948, both countries began the process of setting up departments of customs and excise to regulate trade along the border. The Indian government set up thirty-nine land customs offices on the Bengal border and twenty-two on the Assam border with East Pakistan.[32] The Standstill Agreement had cautioned against placing customs barriers on a border that had no natural boundary lines and had yet to be demarcated in certain areas. Further, it had noted the difficulty of enforcing measures to prevent smuggling across a border 1,350 miles long, traversed by many waterways, railways, and roads. Despite such warnings, both countries sought to tap the potential for revenue from regulating border trade and thus declared that, for the purposes of customs and excise, the other country would be considered 'foreign' territory.

The imposition of customs barriers had the immediate effect of creating confusion among traders, especially those who dealt in perishable items such as fish, eggs, milk, and vegetables. The Sealdah Fish Aratdars Association made a representation to the local customs authorities about the enormous difficulties experienced by the fish trade due to customs barriers.[33] Permits for export licences, which could only be issued from Delhi, compounded the problem. Such a lengthy process meant that the fish and other perishable items languished at train stations. In an effort to solve the problem, the Indian government quickly declared the perishable items exempt from customs duties.

The expansion of bureaucracy and militia into the border zone meant the disruption of the regular economic activities and social life of those who lived in this area. The case of Dr Gaur Chandra Ray of Fulbari, India, illustrates how the border created barriers in the pursuit of one's occupation. Dr Ray resided in India, while his dispensary was located in Kushtia, Pakistan. On 12 March 1948, while returning home with some medicines, two constables of the Kazipur police camp arrested him and robbed him of his belongings. He was ultimately released upon payment of bail of Rs 2,000.[34]

More frequently, the border severed villages from the markets that served them, forcing villagers of one dominion to cross the border to access items for their daily use. As purchasing supplies in the other country could be construed as anti-national, the routine exercise of going to the market began to assume international significance. The local Muslim League condemned the situation in which the villagers at the Sylhet border had to travel across the international border to the local bazaar at Dawki to purchase *pan* (betel leaf), and orange, pineapple, and rice saplings, where they faced harassment from the Indian border officials.[35] The resolution cited the case of Idris Ali, a tea stall owner, who had been arrested by the Indian police on the accusation that he was a Pakistani spy. In response and as a solution, a local bazaar at Tambil was established and the Additional District Magistrate of Sylhet ordered the villagers from the Pakistani not to go to the Dawki bazaar. However, subsequently, the official order was cancelled and people again started frequenting the bazaar across the border.

The border dwellers circumvented state mechanisms for controlling their movement either by bribing officials or moving their goods clandestinely. For instance, Kalu Muhammad Chaudhuri, a potato dealer from Jagirpara, Dinajpur (Pakistan), had given the Pakistan Police and Muslim National Guards Rs 15 to be allowed to cross to the Sarbamangla Hut in India.[36]

Policies regulating the flow of commodities across the Bengal border were influenced by two considerations, both of which contributed to the development of uncertainty and unpredictability of life at the border. First, the ups and downs of the inter-dominion relationship between India and Pakistan translated directly into changes in policies to allow or boycott certain goods. Second, the lack of centralization meant that officials in Delhi, Dacca, and Karachi had little control over the activities of border officials. Although officials were expected 'to use their discretion and expected that they would use such discretion with imagination and tact',[37] they often resorted to harassment for pecuniary gains. Commodities were confiscated, detained, or purposely lost at the discretion of such officials. For example, in March 1948, when Murari Mohan Dey and Amulya Chandra Dutta were transporting two boats loaded with bell metal utensils from Nawabganj, Pakistan, to Malda, India, Pakistani military patrolmen arrested them despite of the fact that they had a legal government permit to export their merchandise. They and their goods were released only after they paid Rs 500 to the commander of the patrol station.[38]

Traders often had to satisfy different groups of border officials from the same side of the border. In April 1948, the Pakistan border police arrested some cobblers from West Bengal who had crossed over to East Pakistan on a work permit as they were returning home. The police released them after receiving a bribe. Then the Muslim National Guards arrested them again on the same trip and demanded another bribe.[39] Competition over bribes ensured that different state departments at the border did not develop cordial relations with each other, thus further hampering the implementation of any consolidated border policy.[40]

Harassment ranged from the confiscation of both personal and trade commodities to ignominious body searches and the unlawful detention of border crossers. Hindus and Muslims, both post-Partition emigrants and regular travellers, were vulnerable to the whims of the nations' sentinels.[41] Sasanka Bose, like many others, wrote about his grievances to the major newspapers hoping for redress from the concerned ministries. In one such letter, he noted that at Sealdah station, a major railway junction and transit point for post-Partition migrants, there was no list specifying what commodities were not allowed to be taken across the border into East Pakistan. This meant that travellers had little idea of what they could and could not carry in their luggage. Even though passengers were allowed to carry ten yards of cloth, Bose noted that the officials 'were disinclined to allow even a single yard'.[42] He claimed that items of daily use such as soap and razor blades were routinely confiscated. Harassment at the border, according to an Indian intelligence official, had a modus operandi: 'Guards would threaten to search only the women members of the evacuee group trying to cross the border. To avoid the humiliation of their women, male members among the evacuees then purchase exemption from such a search by giving away to them their cash jewelry and other valuable moveable property.'[43]

To address these problems of harassment, India and Pakistan agreed to appoint liaison officers at each customs post who would be in charge of preventing the harassment of minorities.[44] Inter-dominion relationships at the border helped shape the idea of majority and minority identity, as each nation claimed minorities in the other country as their responsibility. As part of the process of regulating the border, India, despite its professed claims to a secular national identity, became accountable for the well-being of the Hindus of Pakistan. East Pakistan, given the logic of its birth as a homeland of the Muslims, found it less contradictory to lay claim to the Muslims who still resided within India's newly formed boundaries.

One of the immediate consequences of the delimitation and regulation of economic goods was the rise in smuggling across the border. Rice, cloth, kerosene oil, and salt were smuggled from India, and jute, betel nuts, and chillies were the main products smuggled from East Pakistan.[45] Partition had placed 71 per cent of jute-growing lands in East Pakistan and all the 104 jute mills and bailing presses in India.[46] Sustenance of the jute mills created a severe demand for the raw material, which was further accentuated by India's imposition of customs duty on that item. Also, both India and Pakistan suffered from severe food shortages in the years after the Partition and were keen to prevent foodgrains such as rice from crossing the borders. Trade agreements placed restrictions on the trade of both rice and jute and these commodities were the most frequently smuggled from respective countries.

In addition to inter-dominion trade agreements, the administrative officials of the border districts in India implemented several measures to check the smuggling of items such as cloth and sugar to Pakistan. The District Magistrate of Nadia issued a directive which forced cloth dealers to sell their merchandise only in the presence of an authorized officer, and in addition, prevented them from selling to persons without ration cards and permits.[47] Similarly, when Nadia district officials discovered that women in Ranaghat were smuggling sugar by carrying it on their heads at night, they prohibited all sale of sugar at night in that area.[48]

For some villagers living in the borderlands, smuggling provided an economic opportunity that they exploited to the hilt. Indian intelligence officials observed in 1964 that smuggling had become a 'normal affair' and 'people living in both sides of the border very often indulge in smuggling which has been a very lucrative avocation for them'.[49] The report concluded that the smuggling was 'carried out under the tacit support of the police'.[50] Border dwellers thus had an ambivalent relationship with the local agents of the state. Although the presence of these officials created an obstacle to normal trade, by enlisting their tacit support through bribes and other favours, the border residents subverted the state structures aimed to control their activities.

Understandably, India and Pakistan were distressed at the loss of revenue resulting from these activities and launched an extensive anti-smuggling drive. Prafulla C. Sen, the Civil Supplies Minister in the West Bengal government, issued a stern warning to all producers and traders that the smuggling of food was a serious crime and that it was their 'patriotic duty' not to undertake such activities.[51] Similarly, S.M. Afzal, the East Pakistani Food Minister, in December 1948, warned smugglers in the border districts that 'they would meet their fate at the hands of the military and civil patrols posted along the borders and for such people there should be no sympathy shown in any quarters'.[52] Prevention of smuggling now became associated with one's national duty, and the border citizens were asked to prove their patriotism by putting a stop to it.

Besides government officials, some citizens of West Bengal also voiced their grievances against smugglers and urged strict actions against them. Shyamapada Bhattacharjee, a Member of the Legislative Assembly (MLA) from Behrampore, Murshidabad, a border district with a Muslim-majority population, combined religion, smuggling, and anti-national sentiments when he claimed that such illicit activities were carried out mainly by the Muslims in the area. He pointed out that while essential goods such as cloth and sugar were not available in Indian markets, such commodities were available in 'good quantities in areas of Pakistan bordering the Indian Union ... these goods are being mostly smuggled by people who style themselves as citizens of the Indian Union'. These smugglers showed a 'total indifference and lack of patriotism' and were 'shamefully denuding the union of its wealth'.[53] According to Bhattacharjee, 75 per cent of the smugglers were Muslims and thus, it was no surprise that they were engaged in unpatriotic activities aimed at the economic debilitation of the Indian nation.

On the East Pakistan side, there were similar associations of smuggling and patriotism. S.M. Siddiqui, a petty merchant based in Dacca, appealed to the East Pakistan Prime Minister to stop the smuggling, arguing that such activities not only were weakening the country financially but also would ultimately result in forcible union with India. According to Siddiqui, the primary duty of every Pakistani citizen was to stop smuggling and urged that it should be one of the first tasks addressed by Prime Minister of Pakistan as a way of establishing his credibility and ability to guide the country economically.[54]

Along with declaring smuggling as 'anti-national' and 'unpatriotic', India and East Pakistan took some concrete measures to curb such illegal activities at the border. As a part of the national defence planning, the Government of West Bengal (GoWB) proposed the construction of three aerodromes in the border districts of Nadia, 24 Parganas, and Murshidabad, along with a road connecting Calcutta to the border. Government officials claimed that these measures, when implemented, would 'provide better facilities of easy communication between the capital and the border regions of the province and put Government in a better position to stop smuggling of various commodities'.[55] Further, concrete pillars would be placed along the border and riverbanks to demarcate the boundaries of the two states. In addition, East Pakistan and West Bengal set up private militias to prevent smuggling as well as instruct border citizens of their patriotic duties. The GoWB announced plans to raise an army of 15,000 men by the middle of 1948 to check smuggling and 'subversive' activities at 600 frontier posts and established a special battalion to guard the 50 mile natural barrier along the river Ganges.[56] B.C. Roy announced that such arrangements would be beneficial 'for training villagers in border areas to defend themselves and to act in collaboration with the police in the neighborhood to assist them in stopping smuggling'.[57]

On the Indian side, semi-military volunteer corps came into being under the patronage of prominent individuals like Uday Chand Mahtab, the Maharaja of Burdwan. Initially registered as the *Bangiya Jatiya Rakshi Dal* (Bengal National Protection Brigade), this non-official association sought to train youths of the seven border districts of Darjeeling, Jalpaiguri, West Dinajpur, Malda, Murshidabad, Nadia, and 24 Parganas to 'protect the frontiers of West Bengal from any aggression by evil minded persons'.[58] A training centre was established at Kanchrapara under a permanent officer of the Indian government with war experience[59] where 1,982 volunteers were trained in 1952. During the period of training, originally sixty days but later extended to seventy-five days, recruits received free accommodation, meals, uniforms, and medical treatment, in addition to an honorarium of Rs 5 per month, making this a lucrative employment for some. Later in the year, this Brigade was incorporated into the West Bengal National Volunteer Force, which the Government of India funded, and was required to function in collaboration with the police in the maintenance of law and order in the province.

In East Pakistan, the state carried out an extensive recruitment campaign and formed the *Ansar Bahini* in early 1948. The name 'Ansar' was adopted as 'expressing within itself the historical and religious significance, the whole ideal of voluntary service to the community and to the nation', while 'Bahini' literally translates to army.[60] Although membership to this organization was open to all male Pakistanis between the ages of eighteen and forty-five, volunteers mainly consisted of Muslim youth who had been in the recently demobilized Muslim National Guards. The mandate of the Ansar Bahini was to help maintain the safety and security in rural areas as well as to mobilize resources to expand the local infrastructure. However, because East Pakistan's civil structure had yet to come into full force, there was a break of communication between higher authorities at Dacca and those operating at the local and rural levels. This disjuncture often led the lower echelons of the Ansar Bahini to use their police powers in an arbitrary and exploitative manner.

In September 1952, East Pakistan promulgated the Prevention of Smuggling Ordinance, and deployed the Pakistan Army to take action against what was termed as 'The Number One Enemy of Pakistan'. The army was authorized to employ extreme measures against perceived smugglers, including the authority to shoot to kill.[61] This initiative was primarily taken to prevent the smuggling of jute and cotton but could possibly encompass other items. An editorial in the *Dawn* reported that 'Numerous imported articles like crockery, watches, fountain pens, and medicines, besides gold and silver bullion were found to be the stock-in-trade of the smugglers. Smuggling of these imported articles to Bharat meant depletion of our sterling and dollar resources for the benefit of Bharat.'[62] The range of these items indicates that migrants and evacuees who crossed the border with all their belongings also came under the purview of the army personnel. Three weeks after the Pakistan army had been deployed at the Bengal border, the East Pakistan government declared the anti-smuggling drive a success with a rise in the prices of jute within Pakistan.

The respective governments intended these militias to deter smugglers, to protect the border, and to imbue the border citizens with the ideals of national citizenship. However, in reality, they often engendered communal antagonism. Allegations were hurled back and forth between India and Pakistan that respective border militias were inducing minority citizens to migrate to the other country. The East Pakistan government claimed that the Santhals[63] of Jagannathpur, Pakistan, had been induced by some Hindus of the Congress to leave their homes and cross over to India where they would be given Muslim houses.[64] After conducting a local investigation, the Indian government denied such allegations. It, in turn, accused the Pakistani border militia of oppressing the Santhals who were then forced to temporarily evacuate their homes. It is impossible to untangle what actually occurred but the given incident provides an insight into the confusion and antagonism that prevailed at the border. The Ansar Bahini were responsible for burning Muslim evacuee houses on the West Bengal side of the border so that Hindu refugees would not be able to use these for rehabilitation. In addition, this ensured that the Muslim evacuee from India would not be able to return to his home in the future, making his/her decision to migrate to East Pakistan a permanent one.[65]

A DOCUMENT REGIME

When it came to Partition migrants, India and Pakistan followed two different policies at their western and eastern borders. In the western frontier that divided the erstwhile Punjab province, both governments sought to regulate the flow of human traffic by requiring them to acquire 'permission' from appropriate authorities to enter either India or Pakistan. In 1948, the Indian government promulgated the Influx from Pakistan (Control) Ordinance, which made it mandatory for border crossers from West Pakistan to acquire a permit.[66] Although it did not explicitly identify who did or did not require a permit, since most of the Hindu migration from Pakistan had abated by the end of 1947, the system, in effect, was designed to prevent the return migration of Muslims who had gone to Pakistan during the Partition violence but now sought to return to their homes in India.[67] An official Indian publication justified such a step thus: 'The return of Muslims will impose a heavy strain upon the economy of the Dominion [India]. Cognizant of this danger, the government of India has recently introduced the permit system to check this movement.'[68] On its part, Pakistan, worried about the strained economic resources facing the new nation, also instituted mechanisms to stem the flow of Muslims from India. In essence, the border on the west was closed and migration across it was regulated through a documentary regime.

The Bengal border, on the other hand, was initially open for migration and people crossed back and forth without any requirement of permits.[69] This permissiveness reflected the official belief that refugees from East Pakistan would return to their homes once local situations improved. For India, refugee rehabilitation on its eastern borders was a financial strain on the provincial and central economies. For Pakistan, the migration of the Hindu refugees signified its inability to provide security to its minorities. By keeping the border open, both governments hoped to restore confidence in the minds of the minorities and induce them to return to their homes. Further, the lack of large-scale violence on the eastern front created the perception among policymakers in India and Pakistan that migration in this region was unwarranted and would abate as soon as the political situation normalized.

The turning point in this policy of open borders can be traced to two major political moments in the region. First, the riots of 1950 in East Pakistan and West Bengal which began as a communist uprising but soon took on communal colors, elicited major cross-border migration. Hindus from East Bengal and Muslims from West Bengal and Bihar moved across the border in record numbers throughout 1951 and 1952. The Delhi Pact of 1950, concluded right after the riots, guaranteed citizenship rights to minorities in each nation, and both India and Pakistan promised to protect evacuee properties in their territories until the return of their owners but the Pact had limited success in promoting a return flow of evacuees back to their original countries. Such large-scale migrations generated increasing support for a closed border, where each nation could regulate and control movement.

Second, the riots in Dacca in early 1952, in protest against the imposition of Urdu as the national language in Pakistan, were widely believed by the central Pakistani high command to have been incited by Indian agents. East Pakistani newspapers such as *The Morning News* published regular articles supporting such theories and urging the closure and regulation of the border.[70] Although there was no merit to such perceptions, such views were influential in deliberations as to whether a permit system needed to be imposed on the eastern border as well. Pakistan took the initiative in announcing that the passport and visa system was the hallmark of a sovereign nation, and thus needed to be imposed on both borders. India followed suit.

The institution of a passport and visa scheme in October 1952 marked the beginning of a documentary regime at the Bengal border.[71] India and Pakistan could now monitor and regulate who could and could not enter their territories, allowing legal passage only to holders of slips of officially marked paper and channelling travel through government-sanctioned points at the border.[72]

It should be noted that both states had already begun to track the movement of minorities across the border as early as 1950. After the riots and the conclusion of the Delhi Pact, each state appointed officials at the two major rail routes—Darsana–Banpur and Benapole–Bongaon—who counted and tabulated the numbers of passengers going across the border. Counting would be conducted from one midnight to another and the tally of passengers from these four stations would be relayed to Dacca and Calcutta for further publication.[73] Such measures were taken in order to evaluate the success of the Delhi Pact and provide information about the return of migrants to their homes. Numbers lent credence to the idea that one state was taking better care of their minorities than the other. However, discrepancies between figures reported by Indian and Pakistani authorities became the norm, and such quantitative methods transformed concern over minorities into games of national one-upmanship. Each state accused the other of either not counting or double counting returning migrants, depending on whether they wanted to claim that political and communal situation in one country was out of control or under control respectively. Numbers differing radically within the same time period were published in official publications as well as in media reports. For example, a memo of the MEA of India noted discrepancies

in the migration figures published by Pakistan since the Delhi Pact and up to April 1951 (see Table 2.1).[74]
The randomness of these numbers indicates that their usefulness was limited to political rhetoric.

Table 2.1:   West Bengal Government's Handout Dated 5/6/51
Tracking Border Passenger Traffic

	Hindu Migrants	Muslim Migrants
1. East Bengal Government's Press Note, dated 20 April 1951	Since February 1950 disturbances and up to 13 April 1951 *(a) 10,74,454 Hindus migrated to India and (b) 16,32,404 Hindus returned to East Bengal.	(c) 13,09,095 Muslims migrated from India and (d) 7,22,656 Muslims returned to India.
Reply to a Question in the Pakistan Constituent Assembly towards the Latter Part of March 1951	Altogether (b) 20,77,504 Hindu migrants had returned to East Bengal.	
Statement made by East Bengal Relief Minister in April 1951, as published in the Dawn on 2 April 1951	This figure II (b) according to the East Bengal's Relief Minister constituted 80% of the total Hindu migrants. The total number of Hindu migrants would therefore be 25,96,880.	16 lakhs Muslim refugees entered East Bengal and (d) 7 lakhs left East Bengal.
Statement made by the Governor of East Bengal in a Press Conference at Karachi towards the End of March 1951	About (a) 20 lakhs Hindus migrated from East Bengal and about (b) 15 lakhs had returned.	(c) 13 lakhs Muslims had entered East Bengal and (d) 4 lakhs had returned to India.

Source: File no. L/52/6568/202 Part II, MEA, Bengal Section, GoI, 1952, NAI
Note: * (a), (b), (c), (d) mark the contradictory figures.

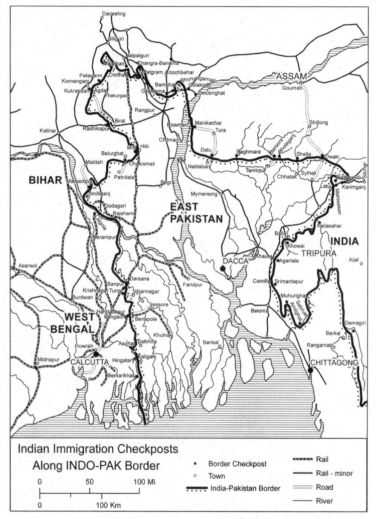

Figure 2.1: Bengal Border Checkpoints

The passport and visa scheme was established to generate more concrete numbers, that is, track people who not only moved through the main rail routes but also travelled on foot and by boat across any one of the numerous outposts that now dotted the border. It was, at least in principle, another tool to control the border and its users. The scheme required border crossers to seek permission to enter from higher authorities in both their own country and their destination, thereby establishing a clear linkage between states and their citizens. They were also required to enter and exit through pre-determined checkposts at the border newly established to control and document movement across the border. In essence, passports and visas introduced a new form of legal tender of citizenship by marking the origination and destination of the passport holder.

Pakistan issued Category A visas for Indian nationals 'who live in Indian territory within ten miles of the East Bengal border and who normally earn their livelihood by working in Pakistan territory within ten miles of the East Bengal border'.[75] This visa was valid for a maximum period of five years and limited the areas to which an Indian national could venture into Pakistani territory. Similarly, India agreed to issue visas to Pakistani citizens who lived along the border. Pakistani cultivators with land situated in an Indian village contiguous to Pakistan, shopkeepers and petty traders with businesses across the border, and agricultural producers dependent on markets in the Indian villages along the border were all required to provide rent receipts of their individual concerns to be eligible for such visas.[76] In the definition of both states, such a borderland stretched 10 miles east and west of the actual line of division. While recognizing and allowing border dwellers to continue their cultivation and other traditional occupations, these regulations arguably represented intensified efforts to identify the citizens of the respective nations.

Although passports and visas were primarily required of travellers, they soon emerged as the principal documents of nationality. The Indian passport scheme declared that those residents of undivided India who had migrated to Pakistan since 1 March 1947, were not citizens of India, and hence were not be eligible for Indian passports. Further, Pakistani nationals would not be able to enter India without Pakistani passports.[77] Those who had migrated to Pakistan after the Partition and after the 1950 riots but now wished to return to India, were unable to do so because the passport system denied that they were 'citizens' of India. According to an Indian government press note, all Indian nationals within East Pakistan territory had to acquire Indian passports and a visa from Pakistan within three months of the beginning of the passport system before they could travel again.[78]

It is unclear as to how the definition of an 'Indian national' was to be determined given that, for many, their birth, work, property, and families were in different countries. Indian nationals who remained within the territory of East Pakistan after the promulgation of the passport system but planned to return to India before the three month period had to obtain repatriation certificates from the Indian High Commission located in Dacca. The passport system turned travellers into citizens and required each of them to make a decision regarding their nationality that would be documented.

Such decisions were not easy as passport rules themselves were confusing and unclear about citizenship and its determinants. For example, after Partition, a large number of Muslim officials had opted to work in Pakistan and had moved to East Pakistan to join mainly the railways and post and telegraph departments. These 'optees' had left their properties and family in India and had been, until the passport policy, travelling freely across the border. An intelligence report of the Indian government noted that there was an increase in the applications for Indian passports from these officials who wanted to establish their Indian nationality and have access to their families and properties in India.[79] These officials feared that if they acquired Pakistani passports, their properties would come under the purview of the evacuee property laws in India which allowed the government to take over the property of those it deemed evacuees. According to the report, these officials intended to return to India before 15 October 1952 and were willing to resign their jobs in the Pakistan government if the Indian government began a policy of denying Indian passports to optees in Pakistan.[80]

In East Pakistan, the leader of the legislative assembly, Nurul Amin, declared that with the advent of passports, there would be no distinctions between majority and minority communities.

The passport does not make any distinction between a Hindu and a Muslim national. All are equal in Pakistan. As soon as a Hindu or a Muslim declares himself as the national of Pakistan he is a Pakistani and he is entitled to all the facilities which his own country can give him. With regard to people living in another country whether they are Muslims or Hindus, they are foreigners and they will be treated equally. Here again, there is no distinction. The distinction is between a national of Pakistan and a foreigner—a national of India. This is the only distinction and nothing more.[81]

Amin argued for a documentary nationality where previously there had been none. Passports, thus, marked the first concrete step towards fixing nationality and consequently, stopping the hitherto fluid relationship between migration and residency.

However, promises of equal citizenship rights did not allay fears of dispossession and displacement in the minds of minorities in either state. In East Pakistan, some Hindu minorities applied for the Indian passports in the belief that they would not be able to move to India unless they were Indian citizens.[82] Others decided on pre-emptive action and crossed the border before the start of the passport and visa system. Indian newspapers reported increase in migration from East Pakistan to India in the days leading up to the 15 October deadline. *The Statesman*, a Calcutta-based English daily, published figures of migration for the month of October when migration from East Pakistan to India through a single border outpost, Bongaon, averaged around 1,000 persons daily.[83] It also reported that 'among the immigrants, is a fair sprinkling of Muslims who appear to be as anxious as Hindus to adopt Indian nationality before it is too late. This fact is interpreted to indicate that the exodus is not altogether occasioned by communal tension.'[84] Both governments monitored foot traffic across the border and tried to assure minorities that their travel would not be hampered by the passport system. On 15 October 1952, newspapers reported that migration had come to a standstill and carried pictures of empty border outposts, implying the complete success of the imposition of documentary control of the border.[85]

The passport-cum-visa scheme was viewed by Hindus in East Pakistan as yet another obstacle in maintaining their economic and social ties with India. Bhabesh Chandra Nandy, member of the Constituent Assembly of Pakistan, asserted that the passport and visa scheme did not solve any border security issues in East Pakistan because 'the boundary line sometimes divided the same house, the outer portion coming within Pakistan and the inner portion of the house falling in the Indian Dominion'.[86] Further, the reduction in the number of migrants also affected the local economy in the border region.

In every railway and steamer station such as Goalondo, Chandpur, Narayanganj, thousands of passengers used to come and go and hundreds of people as porters or business men were earning their livelihood. Some were running small hotels and restaurants, some were selling *pans* (betel leaf), cigarettes and *bidis* (indigenous cigarettes), and some were working as coolies. Now as the number of men going by steamers and trains have reduced ... these people have lost their earning and are now starving.[87]

For Nandy, the introduction of the scheme thus was 'impracticable and a most costly project'.

Officials on the Indian side agreed that the passport-cum-visa system had 'caused considerable hardship and difficulties', not because of the effects of passport regulations but in terms of 'the inevitable delays involved in dealing with a prodigiously large number of applications for visas, repatriation certificates and migration certificates from single visa offices in Dhaka and Calcutta'.[88] Within a month of the start of the passport system, the Indian authorities had received requests for 18,972 visas, 9,607 repatriation certificates, 1,985 migration certificates, and 9,134 passport applications.[89]

To 'alleviate the hardships' of migrants due to such documentary requirements for travel, the Indian government initially announced that migrants from East Pakistan would not require a Pakistani passport but only needed to obtain a migration certificate from the Deputy High Commissioner for India in Dacca. To acquire such a certificate, the intending migrant would have to write to the visa officer in Dacca, providing details about himself and his family members and the reasons for migration to India. In addition, to prevent impersonation, he was required to provide photographs of himself and all his family members who would be migrating with him.[90] The process was intended to be simple and cost effective by not requiring the applicant and his family to travel to Dacca. But in practice, it was not very easy to acquire migration certificates which were issued at the discretion of specific officials stationed at each High Commission at Dacca and Calcutta, who were instructed that 'facilities for migration should be given in all *genuine* cases but should not be available to every member of the minority community regardless of the merits of the case.[91] Those who had landed property or any business in East Pakistan were not entitled to procure a migration certificate 'unless there was a danger to their life', or in cases involving 'danger to the honor of women folk'.[92] Economic distress was not a valid reason for migration since it was not confined to the minority community but affected all Pakistan citizens. Further, the Indian government argued that if 'the members of the minority community were to be encouraged by us to migrate because of economic distress in the country (East Pakistan) we will only be providing justification for Pakistan propaganda that the Hindus in East Bengal are only 'shadow Pakistanis'.[93]

However, for some Indian officials, such a policy was too narrow in definition and requirements for intending migrants. A.C. Guha, the Minister for Revenue and Defence Expenditure, pointed out that East Bengal had been suffering bad harvests and critical food crisis in the past few years, which made it difficult for small land or business owners to maintain their families. He claimed that the East Pakistani government was biased in its dispersal of relief measures towards its Hindu and Muslim citizens such that 'The middle and lower class Hindus have now got no means of livelihood. The only alternative for them to save their life is to migrate.'[94] Although Guha was making a clearly communal argument, it struck a chord with the higher authorities in Delhi. The Indian government did not change its policy but instructed its high commission to relax its guidelines and issue migration certificates where it would remove genuine hardship.

It is important to note that with the surfeit of different documents controlling movement, the act of migration itself changed, at least in the official perception. It was no longer necessarily the result of a momentous decision taken due to fear of life and well-being, but rather a premeditated move influenced by economic considerations. Consequently, those who acquired migration slips and visas under these circumstances could not claim victimhood and refugee status and were not eligible for relief from the Indian state's relief and rehabilitation schemes.

The bureaucratic regulation of the border gave rise to a cottage industry of preparing false visas, passports, and migration certificates in Dacca and Calcutta. In an attempt to curb such practices that prevented the governments from identifying their legal citizens, photographs became a key requirement for obtaining official documents. However, such requirement often involved long treks to the nearest town for those applicants who resided in rural villages of East Pakistan and additional expense to those who often had limited means. In an attempt to relieve this situation, the Indian government proposed that the requirement for photographs be limited to the male members of the family. Such gendered concerns were also embedded in the process of acquiring passports in East Pakistan. The Pakistani passport scheme had a separate provision for mainly Muslim women who observed the purdah by excusing them from having to submit photographs. A passport officer in Faridpur, East Pakistan, noted, however, that a 'number of Hindu gentle men were coming up with the request that their women folk should be exempted from the necessity of submitting photographs because they were *pardanashin*'.[95] The officer informed the higher authorities in Dacca that very few Hindu women in East Pakistan observed purdah and that the Hindu men were requesting an exemption only because they wished to avoid the expenditure on photographs for passports.

The establishment of a documentary regime at the border allowed India and Pakistan to regulate border traffic and decide who would be allowed to cross the border either as legal visitors or potential citizens. Border travellers were required to carry their passports and visas at all times, and those travelling from East Pakistan to India with migration certificates were required to have three copies, one for the Pakistan outpost, another for the Indian outpost, and the third for Indian authorities at their destination.

India and Pakistan had different reasons for adopting the documentary control of their mutual border. While both wanted to mark their sovereign territory and regulate travel, for Pakistan, the passport system was, first and foremost, a sign of sovereign statehood which had hitherto been delayed by free travel across the Bengal border. The power of granting visas to travellers allowed it to posit itself as a nation and differentiate its citizens from foreigners. For India, unwilling at first to impose the system, it very soon became a means of preferentially allowing certain groups of people the right of entry.

While documentary control of the Bengal border evolved to define the jurisdictional and economic limits of each nation, such limits were continuously tested by the movement of illegal goods and by people who circumvented the government channels of migration certificates and passports. The establishment of regulatory institutions at the border failed to prevent the development of a subversive border economy. In fact, over the years, officials of the state often became participants in such economies, turning a blind eye or accepting a bribe to accommodate the illegal movement of goods and people.[96]

In some ways, the establishment and operation of the Bengal border offers a more accurate description of the impact a problematic dividing line would have on an undivided region than the highly surveilled border between India and West Pakistan. Officially, it remained somewhat open to people and goods until the establishment of the passport and visa scheme in 1952. While routine border disputes allowed the new states to *practise* international diplomacy and demarcate their sovereignty over territory and its inhabitants, they primarily ensued due to the intrinsic faults with the boundary award. It was at the border that competing nationalist projects met and the inhabitants at the border were drawn into the centre of the post-colonial endeavours of national identity formation. Although their respective states sought to identify them as Indian and Pakistanis, the border citizens often had ambivalent attitudes about such impositions. Moreover, the illegal movement of goods and continuous flow of people without appropriate documents was a constant reminder of the limits of state authority at the periphery.

NOTES

1. Letter from Deputy Secretary Home Political to, Government of East Bengal (GoEB), dated 9 July 1952, File no. L/52/1934/202, 1964, Ministry of External Affairs (MEA) (Secret), Bengal Branch, National Archives of India (NAI).

2. Willem Van Schendel, 2001, 'Working through Partition: Making a Living in the Bengal Borderlands', *International Review of Social History*, vol. 46, no. 3, p. 408.

3. The all-India Border Security Force (BSF) replaced these fragmented units in 1965.

4. By 1970, incidents of disappearing boundary pillars were quite common. Telegrams between India and East Pakistan accused nationals of the other country for the thefts. See File no. PI/108/20/70, Pak I section, MEA, GoI, 1970, NAI.

5. Although Radcliffe used a map prepared by the Bengal Drawing Office in 1944, the map itself was drawn on the basis of a survey in the year 1915–16.

Government of India, 1958, *Decisions of the Indo Pakistan Boundary Disputes Tribunal, 1949*, New Delhi: Government of India, p. 19.

6. Letter dated 11 September 1947, from Secretary, New Bengal Association, Mehrpur and Nadia, to Acharya Kripalani. This issue was resolved with the Algot Bagge award of 1950 where the starting point of the river was fixed at a point in the Ganges south-west of Jalangi River. File no. G-33/1947–48, *All India Congress Committee (AICC) Papers*, Nehru Memorial Museum and Library (NMML).

7. Secret fortnightly report of first half of April 1957, *Reports and Returns: Fortnightly Reports of West Bengal—1957*, File no. 4/2/57-Poll-II, Ministry of Home Affairs, GoI, 1957, NAI, New Delhi.

8. *Ibid*. The report pointed out that 'the main stream of the river between Sodepur in the Indian union and Bhatchhala in East Pakistan passes through Pakistani territory at the time of the ebb-tide due to the formation of a char near the Sodepur side of the river and that during ebb tide all river craft plying in the river have to go along midstream on the Pakistan side'.

9. *Hindustan Standard (HS)*, 1 January 1948, p. 1.

10. Secret fortnightly report of first half of November 1957, *Reports and Returns*.

11. Radiogram dated 27 July 1948 (draft) to East Bengal from West Bengal, File no. P184/48, Home Police Confidential Records, GoWB, 1948.

12. *Ibid*. Letter dated 22 July 1948, to B.K. Acharya, Additional Deputy Secretary to GoWB, Home, from A.S. Roy, Camp Nimtita, Suti PS.

13. Most of these were termed as 'frontier incidents' and they happened on a daily basis. File no. L/52/1934/202, Secret, MEA, Bengal Branch, GoI, 1952, NAI.

14. File no. PL/108/23/64, MEA, GoI, 1964, NAI.

15. 'Proceedings of the Border Conference held at Fulbari PS, Raiganj District, Jalpaiguri (India), 8 April 1953', File no. 3/21/55-BL, MEA, Pakistan Division, BL Section, GoI, 1955, NAI.

16. Official memo from SB Maitra, Assistant Secretary to GOWB to Under Secretary GOI MEA, New Delhi dated 2nd March 1964. File: PL/108/23/64, MEA, GOI, 1964, NAI.

17. *Ibid*.

18. Upon getting the permits, the applicants were then required to take it to the officer-in-charge of the nearby border outpost who would determine the date, time, and place of grazing. *Ibid*.

19. Proceedings of the Conference on Influx of Pakistani Muslims held at the Cabinet Room, 12 September 1949, No File no., Home Political (Secret), West Bengal State Archives (WBSA). Conference members included the chief secretary, home secretary, inspector general of police, and the district magistrates and subdivisional officers of the border districts of West Bengal.

20. Sukumar Sen, Letter to C.C. Desai, 6 September 1949 (*Ibid.*, p. 5).

21. *Ibid.*, p. 4.

22. File no. JDM 868/49, Home Political (Secret), 1949, WBSA, p. 3. A high-level official meeting took place on 4 November 1949 in Shillong on the subject of restricting immigration of persons from East Bengal to Assam. Participants included N. Gopalaswami Ayyengar, Sri Prakash, Governor of Assam, B.C. Roy, Chief Minister of West Bengal, G.N. Bardoloi, Chief Minister of Assam, Sukumar Sen, Chief Secretary of West Bengal, and others.

23. *Ibid.*

24. *Ibid.*, p. 3.

25. In East Pakistan, the government followed a policy of disarming minority Hindus who lived near the border. For details, see Willem Van Schendel, 2005, *The Bengal Borderlands: Beyond State and Nation in South Asia.* London: Anthem, pp. 98–100.

26. In the first session of the Parliament in 1950, Gopalaswami Ayyengar, the Minister for Transport and Railways in the central government, admitted 'nearly four and half lakhs of Muslims have entered into the state of Assam alone between 15 August 1947 and beginning of November 1949'. See GoI, 1958, *Parliamentary Debates Official Report (Questions and Answers), Vol. 1,* 1 February 1950–13 March 1950, Delhi: Manager of Publications, p. 20.

27. In answering a query by parliamentarian B.S. Mann, on whether Muslim emigrants from East Pakistan had occupied any lands, Gopalaswami Ayyengar replied that 'There is no particular part of territory which these people have occupied … they have come in driblets, and nothing like an invasion across the border all along the line has taken place' (*Ibid.*, p. 20).

28. *Ibid.*

29. 'The complementary nature of the economies of the two Dominions therefore renders it necessary that, pending the negotiations of long term agreements, steps should be taken by both Governments to ensure that supplies of goods are distributed throughout the two Dominions more or less as they are at present when they form part of a single state'. See 1970, 'Report on Standstill Agreement with Pakistan', in S.L. Poplai (ed.), *India 1947–50, Select Documents on Asian Affairs, Vol. II* (External Affairs), New York: Oxford University Press, p. 124.

30. Proceedings of the Inter-Dominion Conference held at Calcutta, 15–18 April 1948, No File no, Home Political (Secret), 1948, WBSA.

31. Conference of Representatives of the Governments of East Bengal and West Bengal at Dacca on the 14th of February, 1948, File no. 62/1948, Home Political (Secret), 1948, WBSA.

32. *HS* (Editorial), 6 March 1948, p. 4.

33. *HS*, 5 March 1948, p. 3. Calcutta, one of the main clearing centres, usually received more than half of the fish from East Pakistan.

34. Incident on 12 March 1948, File no. 1I-45/48, B Proceedings 216–17, Home Political, August 1949, Bangladesh National Archives (henceforth BNA).

35. Resolution dated 3 April 1948, File no. 5M-4/1948, B Proceedings 402–8, Home Political, July1949, BNA.

36. Incident on 24 March 1948, File no. 1I-45/48, Home Political B Proceedings 216–17, August, 1949, BNA.

37. Home Political (secret), 1948 *Conference of District Magistrates of West Bengal held at Writer's Building, Calcutta, 7.9.48*, WBSA.

38. Report dated 24 March 1948, File no. 1I-45/48, Home Political B Proceedings 216–17, August, 1949, BNA.

39. *Ibid.*, p. 3.

40. For more examples, see Schendel, *The Bengal Borderland*, p. 150.

41. Pakistan newspapers regularly reported harassment of Muslims who travelled from East Pakistan to India by the Indian authorities. *Dawn*, 10 October 1952, p. 6.

42. Sasanka Bose, Letter to the Editor, *HS*, 3 November 1948, p. 4.

43. Note dated 30 April 1964, File no. 396/64(II), 1964, West Bengal Police, Intelligence Branch Archives, Calcutta. Similar incidents were reported in Cooch Behar–Rangpur border where Muslim women migrants were molested and deprived of their jewellery. *Dawn*, 12 October 1952, p. 4.

44. File no. 1/41/61-FIII, 1961, Ministry of Home Affairs, GoI, NAI.

45. Fortnightly report for the first half of May 1957, *Reports and Returns*.

46. *HS*, 1 August 1948, p. 4.

47. *HS*, 9 May 1948, p. 6.

48. *Ibid.*

49. Note dated 30 April 1964, File no. 396/64(II), 1964, West Bengal Police, Intelligence Branch Archives, Calcutta.

50. *Ibid.*

51. *HS*, 5 March 1948, p. 3.

52. *HS*, 17 December 1948, p. 6.

53. *HS*, 1 April 1948, p. 4.

54. File no. 3L-3/1951, B Proceedings 529–55, Home Political, April, 1952, BNA.

55. *HS*, 28 January 1948, p. 1.

56. *HS*, 4 January 1948, p. 1.

57. *The Statesman*, 4 February 1948.

58. *Memorandum of Association of Bangiya Jatiya Rakshi Dal*, No File no., Home Political (secret), GoWB, 1948, WBSA.

59. File no. 10/19/49, Police I, Ministry of Home Affairs, GoI, 1949, NAI.

60. James Buchanan, 1948, 'First Annual Report on the Ansars', File no. P10A-76/49, Police, Government of East Pakistan (GoEP), quoted in Schendel, 'Working through Partition', p. 407.

61. *Dawn*, 4 and 5 September 1952, p. 1.

62. *Dawn*, 28 September 1952, p. 4.

63. One of the main tribal groups in Bengal.

64. File no. II-228/1948, Home Political B Proceedings 361-9, July 1949, BNA.

65. Joya Chatterji, 1999, 'The Fashioning of a Frontier: The Radcliffe Line and Bengal's Border Landscape, 1947-52', *Modern Asian Studies*, vol. 33, no. 1, p. 237.

66. *HS*, 4 November 1948, p. 4.

67. For an elaboration of this argument, see Vazira Zamindar, 2007, *The Long Partition and the Making of Modern South Asia: Refugees, Boundaries, Histories*, New York: Columbia University Press.

68. India (Dominion) Ministry of Information and Broadcasting, 1948, *After Partition*, Delhi: Publications Division, Government of India, p. 74. For more on the mechanisms of the permit system, see Zamindar, *The Long Partition*, pp. 79-119.

69. Interestingly, West Pakistani citizens who wanted to enter India through the Bengal border were still required to have permits. It is unclear, in the absence of any documentary identification, as to how border authorities hoped to differentiate between West and East Pakistani citizens. There are several reports of Indian border police holding up East Pakistani Muslims who did not require permits and accusing them of actually being West Pakistani citizens. For example, see *Dawn*, 10 October 1952, p. 6.

70. File no. L/52/1321/202, MEA, GoI, 1952, NAI.

71. The passport system came into force on 15 October 1952 for India and on 17 October 1952 for East Pakistan.

72. There were fifty-four approved routes to enter India from East Pakistan. These were publicized in major newspapers in India. See *Amrita Bazar Patrika*, 4 October 1952.

73. File no. L/52/6568/202, Part II, MEA, Bengal Section, GoI, 1952, NAI.

74. *Ibid.*

75. File no. 2B-17/1952, Home Political B Proceedings 968-72, March 1953, BNA.

76. *The Statesman*, 17 October 1952, p. 1.

77. *The Statesman*, 15 October 1952, p. 1.

78. Indian government press release published in major Indian and Pakistani newspapers, for example, *Dawn*, 8 October 1952, p.4.

79. Note dated 15 September 1952, File no. L/52/1321/202, MEA, GoI, NAI.

80. The same source reported that around 1,000 optees of East Bengal Railways had resigned their jobs and gone back to India before the passport system came into force (*Ibid.*).

81. *Dawn*, 15 October 1952.

82. Note dated 30 September 1952, File no. L/52/1321/202, MEA, GoI, NAI.

83. *The Statesman*, 8 October 1952, p. 8.

84. *Ibid.*, p. 1.

85. *Amrita Bazar Patrika*, 16 October 1952, p.1.

86. See 1953, *Constituent Assembly (Legislature) of Pakistan Debates, Vol. 1, No. 14*, Government of Pakistan, 25 March, p. 716.

87. *Ibid.*, p. 717.

88. Note dated 23 November 1952, File no. L/52/1321/202, MEA, GoI, NAI.

89. *Ibid.*

90. *The Statesman*, 15 October , p. 1.

91. Memo dated 27 August 1956, File# 1/22/56-FIII, Ministry of Home Affairs, GoI, 1956, NAI.

92. Ibid.

93. K.M. Kannampilly, 27 August 1956 (*Ibid.*).

94. A.C. Guha, 'Note on the Migration from East Bengal', 22 August 1956 (*Ibid.*).

95. Passport Officer, Faridpur, Memo no. 74-PF, 6 November 1952, File no. 18P-54 /1952, B Proceedings 253–5, Home Political, July 1953, BNA.

96. For an elaboration on the unregulated border economy, see Schendel, *The Bengal Borderland*, pp. 147–90.

II

Citizens

3

Home and Hearth

n the summer of 1947, Safdar Ali Khan, a guard in Moradabad, Uttar Pradesh, was in two minds about whether to remain in India or make the journey to Pakistan. He, like other employees of the recently dismantled British government, had the option to decide his future employment with either the Indian or the Pakistani government.[1] For Safdar Ali, the initial decision to join the Pakistan government reflected his anxieties about being a minority in a majority Hindu country. His co-workers may also have coerced him into the decision. However, the logistics of moving to a new country very soon made him realize that he would prefer to remain in India. Further, his ailing mother did not want him to leave her. So, Safdar Ali applied to the Indian government to revoke his earlier application in which he argued,

It is useless and self-contradicting if I claim to be a patriotic son of India which I have blundered [sic] in favor of Pakistan. Really speaking, as I have stated above, the decision was not my own but I made under compulsion. I am an Indian first and an Indian last. I want to live in India and die in India. So I must serve in India.[2]

His second application made a point in emphasizing his loyalty to one particular nation in case the Indian authorities viewed his earlier decision as anti-national. The Government of India judged his petition within the narrowest terms of the law by pointing out that there had been a gap of more than six months between Safdar Ali's first and second application. Thus, Ali's application to opt for India could not be entertained and he would have to adhere to his first option and move to Pakistan. In the official mind, there should be no room for indecision, and six months was ample time to make critical choices about the future of one's residence and citizenship.

What did it mean for Safdar Ali and people like him who had to choose between their home and their loyalty to a particular state? The logic of the creation of new nation states necessarily demanded that residence and national identity now were at odds with each other for a particular group of people in each state. Both India and Pakistan, in their initial policies, implicitly assumed that religion would be the primary motivator in the decisions of these minorities as they debated whether to stay or leave. Thus, Hindus and Sikhs would automatically choose to live and work in India, while Muslims would express a desire to remain or migrate to Pakistan. Although those who worked for the erstwhile colonial state were given the option to choose, such choices were illusory as neighbours and co-workers often intimidated those who belonged to the minority communities in India and Pakistan to migrate across the border.[3] Minorities, who were not state officials, faced no less intimidation.

The common assumption implicit within studies of the Partition has been that the large-scale migrations after 1947 occurred due to violence and a desire among minorities to search for safety among their numerical majority. Partition was, in this understanding, a kind of demographic 'balancing act', and successive censuses in India and Pakistan gave credence to this. But what about those minorities in the partitioned areas who did not want to move and/or viewed their move as temporary? In Bengal, a large number of Hindu and Muslims minorities continued to remain in their ancestral homes and assumed the citizenship of the country within which they resided. They found no dichotomy between their religious and national identity.

In the post-Partition period, such decisions to remain became problematic as India and Pakistan began to implicitly assume, in their respective policies towards minorities and refugees, that there was a linear equation between nation, religion, and residence. The question that animated the official and public debate on citizenship in each state was whether a minority could also be a true citizen of the state. Could a Muslim be an Indian or could a Hindu be a Pakistani? The debates within India, on what constituted the moral nation, tended to identify Hindus and Sikhs as 'natural' citizens and by default, the Muslim minorities as 'naturally' belonging to Pakistan.[4] In Pakistan, especially in its eastern wing, Hindus were deemed to have a 'natural attraction' to India. Migration of minorities, initially temporary, thus reflected their attempts to find security and negotiate this 'natural' ascription of their identities as national citizens. However, for those minorities who continued to stay behind in their ancestral homes, citizenship remained imbricated within layers of past social and economic relations. Loyalty, for these minorities, was an attendant corollary to continued residence.

This chapter expands on the ideas of proxy citizenship by examining the legislation on evacuee properties and how it impacted the Hindu minorities in that region. Primarily in response to the large-scale migration after Partition, both India and Pakistan passed several laws which assured the minorities in each state that their property and citizenship rights would be guaranteed if they returned back to home and hearth. The permit system in 1948 and the passport and visa scheme of 1952, as discussed in Chapter 2, were geared towards regulating and stopping the flow of migrants across the international borders. In addition, they urged their respective minorities to remain at home and guaranteed to take care of their property in case they have temporarily moved across the border. The states identified these migrant–residents as 'evacuees' and began a process of guardianship of their properties. As we shall see, in the case of East Pakistan, such legislations helped resolve their needs to rebuild a post-Partition national order. In the process, citizenship within the new nation state often became conditional on continued residence in one's home and property ownership.

PROTECTION VERSUS REQUISITION

Both India and Pakistan established complex structures headed by a Custodian-General[5] in each country to protect minority properties and guaranteed the return of such property to the rightful owners upon their return. Both states set up Evacuee Property Management Boards in the areas of East and West Bengal that had experienced mass migration.[6] They stipulated that these boards would function only on the definite request of individual property owners. However, such 'management' of property soon became intertwined with the nation-building project, especially in East Pakistan, where forthcoming requisition of property acts would influence protection of evacuee property.[7]

In India, the Evacuee Property Act of 1948 specifically did not include the regions affected by the Partition in the east. The Act focused on protecting property and agricultural lands in northern India, ostensibly for the return of their Muslim owners, but, in reality, for the purposes of refugee rehabilitation of those Hindus coming from Pakistan. Such a differential policy stemmed from two implicit assumptions on the part of the Indian State. First, that there were no *real* reasons for the migration of people in the east and thereby it was temporary. Second, those Muslim minorities who left India from this region were mainly non-property owners and thus, legislation was not required. Both assumptions influenced how the Indian State addressed the issues of refugee rehabilitation in this region.

In East Pakistan, the need for rehabilitation of Partition refugees guided the controversial legislation that sought to acquire property of those who had left for India. Initially to be in effect from 1948 until 1951, the East Bengal (Emergency) Requisition of Property Act (Act XIII of 1948) gave the provincial government power to acquire, either on a temporary or permanent basis, any property it considered necessary for the establishment of offices and residences for the officials of the new state.

Hindu political leaders in East Bengal such as Manoranjan Dhar, Pravash Chandra Lahiry, and Ganendra Chandra Bhattacharjee strongly criticized the Act as a tool of minority persecution both in the East Bengal Legislative Assembly (EBLA) and the Constituent Assembly of Pakistan (CAP).[8] By 1951, Pakistani authorities admitted to misjudging the provisional aspect of the law. In a private memo, the Joint Secretary of the Finance and Revenue Department (Requisition) in East Pakistan admitted that the estimate of three years had not been adequate to rebuilding the provincial and central government buildings. He indicated, 'it is found now that schemes for construction of permanent buildings for their offices and officers have not been taken up seriously yet by many of the Departments concerned'.[9] Further, the memo continued,

About 5,000 premises have already been requisitioned in the province and demands are still coming from different Government departments for further requisitioned accommodation. But there is no scope for further requisition in any district. All the available accommodation has already been requisitioned and there is on the other hand, persistent demand and clamour from the owners of the requisitioned houses specially from returned emigrants, the Muhajirs (Muslim refugees from India) who have acquired houses here by purchase or by exchange with their residential house in West Bengal In most cases their demands are found to quite reasonable and equitable and a great hardship is being caused to them by the operation of the Requisition Proceedings.[10]

Given that such a situation was 'detrimental to the normal development of the province', authorities directed civil departments and private companies to build alternative accommodations within the next six months.

Such a short time limit was unrealistic and the East Bengal authorities decided to continue the earlier law under a new name and with slight modifications in its terms of operation. Under the East Bengal Evacuee Property (Restoration of Possession) Act 1951, a person (including his legal heirs) who was ordinarily resident of East Bengal and left for any part of India owing to the communal disturbances, or fear thereof, after 15 August 1947 would be considered an 'evacuee'.[11] The Government of East Bengal set up an Evacuee Management Committee that could take charge of any abandoned property, either on the basis of an application from the owner or by its own volition. This Committee had the authority to grant leases or to rent such properties as it deemed necessary. For the first time, the district civil court was restricted from challenging any order or any action that the Committee undertook.

An 'evacuee' was a 'person ordinarily resident in East Bengal, who owing to communal disturbances, or fear thereof leaves or has, on or after prescribed date, left East Bengal for any part of India and includes the legal heirs of such person'.[12] It is important to note that the law sought to identify both those residents who had left and their legal heirs as 'evacuees' as people who had evacuated, showing clear intention, rather than abandoned their homes. The assumption of voluntary action on the part of these citizens was critical in the state's requisition process of their homes in their absence. The East Pakistan authorities, faced with the scarcity of housing for their new government and its employees, frequently assumed intent to evacuate as indication of permanent departure.[13] The Government of Pakistan debated on creating a further category of 'intending evacuees', comprising of minorities whom officials perceived to be at risk of flight. To avoid being labelled as such, one had to provide a written statement of one's intention to stay to local district authorities. The linkages between evacuee property and requisition of property ensured that the *intentions to migrate* continued to influence decisions of local authorities in East Bengal. The operation of the requisition laws created, sui generis, the category of 'evacuees'.

Although laws had clear definitions and guidelines for the protection of evacuee property, their terms were open to interpretation at the level of implementation. As the local authorities went about identifying 'evacuee' property and houses that could be requisitioned, they exercised their power and judgement that sometimes bordered on the indiscriminate. Identifying abandoned houses of minorities as 'evacuee' property, and taking control of it 'to protect' the property till the evacuee's return, was the first step in the requisition process. An appointed government official would personally inspect the property and conduct local enquiries regarding the owner's intention to return home. Subsequently, the local authorities served a notice of requisition and earmarked the property to house government offices or officials.[14] Such a notice of requisition did not require anyone to be present within the house as long as the notice was affixed 'to some conspicuous part of the premises in which he [the owner] is known to have last resided or carried business or personally worked for gain'.[15]

Such a process did not provide any opportunity for direct enquiry of the evacuee owner's intentions until the requisition notice had been served. The property owners were given only fifteen days from the publication of the requisition notice to appear before the local district authorities to state their objections to the requisition or to claim their compensatory rent for the property. Furthermore, the East Bengal government expected all minorities to return to their residences within six months.[16] Failure to return was taken as a sign of the evacuees' abandonment of their property and their preference for residence across the border. Manoranjan Dhar, a member of the EBLA, protested against the imposition of the time limit for the return of evacuees arguing that the essence of the bill 'is how to get evacuees back'. Moreover, he warned, 'some evacuees who want to come back to East Bengal may find that they have no accommodation to take shelter, because most of their houses have been requisitioned or disposed of.[17] Anticipating the bureaucratic hassles that they would have to undergo to regain ownership of their requisitioned property, many Hindu owners began to entrust their houses to the care of close relatives, tenants, or caretakers. Although clear guidelines prevented evacuee property from being requisitioned if family members or caretakers were present, a definite disjuncture between prescription and practice existed.

The law sought to define what constituted 'property' and divided them into two large categories: moveable and immoveable. While land and houses were clearly of the latter kind, what comprised as 'moveable' remained open to interpretation. By 1953, representatives of India and Pakistan decided, in a meeting at Karachi, that evacuees would be allowed to remove all 'personal and household properties' to the other country without having to pay custom duties or export–import duties.[18] However, evacuees could not move machinery or machine parts,[19] merchandise and trade goods, unsown cloth that was in excess of personal needs, cattle, cash in excess of permitted quantities, and bullion. For all these items, evacuee owners were allowed six months from 1 March 1954 within which to claim restoration or dispose of their moveable property within the country of their original residence.

Evacuees who carried more money than the stipulated amount were deemed to be shifting capital from one country to the other, sometimes perceived as a deliberate effort to sabotage East Pakistan. Such suspicions were voiced even before the Partition. An article in the *Dawn*, a Muslim League paper, published from Karachi, claimed that minority Hindu businessmen had shifted approximately 200 crores in capital to India by early July 1947. The article identified this alleged transfer of capital as 'Hindu hostility … motivated by a desire to hit the Pakistan Exchequer by denying it a big source of revenue'.[20] Although the prescribed amount of money changed over the years, the perception that the minorities were complicit in such 'anti-national' transport of capital gained ground, especially as migration continued unabated over the next three decades. The very definition of moveable property was redefined thus and impinged with nationality as property, which had hitherto been owned by individuals, now came to be seen as belonging to the nation. Moving them across the border along with oneself was thus an 'anti-national' act. These legislations, in their effort to protect the possessions of the evacuees, *nationalized* moveable property and sought to align the ownership of immoveable property with permanent and continued residence.

NATIONALIZING PROPERTY

In East Pakistan, complaints against the Requisition Act quickly accumulated after the promulgation of the law in 1948. East Pakistani citizens, especially those who belonged to the minority Hindu community, perceived these regulations as forms of state intervention that robbed them not only of residential space but also of ownership rights. Minority Hindu citizens, who continued to reside and maintain ties with their ancestral homes, identified their citizenship within the East Pakistan state with such physical ties. Requisitioning of houses where some family members resided was then perceived as the state's lack of faith in its minority citizens or as attempts to oust them.

For instance, Gour Chandra Chakrabarty, a retired government servant of undivided India, who had become a pensioner of the Pakistan government after 1947, found his only residence in Kaliajury, Comilla, requisitioned during a temporary absence.[21] His petition began with the assertion that he was a 'loyal subject of the Pakistan government' and outlined in detail the reasons for his absence. He had gone to Kharagpur in West Bengal to perform the marriage of one of his daughters, and subsequently had become ill and vacationed in Puri, Orissa, to recover. Meanwhile, the local authorities had requisitioned his house, allegedly without notice. When Chakrabarty returned to his home, it had already been allotted to a government servant. He assured the district authorities that he intended to 'spend the rest of his life at his village home at Kaliajury and God willing, to die here'.[22] Chakrabarty hoped that such a promise of continued residence would elicit a favourable response. However, after an enquiry, the district magistrate noted that, 'It does not appear that he [Chakrabarty] has any bonafide intention to stay in Comilla as it is understood from local evidence that he had removed all his moveable belongings to West Bengal'.[23] An additional factor meditating against the return of his property was that both of Chakrabarty's sons worked in West Bengal. The house remained requisitioned and Chakrabarty probably was forced to live with his sons in West Bengal.

In 1950, immediately after the Khulna–Barisal riots, the East Bengal authorities requisitioned the house of the Barman family in Kishoreganj, Mymensingh district, when family members had gone to Calcutta for medical treatment. Ironically, Suresh C. Barman and his brother, K.C. Barman, the Deputy Secretary of Land and Land Revenue Department in West Bengal, a department intimately connected with refugee rehabilitation and requisitioning of property, jointly owned the house. While Barman had opted to join the civil service in West Bengal after 1947, Suresh had continued to reside in their ancestral home. When Suresh and his wife went to Calcutta for the latter's medical treatment, local authorities deemed the house to be vacant and available to be requisitioned even though the couple had left a caretaker, Sivacharan Das.[24] As part of the usual course of action, the Barman family had lodged a request with the East Bengal authorities to derequisition their house. However, Suresh Barman did not get back the house even though official policy promised such derequisitioning to returning evacuees.[25] The needs of the state gained precedence over the individual citizen's rights of ownership in this case. The local subdivision officer (SDO) at Kishoreganj reported, 'The brothers are evacuees ... the story that Suresh went only for the treatment of his wife cannot be believed. Not a single member of the family was in the house.'[26] The subsequent documentation is unclear whether Suresh Barman had really left East Bengal for his wife's treatment or whether he was already an 'evacuee'. However, from the state's perspective, ownership rights could only be recognized as long as one continued to be physically present within one's house. Absence could and often would be interpreted as intent, and the state felt it legally correct to take over the rights of that house, ostensibly to safeguard it on behalf of the evacuee, but in reality, to serve its own infrastructural needs.

Highlighting the arbitrariness of the law, Nirmal Kumar Choudhury, a correspondent for the *Ananda Bazar Patrika* and stationed in Patna, India, read about the requisition of his property in another newspaper. The *Hindustan Standard* in July 1950 reported that:

With 24 hours notice the residential house of Shri Bimal Kumar Choudhury of Panchbibi (Bogra) has been requisitioned by the Pakistan Government. Bimal Babu's mother and sister are living in the house. They have got a few hundred *maunds* (around 82.6 pounds) of paddy in their '*gola*.' They and the other gentlemen of the locality prayed for time but the Circle Officer who came to take possession of the house is said to have given them a rude reply advising them to move the higher authorities.[27]

To the readers in India, Choudhury's predicament was yet another sign, at best, of East Pakistani state's inefficiency and, at worst, another instance of minority persecution. However, in his letter to his friend, A.M.A. Azim of the *Associated Press of Pakistan* in Dacca, Nirmal Choudhury showed complete faith in the process that, in his view, had *mistakenly* requisitioned an occupied house.[28] He assured the authorities that his brother had temporarily gone to West Bengal for medical reasons and had already returned home. In this case, the problem arose from the government's interpretation of 'family' that did not take into account the presence of an extended family in residence.

A common thread that runs through these petitions that represent more than a hundred retained in the files of the Revenue Department of East Bengal is the *intentions to stay*. Although many of these migrants may have, in reality, fled their homes in the wake of the riots and political uncertainty, their migration was temporary. Most petitions highlighted that the owners had left their homes temporarily, often to visit relatives, to attend social functions, or to keep medical appointments. Thus, the writers argued, temporary absence did not and should not define intention to evacuate and their property should not come under the purview of the requisitioning authorities. The petitioners left behind family members or caretakers to prevent their properties being declared 'evacuee' property and they returned once they felt that the political climate had stabilized or their medical treatment was completed.

Further, there had been a tradition of migration from rural eastern Bengal to the urban centres of West Bengal, mainly Calcutta, to obtain higher education or work.[29] Although Partition divided this region into two new states, such patterns of temporary migration and divided families continued within the existing networks of kinship relations and economic associations. Traditionally, family members had continued to remain in the ancestral home while the urban, educated males worked in western Bengal and returned home during family celebrations and religious holidays. After 1947, such patterns of mobility became invested with signs of citizenship whereby the very act of leaving one's residence, for whatever the reason, was interpreted as intent to migrate.

When the evacuees returned and demanded their homes from the government, their requests became entangled within the nation-building project and definition of national loyalty. The issue debated within official circles was whether these returning evacuees were petitioning their homes for continued residence or for financial gain through the sale of their property to the highest bidder,[30] or worse, as an attempt to somehow sabotage the state-building process. The East Pakistan government did derequisition some property. But a substantial portion was not derequisitioned because the government could not build alternative houses and office buildings as quickly as needed.

Some officials in East Pakistan thought that it was only a matter of time before the minority Hindu citizens migrated to India. During the riots of 1950, Surat Lal Roy, a resident of north Nawabpur in Dacca, had moved his family to another part of the city for safety. After the political environment had stabilized, he returned to find that the East Bengal authorities had requisitioned his house. In addition, some unauthorized muhajirs[31] were living in his house. After petitioning for derequisitioning, he succeeded in obtaining his residence.[32] However, in his report, A. Khaleque, the local police sub-inspector who had conducted the local enquiry to establish the validity of Roy's petition, suggested that 'Order may kindly be passed to return the house to the petitioner after taking an agreement that if he goes away to West Bengal, the house may be surrendered to the Govt [sic]'.[33] The official clearly expected Roy to ultimately leave for India.

The needs of the state sometimes circumvented the rights of ownership as properties that were not 'empty' were served with requisition notices. The petition of the Sutradhar family in Comilla illustrates the complexities involved within the process at the local level. The story began in October 1948 when the district government at Comilla requisitioned the Royal Hotel, situated in the town centre, in order to establish a police club within its premises. Prabud Chandra Sengupta, the owner, filed an objection towards this requisition noting that although the authorities had provided him with an alternative building for his hotel, relocation would be a financial drain. He emphasized that his boarders, both Muslims and Hindus, were already in residence and it would be difficult to move them.[34]

Superficially, here is another instance of the local authorities acting arbitrarily. However, matters were complicated when the district authorities requisitioned the house that the Sutradhar family jointly owned, as the alternative accommodation for the Royal Hotel. Not only had the family been residing in their house, they also conducted a successful timber and furniture business from within the compound of the house. In her petition protesting the requisition, Ashubala Sutradhar noted that she had to support her ailing husband and her 80 year old mother-in-law, who were both residents of the house in dispute. Moreover, their second house, which was situated outside of Comilla township, had already been requisitioned earlier, leaving the family without any residence. Ashubala also sent her petition against the requisitioning to the District Minority Committee, seeking some political support. The district authorities discredited her petition arguing that her husband's illness 'is neither recent or acute. At least it has not prevented him from moving about.'[35] In addition, the land acquisition officer reported that the Sutradhars had begun their business after the requisitioning notice had been served 'for the purposes of defeating the requisition'.[36] For local officials, her petition was yet another instance of minority citizens raising objections on 'false or fictitious grounds' to disrupt the formation of the new government.[37]

Fortunately for Ashubala, Tafazzal Ali, the then Minister-in-Charge of the Revenue Department, took up her case. Ali noted that the East Pakistan government had issued a ban against the requisition of houses for non-officials. The district authorities should have applied for permission from the government before they decided to requisition Ashubala's house for relocating Prabud Sengupta, the owner of Royal Hotel. Concluding that the district magistrate had acted in a prejudicial manner, Ali approved the derequisitioning of the house.

One did not have to be a property owner for the long arm of the requisition law to displace a minority resident. Amrita Lal Bhowmick, an accountant in the Chittaranjan Cotton Mills in Dacca and a tenant in a non-owner occupied family house in Gandaria, Dacca, found his quarters requisitioned in July 1950.[38] He had been a resident in Dacca since 1947 and had been residing in the house with his family. Bhowmick, a relative of the owner, had been allowed the use of the property while the owner searched for a suitable property to exchange or a buyer for his property. On the particular day of the requisitioning, authorities had arrived at the house while Bhowmick was at his office, served his maid the notice of requisitioning, and locked up the house. When he returned home, Bhowmick could not enter his house, nor could he collect his clothes or money. Bhowmick successfully petitioned to the higher authorities and the property was temporarily derequisitioned.[39]

A narrative of suffering and a debate on the rights of residence were embedded within this success story. When his house was requisitioned, Bhowmick had supplied the authorities with rent and municipal tax receipts and provided details of his ration card that proved his tenancy. However, the authorities concluded that his personal relationship with the owner made him a *caretaker* of the house rather than a *tenant*. This was a critical distinction. At one level, such difference alluded to the fact that the actual owner had intentions to evacuate providing the pretext for requisitioning. Second, the differentiation between Bhowmick as caretaker rather than a tenant enabled the local authorities to project themselves as the official custodians of this evacuee property. Consequently, in this particular case, the act of requisition would not involve the disenfranchising a tenant.

The Government of East Bengal had defined guidelines for the compensation of both moveable and immoveable property that was requisitioned. Both the government and the owner were to agree on the compensation. If such agreement was not reached, the East Bengal government would nominate a person having expert knowledge on the property to be acquired.[40] The owner could also appoint his own assessor and a government-appointed judge would arbitrate the case in the district high court. The market value of the property was fixed equal to its value on or before 14 June 1947. This assessment applied to all houses within a radius of 20 miles from the New Government House at Ramna, in the capital of Dacca, and within 20 miles from the court in the district of Chittagong. However, the rules for compensation were not clear for requisitioned houses that were beyond the 20 mile radius of these two cities and in other districts of the province.

Over the years it became difficult to transfer the rent to the owner, who may have moved to India, then the rent had to be channelled through bureaucratic institutions that regulated the transfer of money between the two countries. For example, in his petition for adequate compensation for his house in Dacca, N.C. Chakravarti, a civil servant in the West Bengal government and then a resident of Calcutta, noted that he had been earning Rs 50 as rent before his house had been requisitioned.[41] He protested against the official estimation of rent at Rs 30 which, along with an exponential rise in municipal taxes after the Partition, meant that he 'was denied any practical benefit'.[42] Moreover, he requested the government to send his rent by money order to Calcutta since the 'cost of the journey will exceed the compensation'.[43] Although his rent was revised and raised to Rs 50, it is unclear whether the East Bengal government was prompt in sending any money order to Calcutta. Most likely, Chakravarti, like the cases cited earlier, had to wait years to obtain any compensation for his property.

HOME AND THE NATION

Both the Evacuee Property Act and the Requisition of Property Act, in their implementation, highlighted the interconnections between location, residence, and citizenship. Since Pakistan had yet to formulate specific laws defining citizenship, residence and religion were often the basic denominators that defined national belonging. As people continued to move back and forth across the new border, definitions of such belonging remained unstable. With regard to the operational aspects of these two legislations, the critical question that confronted both the state and its minority citizens was: whether a person who had left the jurisdictional boundaries of one nation where he owned property, could continue to be the legal owner even though he may have adopted a foreign nationality? Did residence and property ownership imply nationality and did the act of migration imply intent to reject that nationality? More importantly, could an evacuee be loyal to the nation where s/he was born?

These were central questions for the employees of the Government of East Bengal who had opted to join service in East Bengal while retaining their properties in West Bengal. Low pay in government service and the lack of housing in Dacca had ensured that these optees had to leave their families in West Bengal and continue to supplement their incomes from their properties there. But now, with the imposition of a document regime at the border after 1952 that required them to acquire passports and visas, movement between the two states had become difficult. To address these issues, the East Bengal Secretariat Association, formed in 1947 in Dacca, framed a memorandum to the East Bengal authorities in September 1953 which began by emphasizing that:

The Government employees who opted to serve East Bengal at the time of Partition have become Pakistanees [sic] irrespective of the fact that some of them originally belonged to territory now falling in India ... when the Optees came to serve the Government of Pakistan the Optees naturally expected that this would not jeopardize their right and title to their properties in India.[44]

The authors of the memorandum urged the East Pakistan state to provide facilities which would enable them to dispose or exchange their property in India and to take steps to counter the 'propaganda not to purchase Muslims property' in India.

The matter became complicated, as the memorandum pointed out, in the case of the family members of deceased optees, who, having no recourse to income, were forced to return to India. However, 'the door to returning to India ... has now virtually been closed with the introduction of Passport system as a Pakistani Muslim can never expect a fair deal and scope to resettle in India on return from Pakistan particularly in the absence of any guardian.'[45] In effect, the memorandum was requesting the East Pakistan state to act as the male provider to the family of deceased optees.

The memorandum points to two prevailing assumptions about Partition migration and property belonging to minorities in each state. First, even though both India and Pakistan had put legislations in place to guard evacuee property, often this was logistically impossible. Refugees and local citizens looking to make good on empty houses, often encroached on such property. It was also difficult to sell off property and get a good price for it if people knew that one was planning to move across the border. Second, while the permit system was not applicable at the eastern border and the passport–visa regulations did not specify whether a particular community could or could not cross the border legally, the return of minorities was often subject to suspicion.

But for the writers of this particular memorandum, the central issue was whether they would have rights to their property. The argued that although by choosing to serve in East Pakistan 'they had burnt their boats and they did not want to go back', they were also prepared to 'try to get Indian nationality in the interest of their properties in India ....'[46] For them, nationality was utilitarian, providing them access to their property. While they did not want to return to India, they found no contradiction in acquiring Indian citizenship if that was the only way they could retain hold of their property.

In East Bengal, even as houses came to be *nationalized* in the efforts to meet the demands of state building and refugee rehabilitation, some minorities did not perceive the contradictions between citizenship within one country and continued ownership of property in the other country.

Some of those who had moved permanently to India now requested the Indian government to ensure that they received compensation from the East Pakistan government for their requisitioned property. An anonymous letter writer outlined his grievances and demands to the editor of *Hindustan Standard* thus, 'Our house was taken up in August 1947, another August has passed and the year is drawing to a close, yet we have not received any sum by way of compensation'.[47] After sending a number of letters to the East Bengal government enquiring how and when the owner could collect compensation, he had received a short letter noting that the rent had been fixed at Rs 25 instead of the earlier rent of Rs 40. The writer exhorted the West Bengal government that 'It is the incumbent duty of the state to offer protection to our properties in foreign lands i.e. Pakistan. This is not a new or abnormal demand, nor is it being prompted by sabotage motive [*sic*]'.[48] Rather, the writer urged the West Bengal government to advise all the new citizens to apply for compensation to the High Commissioner of Pakistan to assuage any suspicions of disloyalty.

Although the requisition drive and petitions protesting its operation created a space for the articulation of citizenship rights through ownership and proof of residency, the issue of compensation introduced a new factor in the negotiations. This new element concerned the rights of arbitration as some minority Hindus began to send their petitions to the Indian High Commission at Dacca. East Pakistani authorities viewed such actions on the part of their citizens as undermining their authority. Aziz Ahmed, the Chief Secretary to the East Bengal government, in his letter to Muhammad Ikramullah, Foreign Secretary of Pakistan, noted, 'There is an almost universal tendency on the part of the Hindus in this province to look upon the Deputy High Commissioner as a sort of appellate authority and a protector of their interests—an impression which the Deputy High Commissioner himself does little or nothing to discourage'.[49] Ahmed was only stating what was a common perception at the time. He went on to clearly stake a claim on East Bengal's minority citizens by urging the Indian High Commission to forward only cases that concerned Indian citizens. On his part, Santosh Basu, the Deputy High Commissioner of India, clarified that most of the petitions directed towards Indian authorities in Dacca were from those who had migrated to India and their petitions were postmarked from that side of the border. Further, he cited the recent inter-dominion agreement reached between representatives of both countries in Delhi which provided space for *both* countries to create 'possible conditions which would infuse confidence into the minds of those citizens who have migrated to the other dominion with a view to their return to their original homes'.[50] Hence, according to Basu, rather than undermine East Pakistan, in taking up cases of non-payment of compensation, Indian authorities were only assisting evacuees to enable them to return to their original homes. However, for Ahmed, East Pakistan's jurisdiction continued to extend to those who had migrated to India but not yet adopted Indian nationality. This debate on rights over minority citizens was crucial to the evolving self-definition of both India and Pakistan.

GOD AND THE NATION: A DISCOURSE OF DISPOSSESSION

The arbitrariness of the requisition operation had the immediate effect of producing a perception of minority oppression. The fact that most requisitioned houses belonged to Hindus led to the belief that the East Pakistan state was deliberate in its attempts to dispossess its minority citizens.[51] For example, Bimalananda Dasgupta, the ex-Chairman of the Dacca municipality, in outlining the different problems generated because of requisition laws, stated: 'Enough has been said and ventilated through the press over this procedure of the Pakistan government to oust people who sincerely want to cling to their paternal homesteads but it seems yet very little or no impression has been made on the authorities.'[52] Similarly, Samar Guha claimed: 'For East Bengal, Pak [*sic*] Government is not likely to undertake any large scale scheme for house building as requisitioning of Hindu houses serves their double purposes, ousting of undesirable middle class Hindus from the urban areas and housing the Muslims in them.'[53] This hypothesis of calculated dispossession found ready reception within the evolving discourse of persecution that, by now, included protests against gun control, forcible donations for the

Jinnah Fund, and arbitrary jailing of some prominent leaders on charges of anti-state activity.

The East Bengal government, aware of the dangerous potential for religious discrimination within the requisition process, had clearly outlined in its promulgations that places of worship would be out of bounds of requisitioning. Thus, while the government had full powers to requisition any property deemed necessary for state building, it also provided that 'no property used by the public for the purpose of religious worship shall be requisitioned'.[54] In their multifarious attempts to counter the requisitioning process, minorities found this clause useful as it became common practice to associate one's residence with one's places of worship. For instance, when Nagendra Saha, a resident of Jessore, sent an express telegram in March 1949 to the Chief Secretary of East Pakistan, he worded his protest thus, 'Our residential building at Lakshmipasa with family deity installed temple inside for years requisitioned under orders of district magistrate for circle officers residence daily worshipping by permanently retained *purohit* [priest] will be stopped family members stranded without shelter pray intervention.'[55] Saha's telegram identifies the loss of access to the 'family deity' as primary reason for his objections to the requisitioning order. In an attached letter, Saha also pointed out a set of other grounds for objection such as continued residence of family members and that the family had no other alternative residence in the area. In support of Saha's petition, the President of the District Muslim League, Narail, Maulavi Abdul Aziz, gathered more than twenty-five signatures from prominent men of the area, most of who belonged to the local branches of the Muslim League. Aziz, in his petition to the Tafazzal Ali, who was also the Chairman of the East Pakistan Minority Board, noted that due to the requisition order, not only had Nagendra Saha and his family been left without a residence, but they also had no access to the 'Siva temple' situated within their house. Such a situation 'had created great unrest amongst the Hindu and Muslim citizens of the locality'.[56] Thus, Aziz urged Ali to take action in favour of the derequisitioning of Saha's house in the interest of maintaining communal harmony.

Saha's example was one among many instances of disputed requisitions.[57] The official response was to discredit the grounds of his petitions. Local authorities reported that only three members of the

Saha family were residing at the house at the time of requisition, 'the other 4 brothers, Haren Babu, Jiten Babu, Anil Babu and Susil Babu were all living in the Indian Union with their family and all belongings since the birth of Pakistan'.[58] In the eyes of officials, this fact of a divided family established *intent to migrate* on the part of Nagendra Saha, and accordingly justified the requisition. To add insult to injury, the officials also stated that contrary to rules, the family had removed a DBBL gun and a radio to the Indian Union, and upon being informed about the requisition order, the family imported a 'good number of women and children'[59] to contest the requisition order. Thus, not only had the Saha family been engaged in what could be interpreted as seditious acts, but had moved family members to their residence for the purposes of contesting the official order. A confidential memo to the District Magistrate of Jessore argued that 'there is no temple in the house in the true sense but there is a small memorial of the deceased parents of Nagen Babu, where photos and a *Siva linga* are placed'.[60] Since the memorial was situated away from the main building, local authorities proposed fencing off the area to separate it from the requisitioned house and thereby ensure continuation of worship. Such a resolution would answer any contentions on grounds of religious rights and still allow for the requisition of the house. In spite of multiple petitions, the requisition of Saha's house remained in force in 1949.

Religion and requisition became visibly entangled with well-publicized cases such as the one concerning the requisition of property of the Raja of Bhawal.[61] East Pakistani authorities had requisitioned the Jaidebpur Palace in January 1948 to accommodate the office of the Government Forms and Stationeries. Although Kumar Ram Narayan Roy Chowdhury, the Raja of Bhawal, had objected to the requisition claiming, 'there are temples of our family deities in different parts of the Palace compound',[62] his petition to Nazimuddin was not successful. Given that a requisition was fait accompli, Ram Narayan then called 'on your [Nazimuddin's] personal assurance as a premier, for protection of our interests, during our last meeting, *we as loyal subjects of the state* co-operated with the government and handed over the possession of the rooms requisitioned in the Palace'.[63] However, problems cropped up immediately after the requisition because, contrary to expectations, sections of the Palace were also converted into a boarding house for the employees of the Department of Forms and Stationeries. Ram Narayan claimed that the occupants 'often cause troubles during the performance of the daily *pujas* of the deities',[64] and also, 'do not take care of the house and *owing to their willful negligence the Palace has been greatly damaged and made filthy*'.[65] Thus, not only had the East Bengal government reneged on its promise that despite the requisition, normal religious activities at the Palace would continue but had also used the building for different purposes than stated earlier.

The allegation that the boarders were deliberate in their neglect of the Palace can be read as an expression of communal antagonism. Such communal rhetoric may seem misplaced given the demographic statistics of the area. Muslims comprised nearly 60 per cent of the population and the rest were of lower-caste Hindu peasants, Rajbanshis, and a tribal group called Banua.[66] But given the active mobilization of lower-caste groups along communal lines before the Partition, Ram Narayan's letter and newspaper reports easily made the connections between communal identity and citizenship in East Pakistan.

Matters came to a head when the *Ananda Bazar Patrika* reported an incident of cow slaughter (*Bhowal Prashadey Garu Jabai*) within the Palace grounds. The report also alleged that on 8 June 1948, 'the meat of the slaughtered cow was cooked and served to the Muslim boarders. In this way, they [the boarders] had defiled the most ancient Hindu zamindari. The adjacent pond, whose water was used for the *Puja*, had also been defiled.'[67] This report projected all the cultural and religious fears of the Hindus onto a physical institution. The 'cow slaughter' incident gained additional importance because of where it took place and became symbolic of all real and perceived minority persecution within East Bengal. Accordingly, the *Ananda Bazar Patrika* reported that the 'Hindus of Bhowal have again become frustrated and panicky' as a result of this incident.[68] For Ram Narayan, this incident provided the pretext to request the derequisitioning on the grounds that the East Bengal state had reneged on its promises to guarantee minority religious rights.

After investigating the incident, M. Siddiqui, the Under Secretary to the Government of Pakistan at Karachi, confirmed that some 'laborers' had indeed slaughtered a cow within the palace premises.[69] They had been 'severely warned' against repeating such an incident. However,

Siddiqui perceived anti-state rhetoric within the complaint made by the manager of the estate and noted:

Either allegations made by the manager of the estate, as indicated in the enclosure to the above letter, regarding interference by the Press staff with religious performance during *Puja*, conversion of major portions of the palace into a boarding house, and damage to the property are not correct and *appear to have been brought up along with the 'cow' incident merely for the sake of propaganda against Pakistan government*. The Pakistan government therefore refutes these allegations and would request the provincial government to send a note to this effect to the property owner, if there is no objection.[70]

Any complaint which centred on minority, and hence religious issues, was, as in this case, interpreted as a criticism of the legitimacy of the Pakistan state.

As the East Pakistan state tried to resolve the debate on whether the state would be a democracy or theocracy, the requisition process, more than any other factor, linked the issues of citizenship and religious rights. Notions of belonging and citizenship were embedded within one's place of residence in the pre-Partition era. However, specifically for the minorities, the requisition process intruded and tore apart this association. In such circumstances, their petitions interwove their dispossession within rhetoric of loss of religious rights and diminished cultural citizenship within the nation. Most petitions, thus, repeatedly identified individual homes as the abode of the *kuladevata* (family deity).[71] Thus, when Amrita Lal Bhowmick protested against the requisitioning of his house, he added that 'the room in which sits my family deity has also been locked up and I have thus been stopped from my daily Puja'.[72] Not only had he become displaced within his original locality but also his words reflected a cultural dispossession.

Why did minorities intersperse their complaints with such religious associations? These demands may indicate a continuation of Hindu communalism at play. However, in the project of creating national identities, both India, a declared secular state, and Pakistan, an Islamic Republic, continued to identify their citizens in terms of 'majority' and 'minority' citizens. Rather than an inherent identification with religion, the petitioners' use of religion was a tactical measure to strengthen their claims within the dynamic political and social environment after the Partition. This alliance between religious identity and residence contributed to the discourse of religious persecution that circumscribed the nation-building project in both countries.

It maybe fruitful to examine whether the East Pakistan state made any deliberate attempts to dispossess its minority citizens. Certain elements within the local administration definitely harboured anti-minority attitudes and/or interpreted the law to justify indiscriminate requisition. However, in general, the East Pakistan government was fully aware of the ramifications of such requisitions where the majority of property owners were Hindu, especially in the new capital of Dacca. In general, the government recruitment targeted all property owners irrespective of their religion. The B Proceedings of the Revenue and Finance Department, which contain petitions relating to the requisition process, reveal that several Muslim property owners faced similar problems to those of their Hindu counterparts. The following table (Table 3.1) gives a sample distribution of requisitioned houses between 1947 through 1950 in the three main administrative divisions of Chittagong, Rajshahi, and Dacca.[73]

Table 3.1 does not aim to be a comprehensive account, nor does it include these petitions surviving in official files uncritically. However, it indicates that the requisition process targeted houses rather than religions. The needs of state formation rather than minority persecution accounted for its arbitrariness. The Pakistan state viewed these houses as potential infrastructure that could speed up the establishment of the new nation. However, the owners of these properties regarded these spaces as their symbolic homeland and private property to which they alone could stake a claim. Thus, embedded within these petitions are the negotiations between personal

Table 3.1: Requisitioned Houses in Chittagong, Rajshahi,
and Dacca between 1947–50

	Hindu	Muslim
Chittagong	487	156
Rajshahi	105	23
Dacca	345	57

Source: Finance and Revenue (Requisition) files, Bundles 1–5, Bangladesh National Archives.

and official claims to what constitutes ownership. Homeowners, irrespective of their religion, viewed the state's inefficiency with regard to paying rent or the very randomness of the requisition process as an infringement of their citizenship rights. For minority Hindus, as the table indicates, such insecurities, generated by the requisition process, simply dovetailed into the existing rhetoric of minority persecution. Simultaneously, these petitions, in addressing their grievances to the Pakistani authorities, acknowledged the legitimacy of the new state rather than undermine it.

THE AFTERLIFE OF THE ACT

Following the riots of 1964 which engulfed large sections of West Bengal and East Pakistan, including the capital cities of Calcutta and Dacca, the Requisition of Property Act emerged in the form of an ordinance under a new name, Disturbed Persons Rehabilitation Ordinance Act of 1964. Although enacted to provide quick aid to the victims of the riots, it also created restrictions on the transfer of immovable property belonging to the minority Hindus without permission from the East Pakistan authorities. The seventeen deputy commissioners in the province were empowered to allow transfer of agricultural land amounting to only 2 acres or a maximum limit of one-fourth of the total landholding.[74] These government officials could sell other properties such as buildings but only at market prices not exceeding 5,000 rupees. The outbreak of war between India and Pakistan in 1965 resulted in the promulgation of the Defence of Pakistan Ordinance (Ordinance XIII of 1965) that authorized the East Pakistani authorities to acquire emergency powers in the defence of the state. A key component under this ordinance was an executive order titled, 'The Enemy Property (Custody and Registration) Order II of 1965'.[75] The immediate impact of this Ordinance was on the properties of those minority citizens who had migrated to India, either temporarily or permanently, and had hitherto continued to retain their rights of ownership. All such property was now identified as 'enemy property' and rights of ownership were transferred to the state.[76] Minority citizens in East Pakistan who had continued to hold property there even though they have migrated to India could no longer be ambivalent about their citizenship. The 1965 legislation directly linked national citizenship with actual residence and property ownership.

That the Bengal Partition engendered a chronic refugee migration lasting nearly two decades was a response to official state policies *after* the Partition. Changing patterns of border control, introduction of new systems of surveillance such as the passport and visa scheme, and the arbitrary requisitioning of property emphasized, especially to the minorities on both sides of the border, that these restrictions would cease only with migration. Paradoxically, although prominent leaders in both countries urged each other to create conditions of safety and security in the minds of their minorities, their efforts at nation building were counterproductive to such rhetoric. The evacuee property and requisitioning laws in East Pakistan are a prime example of such a process. As we shall see later in the book, the physical dispossession engendered by these laws fused easily with incidents of small-scale violence to contribute towards a growing rhetoric of minority persecution. Media depictions of minorities as 'fifth columnists' added fuel to the fire, making it difficult for minorities to remain in their homes. They were presented with Hobsonian choice, either to remain minorities in their own countries and face continuous suspicions from the majority community or become refugees in an alien country and face the uncertainty of a flawed rehabilitation policy.

NOTES

1. These 'optees', as they were called, had the right to opt to work permanently or provisionally based on their religious affiliation. Those who decided to exercise the latter option were given the right to revise their decision within six months, and both India and Pakistan guaranteed that they would take back those who revised their provisional decisions.

2. S.A. Khan to A.K. Azad, September 1947, Durga Das (ed.), 1972, *Sardar Patel's Correspondence, 1945–50. Vol. 1-8*, Ahmedabad: Navajivan Publishing House, p. 421.

3. Joya Chatterji alludes to 'a systematic campaign of intimidation launched to "persuade" Muslims in government service to quit West Bengal and go to Pakistan'. See Joya Chatterji, 2005, 'Of Graveyards and Ghettos: Muslims in Partitioned West Bengal 1947–67', in Mushirul Hasan and Asim Roy (eds), *Living Together Separately: Cultural India in History and Politics*, New Delhi: Oxford University Press, p. 230.

4. *Ibid.*, pp. 164–8.

5. In response to incidents of looting and illegal occupations of houses left behind by evacuees, the Joint Defence Council, on 29 August 1947, created the office of the 'Custodian of Refugee's Property' to protect the properties of the

displaced. See 'The Property of Refugees', Minutes of the Joint Defence Council, 29 August 1947, MP File no. 128, Oriental and India Office Collections (OIOC), London.

6. Inter-dominion Conference, 6–15 December 1948, New Delhi, reproduced in Muhammad Ghulam Kabir, 1980, *Minority Politics in Bangladesh*, New Delhi: Vikas, pp. 100–5.

7. Restricted access to sources in the National Archives of India (NAI) in Delhi and the police records of the Intelligence Bureau in Calcutta have prevented a detailed examination of how the evacuee property legislation operated and affected the lives of the Muslim minority in West Bengal. However, a recent article on the condition of Muslim minorities in West Bengal provides an excellent description on the marginalization of the community. See Chatterji, *'Of Graveyards and Ghettos'*, pp. 222–49.

8. East Bengal, Pakistan, 1949, *Legislative Assembly Proceedings: Official Report, Vol. 3, No. 4*, EBLA, Third Session, Dacca: East Bengal Government Press, 5 April, pp. 55–73; also, *CAP Debates, Vol 1 (8 and 9)*, March 1948, pp. 219, 286, quoted in Kabir, *Minority Politics in Bangladesh*, p. 20.

9. Memo no. 6127 (50), 18 July 1951, File no. 1L-3 of 1951, B Proceedings 272, Finance and Revenue (Requisition) Department, Government of East Bengal (GoEB), May 1952.

10. *Ibid.*

11. Ashraf Mohammad, 1957, *Evacuee & Rehabilitation Laws, Containing up to date Central & Provincial Acts and Ordinances…: With Rehabilitation Resettlement Scheme Punjab…& Inter-domain Agreements regarding Evacuees (India & Pakistan)*, Lahore: All Pakistan Legal Publications, p. 368.

12. East Bengal Evacuee Property (Restoration of Possession) Act, 1951, reproduced in Mohammad, *Evacuee & Rehabilitation Laws*, pp. 368–78. The prescribed date in this case was 1 January 1950.

13. See 1951, *Constituent Assembly (Legislature) of Pakistan Debates*, Dhaka: Dhaka University Library, 6 April, pp. 897–923.

14. The East Bengal (Emergency) Requisition of Property Ordinance, 1948, drafted by the Legislative and Judicial Department, Legislative Branch, East Bengal Government, B Proceedings 23, Legislative, May 1950, Bangladesh National Archives (BNA).

15. *Ibid.*

16. The time limit of six months was measured from the date on which the provincial government made a proclamation in the official gazette that normal conditions had been restored in the province.

17. East Bengal, Pakistan, *Legislative Assembly Proceedings*, p. 57.

18. Press Note on Moveable Properties of Displaced Persons, Ministry of Rehabilitation (*ibid.*, pp. 562–3).

19. Machines such as typewriters, sewing machines, bicycles, refrigerators, radios, cars, gramophones, musical instruments, electrical goods, and professional apparatus were allowed for removal to the other country (*ibid.*, p. 562).

20. *Dawn*, 11 July 1947.

21. Petition, 15 February 1949, File no. Tr-9/49, B Proceedings 966–81, Finance and Revenue Department, August 1954, BNA.

22. *Ibid.*

23. District Magistrate to Deputy Secretary, GoEB (*ibid.*).

24. Barman also alleged '50 houses in Kishoreganj, about 30 houses at Bajitpur and a large number of houses in Netrokona and Mymensingh have been similarly requisitioned inspite of the fact that most of them were occupied by the owners or their members/men'. File no. My-55/50, B Proceedings 518–29, Revenue (Requisition) Department, August 1954, BNA.

25. In a press note issued from Dacca in August 1950, the Government of East Pakistan had assured minorities that 'it is not the intention of government to requisition any houses in which the owner or relatives of the owner are still living, and if a migrant who has left after the disturbances wishes to come back to reside in the province, his house, if requisitioned by the government will be derequisitioned forthwith' (*ibid.*).

26. Extract from report of SDO Kishoreganj to District Magistrate Mymensingh, 19 August 1950 (*ibid.*).

27. *Hindustan Standard* (*HS*), 12 July 1950.

28. File no. Br-24/50, B Proceedings 3040–6, Revenue (Requisition) Department, August 1954, BNA.

29. Several memoirs of well-known Bengali intellectuals allude to the traditional economic connections between eastern Bengal and Calcutta. See Nirad C. Chaudhuri, 1951, *The Autobiography of an Unknown Indian*, London: Chatto and Windus; Tapan Raychaudhuri, 1993, *Romanthan Athaba Bhimratipraptar Paracharitcharcha*, Calcutta: Ananda Publishers.

30. File no. Da-321/50, B Proceedings 1574–84, Revenue (Requisition) Department , August 1954, BNA.

31. Muslim Partition refugees from India referred to themselves as muhajirs. The term highlights the act of migration.

32. File no. Da-327/50, B Proceedings 1585–99, Finance and Revenue (Requisition) Department, August 1954, BNA.

33. Report dated 2 August 1950 (*ibid.*).

34. Petition to Deputy Secretary, Revenue (Requisition) Department, 31 October 1948, File no Tr 1/49, B Proceedings 938–54, Revenue Department, Requisition Branch, July 1954,BNA.

35. *Ibid.*

36. *Ibid.*

37. The district magistrate wrote, 'We are facing the same difficulty in taking possession of the houses under requisition. There are 402 cases of requisition of which only 80% of the houses were taken over possession and the rest could not be taken over due to objections after objections on false or fictitious grounds. It is the habitual tendency of the owners of the houses under requisition, inspite of realizing that these houses were being requisitioned under the painful necessity of the government to provide officers with accommodation' (*ibid.*).

38. File no. Da-302/50, B Proceedings 1550–7, Revenue (Requisition) Department, August 1954, BNA.

39. *Ibid.*

40. The East Bengal (Emergency) Requisition of Property Ordinance, 1948, drafted by the Legislative and Judicial Department, Legislative Branch, East Bengal Government, B Proceedings 23, Legislative, May 1950, BNA.

41. File no. Da-52/49, B Proceedings 99–101, Revenue (Acquisition) Department, July 1954, BNA.

42. *Ibid.*

43. *Ibid.*

44. File no. 8A-28/52, B Proceedings 1298–9, Home (Political), GoEB, April1953, BNA.

45. *Ibid.*

46. *Ibid.*

47. *HS*, 24 November 1948, p. 4. The concern over properties left behind and whether they would get any compensation was central in the minds of those who migrated to India and was reported regularly in Indian newspapers. See *HS*, 28 June 1948, p. 4; *HS*, 3 September 1948, p. 7; *HS*, 8 November 1948, p. 4.

48. *Ibid.*

49. Letter dated 7 March 1949, File no. 11-241, B Proceedings 8–9, Bundle 49, Home Political Department, August 1949, BNA.

50. *Ibid.*

51. Shyama Prasad Mukherjee was the most vocal critic of the alleged efforts of the East Pakistani state to 'squeeze out' Hindus. See his letter to B.C. Roy, 22 August 1950, *Shyama Prasad Mukherjee Papers* (*SPM Papers*), *Refugees and Minorities, 1950–1951*, File no 39, Index vol. 1, Nehru Memorial Museum and Library (NMML), New Delhi. Interestingly, he also used the same term in his appeals for complete rehabilitation of refugees from East Pakistan. In this case, he interpreted the limited efforts of the Indian government towards rehabilitating Hindu refugees from East Pakistan as 'efforts to squeeze (them) out back into Pakistan'. See his note 'Statistics on Migration', *SPM Papers, Refugees and Minorities, 1949–1950*, File no. 33, NMML.

52. *HS*, 19 December 1947.

53. Samar Guha, 1951, *Non Muslims behind the Curtain of East Pakistan*, Dacca: East Bengal Minorities Association, p. 22.

54. The East Bengal (Emergency) Requisition of Property Ordinance, drafted by the Legislative and Judicial Department, Legislative Branch, East Bengal Government, B Proceedings 23, Legislative, May 1950.

55. File no. Jr-21/49, B Proceedings 737–42, Finance and Revenue (Requisition) Department, July1954, BNA.

56. Letter dated 8 March 1949 (*ibid.*); translation by author.

57. See files of the Finance and Revenue (Requisition) Department, Vols 1–4, BNA.

58. Memo no. 342, 13 April 1949, File no. Jr-21/49, B Proceedings 737–42, Finance and Revenue (Requisition) Department, July 1954, BNA.

59. *Ibid.*

60. Memo no. 113C, dated 26 March 1949 (*ibid.*).

61. The Bhawal estate was situated 22 miles north of Dacca city, within the Madhupur forest region. It was one of the largest zamindari estates in Dacca, although much of the land was not as productive as those of the riverine estates. For more details, see Partha Chatterjee, 2002, *A Princely Imposter? The Strange and Universal History of the Kumar of Bhawal*, Princeton, NJ: Princeton University Press, pp. 15–31.

62. *Ibid.*

63. *Ibid.*

64. The main cause of complaint was the earlier communal issue of playing of music during daily worship. File no. Jr-21/49, 1954, B Proceedings 737–42, Finance and Revenue (Requisition) Department, July 1954, BNA.

65. *Ibid.*

66. Chatterjee, *A Princely Imposter*, p. 16.

67. File no. Jr-21/49, B Proceedings 737–42, Finance and Revenue (Requisition) Department, July1954, BNA.

68. *Ibid.*

69. Memo dated 22 January 1949 (*ibid.*).

70. *Ibid.*, emphasis added.

71. See Finance and Revenue (Requisition) Department, Files no. Da-346/50, B Proceedings 1647–54, August 1954 and Da-71/50, B Proceedings 271–92, July 1954; and File no. 1I-293 of 1948, B Proceedings 16–24, Home Political, May 1950.

72. File no. Da-302/50, B Proceedings 1550–7, Revenue Requisition, August 1954, BNA.

73. Thanks to Irfat Ara for helping me with the compilation.

74. Abul Barkat (ed.), 2000, *An Inquiry into Causes and Consequences of Deprivation of Hindu Minorities in Bangladesh through the Vested Property Act: Framework for a Realistic Solution*, Dhaka: PRIP Trust, pp. 19–20.

75. India was declared an enemy country. The custodian of enemy property took over all interests of the enemy (that is, nationals/citizens of India, those residing in the territory occupied/captured/controlled by India) in firms and companies as well as in the lands and building situated in Pakistan for control or management. The benefits arising out of trade, business, or lands and buildings were not to go to the enemy, so as not to affect the security of the state of Pakistan or impair its defence in any manner.

76. The act had clear communal overtones. An official circular specified that Muslims residing in India, including those who were Indian citizens, would be excluded from the category of the 'enemy'. Further, the properties of such Muslim owners would be handed over to them or their legal heirs upon demand. Although the war ended by September 1965, this act continued to be in force in later years and finally culminated in the Vested Property and Assets Order of 1972 passed by the new Bangladesh government.

4

Citizens of the Nation

The relationships between nation, territory, and citizens were far from resolved after the Partition. Both India and Pakistan were, at least overtly, averse to identifying and equating their citizens along any religious demographic calculus. However, it was difficult to ignore the persistent dilemmas about national identities in the post-Partition context. How was citizenship to be defined? Should a woman's citizenship depend on her marital or birth status? Were Muslims in India (proto-) Pakistanis and Hindus in Pakistan (proto-) Indians? Moreover, the act of crossing the border, even if temporary, served to define one's nationality and permanently marked intent of acquiring a new citizenship and the relinquishing of original identity. Migration ensured that the same person could be designated an *evacuee* in one country and a *refugee* in another. Neither term guaranteed citizenship rights. Even when they were permanent residents without any intention of moving across the border, the perception persisted that Muslim minorities in India were potentially loyal to Pakistan and Hindu minorities in East Pakistan were proxy citizens of India. Then, how did one become a citizen in the post-Partition period?

This chapter examines the processes and legislations in India that sought to clear up such confusions. Although the laws defining citizenship came to be established by the Citizenship Act of 1955, ambiguities about who was entitled to an Indian citizenship continued and the laws were prone to contextual interpretation with regard to those groups who would become 'minorities' within India and

Pakistan after 1947. While in practice, officials often failed to accurately implement equal rights when it came to India's Muslim minorities, concern for Hindu minorities across the border in East Pakistan continued to guide official policy and actions in the post-Partition period. In fact, it was the continuing migration in the east (rather than in the west) that forced the architects of the Indian Citizenship Act to confront specifically the modalities of defining a 'citizen' and to formulate rules for refugees to acquire Indian citizenship.

WHICH NATION DO WE BELONG TO?

Along with territorial negotiations, India and Pakistan were simultaneously confronted with the issues of nationality and citizenship, especially of those people who had now become religious minorities in each of their territories. The large-scale en masse migration of Hindus from West Pakistan to India meant that India and Pakistan's concerns over their minorities focused mainly on the large number of Muslim minorities in India and Hindu minorities who remained in East Pakistan.

Both Nehru and Jinnah were against any mass population exchange, recognizing the economic burden such a process would engender. On the one hand, Jinnah, at a gathering of defence and civilian personnel at Karachi on 11 October 1947, declared that if the 'ultimate solution of the minority problem is to be mass exchange of population, let it be taken up at governmental plane and not be left to be sorted out by blood thirsty elements'.[1] On the other hand, Nehru thought that an exchange of population would 'upset the economy of India', and that 'we will sink as a nation without any resources with a starving and dying population'.[2] They publicly assured their respective minorities of their citizenship rights and the continuation of their religion and culture. In the first session of the Constituent Assembly of Pakistan, Jinnah promised the Hindu minorities that they had nothing to fear and would have citizenship rights equal to those of the majority Muslim citizens. He declared:

Much has been said against it [the Partition], but now it has been accepted, it is the duty of every one of us to loyally abide by it and honorably act according to the agreement which is now final and binding on all ... If you change your past and work together in a spirit that everyone of you no matter what community he belongs to, no matter what relations he had with you in the past, no matter what his colour, caste or creed, is first, second, and last a citizen of this state with equal rights, privileges and obligations, there will be no end to the progress you will make.[3]

He further affirmed, 'You are free; you are free to go to your temples, you are free to go to your mosques or to any other places of worship in this state of Pakistan. You may belong to any religion caste or creed—that has nothing to do with the business of the state.'[4] In later years, both Pakistani officials and Indian authorities often quoted this speech; first, to provide assurance to their minorities that Pakistan was not a theocratic state and second, as an indictment of unkept promises. Similarly, when he addressed the annual Congress Working Committee meeting on 15 November 1947, Nehru asserted:

The Congress wants to assure the minorities in India that it will continue to protect to the best of their ability, their citizen rights against aggression. The central government as well as the provincial governments must accordingly make every effort to create conditions wherein all minorities and all citizens have security and opportunity for progress. All citizens must also on their part not only share in the benefits of freedom but also shoulder the burdens and responsibility that accompany it, and *must above all be loyal to India.*[5]

Implicit within Nehru's guarantee was the notion that minorities had to specially ensure that their loyalty to the nation was above suspicion.

During the summer and autumn of 1947, local and national Congress leaders began to articulate an explicit hostage theory whereby the safety of the minorities of one state would guarantee the security of the other. In July 1947, when urging Hindus to remain in East Bengal, Nalini Ranjan Sarkar boldly declared: 'I have absolutely no doubt that in West Bengal and in the Indian Union the Muslims would get a fair deal, and this cannot but react favorably on the Hindu minorities in Pakistan.'[6] Addressing the annual All India Congress Committee (AICC) meeting on 15 November 1947, the Congress Working Committee President, Jivatram Kripalani, noted:

We should frankly tell the League minded Muslims that though we, Congressmen and our governments are determined to protect them, we can't do so merely on the strength of our police and army ... The safety of the Muslims must come from their Hindu neighbors who form a majority of the population and from whom the majority in the ranks of the police and army must come. These will not be active in affording protection unless they know that *their co-religionists in Pakistan are getting a fair deal.*[7]

Another well-known Congress member and a Muslim, Maulana Abul Kalam Azad, acknowledged that:

It was being openly said in the Congress circles that Hindus in Pakistan need not have any fears as there would be 45 millions of Muslims in India and if there was any oppression of Hindus in Pakistan, the Muslims in India would have to bear the consequences ... It implied that partition was being accepted on the basis that in both India and Pakistan, there would be hostages who would be held responsible for the security of the minority community in the other state.[8]

The parallel riots that engulfed Punjab immediately after the Partition confirmed such a perception in the public mind. Reminiscing in 1968 on the Partition period, Pravash Chandra Lahiry, a Hindu Congress leader in East Bengal, noted that the Bengali Muslims became apprehensive as news of butchering of Hindus in West Punjab reached West Bengal. According to Lahiry, such obvious correspondence was a direct outcome of the Partition that had created minority populations who, almost overnight, had became responsible for the actions of their co-religionists across the border.[9] Lahiry contended that in Bengal, Mahatma Gandhi, who had arrived in Calcutta in September 1947 to calm fears of the Muslim minorities in West Bengal, had forestalled violence in the aftermath of Partition.

Minorities as 'hostages' may have acted as a deterrent to large-scale violence on the eastern border, but they also introduced some basic and difficult questions on citizenship and belonging within the new nation-states. For example, Azad noted that on the eve of independence, 'Jinnah left for Karachi with a message to his followers that now that the country was divided they should be loyal citizens of India'.[10] Such suggestions had left Muslim leaders in minority provinces such as Uttar Pradesh and Bihar which remained part of India with a sense of deception and loss. Azad remarked, '... strange fact that these Muslim Leaguers had been foolishly persuaded that once Pakistan was formed, Muslims whether they came from a majority province would be regarded as a separate nation ... they at last realized that they had gained nothing but in fact lost everything by the partition of India.'[11] Having been numerically and politically weakened, the minority Muslims in India had to confront the difficult question of national loyalty.

Similarly, Pravash Chandra Lahiry's initial reaction to the Partition was one of personal failure and stark alienation. He noted in his memoirs, 'I was a freedom fighter of the Indian nationalist movement. I used to feel proud to be an Indian. But today I still exist but not as an Indian—my identity is that of a Pakistani! There is only one question in everyone's mind—Will we be able to live in a theocratic state with honor?'[12] Samar Guha, the Secretary of the East Bengal Minorities Association, also lamented that Hindus in East Bengal were 'no longer Indians'.[13] Letters to West Bengal newspapers also indicated this sense of confusion over their national identity. Sailendranath Roy from Dhaka wrote, 'A large section of people in eastern Bengal cannot reconcile themselves to the idea that they are no longer Indians or even Bengalis but merely Pakistanis.'[14] Roy echoed the perception of national disinheritance among Hindus in East Pakistan who equated Pakistan with being a homeland only for Muslims. They continued to identify their nationality with India. Even Nehru confirmed such perceptions at a press conference on 15 December 1947 in Calcutta where he noted, 'Even though Pakistan is a separate and independent country—and we must treat it so—I find it a little difficult to think of it as alien to India and of its people as *anything but Indians*.'[15] To be fair, Nehru's vision included both Hindus and Muslims of Pakistan.

The primary issues regarding nationality and citizenship were twofold. First, was it possible for Hindus living in East Pakistan to identify themselves with India even while maintaining residence in East Pakistan? Second, was it possible for minority Muslims in India who had hitherto identified with the Pakistan movement to acquire not only legal but also moral citizenship of India? Although the Constituent Assembly of India, instituted in December 1946 to debate the legal dimensions of nationhood and citizenship and to draft the Indian constitution, decided to grant equal rights to all citizens irrespective of caste and creed, they tacitly required citizenship to be based on residency.

Consequently, Indian authorities expected Hindu minorities whose residences became part of Pakistan to acquire Pakistani citizenship. But minorities in East Pakistan hoped for a different declaration and had begun the public debate on such issues even before the Partition. Major English and Bengali newspapers published letters from their readers expressing concern over the future nationality of Bengali Hindus.[16] A letter from Faridpur urged the exchange of population and questioned higher authorities, 'What will be the position of the Hindus in Pakistan Bengal? If they are given the right of citizenship of the Hindustan union they will be *treated as aliens* in Pakistan Bengal. There is the same risk if they accept the right of citizenship of Pakistan dominion.'[17] In June 1947, the local branch of the Hindu Mahasabha, in the Munshiganj district of Dacca, passed a resolution which demanded 'the right of citizenship or equal rights and privileges be conceived to the Hindu population of Eastern Pakistan in the West Bengal province [*sic*], as such no passport be required for Hindus of eastern Pakistan to go to Indian union'.[18] The resolution, even while anticipating the imposition of certain documentary criteria for Bengali Hindus, did not foresee that minorities would be forced to move after Partition. Thus, it was not unimaginable to continue to live in one country and be a citizen of another.

This question of nationality for minorities residing on the 'wrong' side of the border was fundamental both in the debates leading up to the Partition and in the public mind, after the division, as respective governments attempted to articulate clear guidelines. Amrendra Nath Mukherjee, in an article published a month after the Partition in the *Modern Review*, a nationalist journal published from Calcutta, debated whether Indian nationality should be conferred on the basis of *jus soli* (law of soil) or *jus sanguinis* (law of blood).[19] He argued that all minorities, especially the Hindus in East Bengal, should not be deprived of their Indian nationality on the basis of their residence outside of the new political boundaries. Rather, minority Hindus should be accorded a 'double nationality'. Although Muslims of Pakistan should also be allowed to adopt Indian nationality, Mukherjee assumed that 'Muslims of Pakistan feel glory in their separate nationality and would reject any offer of Union (Indian) nationality even if it was conferred upon them'. But the Hindus in Pakistan 'would feel glory in their mother State ... and submit to Pakistan nationality with reluctance and under pressure of circumstances.'[20] If hostilities occurred between the two countries, Mukherjee continued that persons with such dual citizenship would declare their loyalty to one country even if they may reside in the other. Such a declaration of allegiance would suffice to prevent any accusations of treason.

Mukherjee was not alone in advocating such simplistic formula ensuring Indian citizenship to the minority Hindus in East Bengal. In a letter to the *Amrita Bazar Patrika* of Calcutta, a correspondent identified only with the initials C.L.C., demanded that the constituent assembly should ensure that 'the people of minority communities in Pakistan if they so choose can elect India citizenship by virtue of their citizenship of pre-partition India, while residing in Pakistan and will thus forfeit their claim to Pakistan citizenship ...'.[21] Although this legislation would result in making the minorities 'aliens in their country of residence, the statutory provision will create the necessary psychological atmosphere by removing their sense of being left in the lurch'.[22] Further, the writer asserted that such a provision would enable India 'to intervene through constitutional means in case Pakistan continues in its policy of persecution of minorities who by virtue of their electing Indian citizenship will then be Indian nationals'.[23] For both these individuals, a seamless interface between national identity and loyalty to the nation did not involve a change of address. Pre-Partition social ties and residence rather than post-Partition domicile were the determining factors in attaining Indian citizenship. However, for minorities in West and East Bengal who continued to reside in their ancestral homes, such ingenuous formulations of nationality became complicated with residence and property ownership.

Nehru, at the plenary session of the Congress in 1948, vetoed the theoretical possibility that Hindu minorities could remain in East Bengal but become citizens of India, as impractical and disastrous. Rather, he clarified, 'The only right course for those who live in the Indian dominion is to be loyal to the Indian dominion and similarly this should apply to the other side, because there is no other way of approach to the problem.'[24] Nehru's declaration contradicted the hopes of Hindu minorities in East Bengal for whom inclusion within the imagined national community through constitutional means was not based on their current residence.

THE CASE OF MINORITIES' LOYALTY TO THE NATION

For those who were on the 'right' side of the border, becoming Indians and Pakistanis respectively, after Partition, did not elicit a similar dilemma between their national identity and citizenship. However, for those who became minorities, nationality became a key issue determining not only residency but also loyalty. For Muslims in West Bengal, the communally charged environment of India's relations with the princely states of Kashmir and Hyderabad assured that they became the quintessential representatives of the whole community in their localities.[25] As members of a community which had been closely connected with demand for Pakistan, the Muslim minority in India became the usual suspects of anti-state activities. A letter to the editor of *Amrita Bazar Patrika* is emblematic of the general feeling towards the Muslim minorities in the region. Written in the aftermath of the riots of 1950, the author, S.C. Chatterjee, asserted that:

Muslims having achieved their first objective—Pakistan, are busy making preparations in that state for the attainment of their next objective, namely Pakistanization [*sic*] of India … we find organized efforts are being made by some Muslims in India to help Pakistan in many ways. This is not *unnatural* for them … They have been advised to keep themselves ready for the appointed day of liberation … the soft hearted treatment of all Muslims irrespective of their real attitude towards India, and the stern attitude towards the Hindus which seem to mark the present administration of our country are all but disconcerting to many sane people. It is as if the time honored maxim of administration namely, *controlling the wicked and protecting the good citizens has been reversed for the time being.*[26]

In addition to arguing that the Muslims were inherently disloyal, Chatterjee deployed the stereotype of the 'wicked' and aggressive Muslim against the 'good citizens' who, by implication, are the Hindus.

The discourse on Muslim disloyalty to the Indian nation was echoed at the national level, especially at the constituent assembly sessions after Partition, as Indian leaders debated the issue of minority rights. Any demand for separate electorates or reservation of legislative seats for the Muslim minority was interpreted as reminiscent of pre-Partition League politics. Vallabhbhai Patel, the Deputy Prime Minister of India, indicated, 'Those who want that kind of thing (separate electorates) to have a place in Pakistan, not here … We are laying the foundations of One Nation, and those who choose to divide again and sow the seeds of disruption will have no place, no quarter here.'[27]

Nehru was aware that the minorities in the new nations would be the first to confront the issue of notional citizenship. At press conference in Delhi in October 1947, he noted that 'there are people for whom the question is not decided in their own minds, and we do not want to force a decision on them. A Hindu for instance, may be in Karachi; I cannot tell him that he cannot become an Indian citizen; if he wants he can be one and we will accept him. But if you live here you owe loyalty to the state you live in.'[28] Nonetheless, he went on to qualify that 'an Indian citizen may live in Pakistan, but he owes allegiance to us and he is not a citizen of Pakistan'.[29] Although at first glance his utterances may seem contradictory, it is evident that for Nehru the primary criterion for citizenship was loyalty to the state, even if one's residence remained on the 'wrong' side of the border. He was, however, against any 'dual citizenship' arguing that once both countries became politically stable, national citizenship would follow suit.[30]

Muslim and Hindu minorities of Bengal who had the means to migrate sought to end their predicament by moving across the border. They hoped that such a move, influenced by unsettled political circumstances, would resolve the immediate differences between legal and moral citizenship. Those who did not migrate had to negotiate the semiotics of religious identity in their daily lives. An editorial in the *Morning News*, published in Dacca, East Bengal, and claiming to represent the viewpoint of the Muslim minority in West Bengal, questioned, 'Do Muslims live here by right or on sufferance? If the Government wants them to live like *shudras* it should not fight shy of saying so, and in that case there would be no need for the Muslim members to pollute the West Bengal Assembly by their unwanted presence.'[31] It is significant that the editor, in indicated the discrimination towards the Muslim minority, adopted the terminology of the caste system in which lowest rung comprised the Shudras. On another occasion, Fazlur Rahman, a resident of Calcutta, wrote to his friend in Dacca in early 1948 describing the situation in Calcutta as no longer conducive towards Muslims. According to Rahman, Muslims in West Bengal could not 'even move freely by wearing a *lungi*'.[32] Further, at the time of Holi, 'colored water was thrown on Muslims and Europeans by saying that those who want to live in Hindustan should have to observe all the Hindu festivals otherwise they may go to Pakistan'.[33] Another anonymous writer described how the Muslims going to East Pakistan were:

... thoroughly searched and those carrying cloth or other prohibited articles are arrested. This is another way how this Hindu government harasses Muslims

... I understand that restrictions are going to be tightened and the public, particularly the Muslims who are the target, will be put to great trouble. In these circumstances he is wise who gets aside before the storm comes with full blast.[34]

Minorities who continued to remain in their ancestral homes thus prepared themselves for flight across border at any hint of trouble. Migration was one of the ways in which minorities in each nation sought to resolve the ambiguities between their religious and residential identities. However, their move across the border served only to confirm the idea that minorities were proxy citizens of the other nation. In the case of Muslim minorities in India who had moved to East Pakistan, their migration had clearly laid out their loyalty to another state that could not be erased even if they returned to their ancestral homes at a later date. An editorial in the *Amrita Bazar Patrika* in July 1948 captured this perception of Muslim disloyalty accurately as it stated that 'A non-Muslim finds it impossible to adjust himself to the political pattern of the ancient Shariat. We do not know how a Muslim in his heart of hearts reacts to the Indian Union.'[35] According to the editorial, the introduction of the 'rule of the Shariat' in Pakistan thus provided a legitimate basis for the Hindu minority in Pakistan to feel alienated, whereas Indian Muslims were taken to be inherently disloyal. The demand for Pakistan and its realization had forever branded the Muslim minority in India as fifth columnists.

The communal logic of the Partition process itself generated automatic linkages between religion and nationality as in the case of the division of personnel from the civil and military services. These Optees had the right to 'opt' for either India or Pakistan, irrespective of where their hometowns were, and could, at least on paper, change their decisions within six months. The general assumption in this division that religion would be the basis of the choice ensured that Hindu and Sikh officers were expected to serve in India and Muslim officers in Pakistan.[36] Further, the element of choice was often illusory as the communal logic of the Partition played a primary role in forcing such decisions. For these minority civil servants caught between serving the state and serving the nation, their decisions to migrate were taken not only because of a general feeling of insecurity but often under coercion from neighbours and co-workers.[37]

In Bengal, Prafulla Ghosh, the Chief Minister of Bengal in 1947, announced that all Hindu officers of East Bengal would be given the option to choose India as their base of operation. Out of the nineteen Muslim Indian Civil Service (ICS) officers in Bengal, eighteen opted to join the Government of Pakistan.[38] All of the Hindu ICS officers opted to serve in India. In effect, for Bengal, which had a high percentage of Hindu officers in the civil bureaucracy, this signified a quasi-state-sponsored official exchange.

Not surprisingly, Ghosh's announcement did not find favour with some of the minority Hindus in eastern Bengal who realized that such a transfer would result in significant concentration of Muslims within higher ranks, thus skewing communal equation against them. At a meeting held on 23 July 1947, some representatives of the Hindu community passed a resolution requesting the West Bengal government to revise its policy. Similarly, a letter to *Hindustan Standard* urged,

Even at the risk of being misunderstood, the West Bengal government ought to make it clear at once that no Hindu officer who is a permanent resident of East Bengal will be allowed to serve in West Bengal as long as it can be shown that his service interest will be safe in the hands of the East Bengal government.[39]

The writer feared,

It is reported that as a result of the choice of the Hindu government employees for West Bengal, the new government of East Bengal will be short of officers in the BCS (Bengal Civil Service) and the BPS (Bengal Police Service) cadres by more than two hundred which deficiency will be met by recruitment of Muslims from outside of Bengal.[40]

He noted that the decision to join the West Bengal government was 'unpatriotic'. In a similar vein, a pamphlet showcasing the minority Hindus' plight in East Bengal claimed that the policy of transferring officials had isolated the community even further.[41]

When each state implicitly conflated an officer's loyalty to the state of his choice with his religion, the difficulties increased. For example, Ghulam Hussain Hidayatullah, the Premier of the Sind province in West Pakistan, allegedly circulated a private note that identified the existing leakages of confidential information with the non-Muslim members of the Pakistani Criminal Investigation Department. He stated, 'I feel compelled to the necessity of placing only Muslims in confidential branches and also in the CID [Criminal Investigation Department] staff.[42] Similarly, in India, Govind Malaviya, the youngest son of the Pandit Madan Mohan Malaviya, a prominent Hindu nationalist and a member of the Central Legislative Assembly, echoed some perceptions about those Muslim officers who had decided to remain in India. In a letter to Vallabhbhai Patel, he voiced his misgivings about these officers:

I have been worried over the report in the newspapers that the personnel of the services are receiving enquiries as to whether they would prefer to remain in Pakistan or in India. Is it contemplated that Muslim officers (and who does not know the part they have been playing during these several months in the secretariat and other offices?) will be allowed to remain with us if they choose to do so? It is a terrible price we have paid for getting rid of this curse of divided loyalties and fifth columnism! Have we still to carry this load round our neck? It may sound a little hard, but the only right and safe course will be that we should ask them *without reservation or exception to move onto their own area.*[43]

Patel replied that once India became independent on 15 August,

The service rules and regulations will be strictly enforced and *no disloyalty will be tolerated.* The oath of loyalty to the Indian government will first be administered to all, and anyone found to have other sympathy or loyalty with any outside agency or organization will have to leave service. You may therefore rest assured that *proper action will be taken to see that all such people are weeded out from here.*[44]

But how did a minority officer show his loyalty if he had decided against migration and remained in his home? Was it even possible to design a process that would measure loyalty to the nation? Nasir Hussain Rizvi, a well-educated Muslim lawyer from Lucknow, proposed an innovative if fantastic idea to counter the 'atmosphere surcharged with suspicion and distrust' in his hometown. In a letter to Patel, he declared,

I come forward to assert my loyalty to my motherland and in proof whereof I beg to offer not only my services but also my life unreservedly and unconditionally in the cause of my country. I am ready to do anything, whether directed against any foreign power or person of my religion. As a guarantee of my sincerity and truthfulness of my assertion I offer my mother and three unmarried sisters as hostages to be held by the Government.[45]

Rizvi's pledge implicitly objectified the women in his family as guarantors of his personal honour. As expected, Patel certified that the Government of India would not take 'hostages' to guarantee loyalty and indicated that Rizvi could give 'positive proof of (his) loyalty' in other ways.[46] Although Rizvi's proposal may seem farfetched, it illustrates the confusion that plagued people's minds with regard to their citizenship and identity in post-Partition India.

REFUGEES OR CITIZENS

The confusion with regard to nationality and citizenship was complicated further in the case of Hindu minorities who continued to cross over intermittently through out the post-Partition period. In the absence of appropriate legislation, these minorities had to negotiate the ambiguities between their migration, residence, and putative and 'natural' national identities. Viewed as 'evacuees' in East Pakistan, Hindu minorities who sought the help of Indian government's relief and rehabilitation measures came to be denoted as 'refugees' after they had crossed the border.

The initial strategy of the Government of India had been to allow citizenship rights to those migrants who officially declared their intention to become citizens of India and later acquired the necessary documentation. Part II (Articles 5–10) of the Indian constitution was the first template on which the rules of citizenship were enshrined.[47] In addition to the criteria of birth and descent, the members of the constituent assembly had drafted special rules of citizenship for those migrants to and from India and Pakistan. In short, for a migrant who had hitherto been a resident of the newly created territory of Pakistan, to be an Indian national, had to show, among other things, that he or she was domiciled in India on 26th of January 1950, had not migrated to Pakistan,[48] and had not acquired the citizenship of a foreign state.[49]

Further, getting one's name on the electoral rolls was one of the primary ways to ensure subsequent citizenship rights. Such strategies presented two contradictory dilemmas for Indian authorities. On the one hand, by allowing any migrant to acquire citizenship, it could limit its rehabilitation responsibilities towards the refugees. On the other hand, the government feared that such a policy might encourage Hindu minorities to continue migration that would create not only an economic strain but also threaten the secular façade of the Indian state. So, the Indian government fixed a time limit by which a refugee/migrant had to declare his/her intention to stay in India,[50] and in the early 1950s, declared that inclusion within the electoral rolls would not guarantee automatic citizenship rights.

The issue of citizenship was primarily influenced by the status of Partition refugees in India. Although most of the national attention was reserved for the relief and rehabilitation of the refugees from divided Punjab, the migration and consequent generation of refugees in this region was short lived. Thus, it was the status of the refugees from the east whose migration seemed never to end that affected and drove the debates on Indian citizenship. Although Nehru's vision of citizenship was linked primarily to territory and loyalty, and the Indian constitution also proclaimed as such, the debates surrounding citizenship were undercut by the assumption that migrating from East Pakistan, in addition to claiming refugee status, also had automatic rights to Indian citizenship. Thus, during a debate on the rehabilitation of refugees in the constituent assembly in 1947, a member argued that the East Bengali minority Hindus were 'natives' of India, 'born of its soil', and had a 'title and a right' to resettlement in the country. He went on to demand that the government avoid using the word refugee which hurt the 'self-respect' of the displaced, and proposed that they be called *pravashi*, which means exile, because the Partition had exiled people who had originally been a part of the Indian nation.[51]

The Government of West Bengal also took up the issue of conferring citizenship and franchise rights to those who sought such rights. In a press conference, B.C. Roy announced that anyone from East Bengal, or from Burma, Ceylon, and Malaya, could acquire citizenship of India if they had resided in the territory of India. For this purpose, the applicant would be required to deposit to the office of a district magistrate, 'a declaration in writing of his desire to acquire Indian domicile',[52] or a letter from the enumerator connected with the preparation of the electoral roll which stated that the applicant 'had been residing in the Indian union and desired to do so in the future'.[53] The only restriction for acquiring such a legal status was that the applicant should not have obtained a foreign passport from any country, including Pakistan, before the date of commencement of the new Constitution of India. In addition, the legal right to vote was conditioned not only upon acquiring citizenship but also by the applicant's residence 'in a place in the Indian Union for 180 days in the financial year ending March 31, 1948'.[54]

Immediately after this announcement, several problems emerged. A *Hindustan Standard* editorial noted that many district magistrates had refused to entertain applications for citizenship and some had insisted on applications written on costly stamp papers. The editorial further claimed that there were no provisions to supply the applicant with any certificate proving his legal status as a citizen.[55] Petitions and letters from refugees also underscored the implicit demand that they had been and were organically connected to India before the Partition and should again be incorporated as citizens of new India. They contained within them a discourse of historic sacrifices for the cause of India's freedom and demanded inclusion within the Indian nation through the insistent claims of a shared political brotherhood. One Radhagovinda Nath, in referring to the problems of evacuees migrating from eastern Bengal, noted, 'It would be *the duty of Government* to see that those members of the minority community who had already migrated from east Bengal or would be migrating in the *future were not deprived of the Indian union citizenship*'.[56] Nath claimed that the refugees had been victims of political choices beyond their control.

It was due to the division of India and Bengal that they had been placed in such a position. At the time when the agitation for the partition of Bengal was being carried on leaders of the country assured members of the minority community of east Bengal that they would receive all sorts of help from the Indian union. That assurance has got to be implemented now.[57]

In addition, some of these petitions also underlined the fact that they were 'victims' of failed promises on the part of the Indian government who had earlier agreed to take care of the minorities in Pakistan. The refugees contended that the Indian government in the post-Partition period had only paid lip service to such promises and had been unable to protect their rights in their home country. As a result they had been 'forced' to migrate, and thus were entitled to become automatic citizens within their 'imagined' nation. For example, one refugee argued:

They [the government] seem to have formed a habit of speaking about the refugees in a patronizing way lacking real sympathy, forgetting that the

East Bengal Hindus have as much right as their compeers in West Bengal to consider this part of Bengal as their home. Whether one likes it or not ... the West Bengal government can hardly escape their responsibility in the matter of absorbing them as citizens of West Bengal.[58]

Others recalled the sacrifices of putative citizens during the colonial struggle and asked for compensation in the form of automatic Indian citizenship. Thus, D.R. Sen argued, 'These Hindus have made sacrifices galore in the cause of Indian Union, and one might say, they have been made the sacrificial goats in the great *yajna* [sacrificial fire] of India's freedom. If even now the government ask [*sic*] them to behave like good boys by staying at home, they might as well ask them to embrace Islam.'[59] Sen demanded action from the Indian government with regard to the Hindus in East Pakistan, extending the idea of proxy citizenship by hinting at the interconnection between nation and religion.

In the absence of specific instructions on the procedures to acquire Indian citizenship, such arguments of historic sacrifices and 'genuine' victimhood were, at best, discursively successful in establishing a claim to the Indian nation. A sure way to ensure citizenship remained, in these early years, to get one's name on the electoral lists for the upcoming general elections of 1952. Prominent leaders in West Bengal, such as Shyama Prasad Mukherjee, argued that the East Bengali migrants, by virtue of a 'Partition covenant' between the Indian leaders and the Hindu minorities that had guaranteed their well-being in India, now had the 'moral right' to claim citizenship in India.[60]

The ambiguities of whether a person was a migrant, refugee, or citizen came to the fore in the case of an unnamed seaman who had applied for relief and rehabilitation in Calcutta after 1947. Born in Sylhet that was included in East Pakistan, this individual had come to Calcutta in 1947 and then left for Rangoon, Burma, in search of a job. After a three year stay, he returned to Calcutta, declared his intentions of remaining there, and had applied for Indian citizenship. His application was rejected on the basis that he could not qualify as a refugee under Article 6 of the constitution that outlined the rules by which East Bengali refugees could acquire Indian citizenship.[61]

THE ACT AND ITS AFTERLIFE

The Indian Citizenship Act of 1955 sought to resolve such ambiguities. The debate over the bill took place in the Indian Parliament in December

1955.[62] According to the joint committee recommendations, Indian citizenship could be acquired through birth, descent, naturalization, and registration. This was in keeping with what had already been laid out under the Indian constitution. A substantial portion of the debates was devoted the status of refugees from East Pakistan and how they could acquire Indian citizenship. The general opinion of the members was that these refugees should be given automatic citizenship by virtue of being 'victims' of Partition high politics and the continuing effort of Pakistan to 'squeeze' out minorities. Further, these refugees had, technically, either been born in undivided India or had parents who could claim such connections. Thus, in addition to 'victimhood', the theories of jus soli and jus sanguinis were also applicable. The main advocates for the cause of refugee citizenship were Thakurdas Bhargava and N.C. Chatterjee, both of who argued that India should grant them automatic citizenship. Thakurdas Bhargava noted, 'Those Hindus living in east Bengal are the potential citizens of this country ... Those persons will be pushed out, if not today, tomorrow or the day after. Pakistan is determined to see that not a single Hindu remains a national of Pakistan and by stages it is giving the push.'[63] In effect, Bhargava echoed prevailing anti-Pakistan sentiments and the belief that the East Pakistan government was deliberately engaged in 'squeezing out' its Hindu minorities.

The arguments in favour of automatic citizenship faced procedural obstacles. By 1955, all those who wanted to acquire Indian nationality were subjected to a document regime. Those migrants who had come to India after the commencement of the constitution had to show domicile and proof of residence for one year and had to register themselves with district-level officials by showing their border slips, migration certificates, or refugee slips. Further, they had to provide an affidavit stating their intention to permanently reside in India and swear an oath of allegiance to the Indian nation.

Critics pointed out that citizenship by registration was troublesome as it involved a substantial cost, travel, and time for those who did not live near district registration offices. H.N. Mukherjee, a member from north-east Calcutta, eloquently took up the cause for citizenship of those migrants who had not or did not have the need to register themselves as 'refugees' after moving to India. He argued:

The right of citizenship is something which raises emotions distinct from those of a resident friendly alien who has got a kind of territorial and temporary association with the country. The citizen has a permanent and personal association with the country and therefore, the very fact of citizenship being more easily available to the refugee would have meant a very great deal. Apart from that, of course, there is a question of registration with all its attendant red-tapish [sic] difficulties. Maybe there are some refugees who will find it less easy to secure citizenship rights in this country on account of this provision— says that there [sic] are a large number of people who did not first register themselves as refugees and did not seek rehabilitation—this class of people will find it difficult to secure citizenship rights.[64]

More importantly, they argued that citizenship by registration was a further affront to the refugees. Thakurdas Bhargava noted, 'Registration is only for those who are not real citizens of India nor are rooted in the land of India nor have a domicile in this country, not wanted to return to any other country.'[65] Registration immediately differentiated the refugee citizens from those who claimed to be Indians by birth and descent because the process required the former to *prove* their intent and swear an oath of allegiance as the manifestation of their loyalty, while for the latter group, such requirements were immanent.

The Citizenship Act of 1955, like the constitution in 1950, made provisions for refugees coming in from Pakistan to become citizens. However, the implicit assumption was that it would be the minority Hindu community who were most likely to migrate to India, assume refugee status, and thereafter demand inclusion as citizens. Although the rules of citizenship did not particularly favour one group of Pakistani migrants over another, official policy acknowledged repeatedly that minority Hindus from Pakistan would get preference since they were most likely to want to become Indian citizens.[66] Underlying such assumptions was the continuing effect of the communal logic of the Partition.

Even after the Citizenship Act was put into place, the practice of granting citizenship to migrants from Pakistan was fraught with complications. For instance, registration policy dictated that migrants from Pakistan had to prove their domicile by staying six months within the territory of India. But to legally migrate, they had to first obtain short-term visas (B and C) from the Indian consulates in Pakistan and also get a passport that immediately documented them as Pakistani nationals. But given the additional length of time each bureaucratic application took to process, often the passports and visas of these

Pakistani nationals would expire and they would have to apply to the Pakistani Deputy High Commission in Calcutta for their renewal. Indian officials noted that such requests were usually turned down on the ground that they have already applied for permanent settlement in India. To make matters worse, Indian authorities would also not extend the visas of these migrants beyond the validity of their passports.[67] These migrants, in their attempt to do everything by the book, were thus caught between the uncertain and contextual interpretations of the law regarding citizenship.

The case of Muslims who had migrated from India and now wanted to return to their natal homes was even more complicated. Indian authorities, in most cases, deemed them to have lost their citizenship rights, and their movement was governed by the permit system instituted in early 1949.[68] Most of them were given temporary permits of three months, which, in effect, prevented them from satisfying the domicile requirement of six months.[69] Thus, when Rab Nawaz Khan arrived in India from Rawalpindi in March 1949, his entry was regulated via a three month temporary permit. In December of the same year, Khan was arrested in Asansol, West Bengal, for overstaying his permit. However, Khan and his lawyers argued that although he was born in West Pakistan, he was actually an Indian citizen because his father had been born in undivided India and owned substantial property in India. Thus, he was, in fact, a citizen by descent and the rules of the permit system need not apply in his particular case.[70] While pending a ruling in his case, the Indian authorities deported Khan to Pakistan.

The beginning of a documentary regime and the establishment of rules for citizenship introduced new set of ambiguities regarding the identity of certain individuals. For instance, a large number of Muslims from Murshidabad, India, who had opted for service in East Pakistan were among many who had to tackle the ambiguities embedded within such legal proclamation. These Murshidabad residents had, in 1947, opted for service in the Pakistan government and had continued to retain both their families and property in India, although for work purposes, their residence was in Pakistan. After the institution of the citizenship rules in the constitution, and the passport scheme, their lives became complicated as the Indian government deemed them to have 'migrated' to Pakistan and not to have been 'domiciled' in

India as of 26th of January 1950.[71] In recourse, these optees had also registered themselves within the Indian electoral rolls. However, when they applied for passports to the local authorities, their requests were denied en masse on the ground that they had opted for service in Pakistan and therefore, cannot be treated as Indian citizens.[72]

Sometimes, Muslim minorities had to negotiate contradictory policies on citizenship at different official levels. For instance, Indian authorities noted that around 200 persons who had gone away to East Pakistan and had become Pakistani nationals, had returned to their homes in Bihar in 1957 and had petitioned the Indian government to grant them Indian citizenship.[73] State authorities concluded that 'While it is possible that a few of them are spies of the Pakistan government, a large majority consists of persons who had fled either from fear or from a false notion of prosperity that might be awaiting them in Pakistan. They have presumably come back to Bihar on finding it more worthwhile to live in this country'.[74] The Bihar government decided to adopt a liberal policy with regard to this particular group of applications because deportation would not serve any purpose other than provide fuel for communal propaganda. Further, they pointed out that 'there were already some Muslims who are Indian citizens but have no great love of this country', and a grant of citizenship might make 'loyal citizens' of these Pakistani nationals.[75] However, the Ministry of Home Affairs, which had the final say, rejected the recommendations of the Bihar government arguing that these Pakistani nationals, by virtue of arriving in India on Pakistani passports and short-term visas, had 'ceased to be citizens of India under section 9 of the Citizenship Act, 1955 and Schedule III to the Citizenship rules 1956'.[76]

In the case of post-Partition India, citizenship followed a different path. In official discourse of both states, the communities who now became a numerical minority came to be classified as 'refugees' and 'evacuees' as they migrated across the border. If they continued to remain, then they came to assume the homogenous identity of 'minorities'. Even as the architects of the constituent assembly of 1946–50 and that of the Citizenship Act of 1955 grappled with the definitions of whom and what constituted a 'citizen' of India, their arguments were primarily influenced by the differential logic of these new identities of refugees, aliens, and foreigners. Further, political authorities in India who crafted the Citizenship Act were substantially influenced by the experience of Partition migrants, especially those from East Pakistan. Moreover, these rules of citizenship, in theory, sought to be inclusive with regard to the Partition migrants, but remained fraught with ambiguities when it came to their implementation. While residence and domicile were key in the determination of citizenship, it was the act of migration to Pakistan and back which became crucial when it came to the actual bestowing of Indian citizenship, especially in the case of Muslim minorities.

NOTES

1. Speech by Mohammed Ali Jinnah, quoted in S. Gopal (ed.), 1990, *Selected Works of Jawaharlal Nehru, Second Series, Vol. 4*, New Delhi: Jawaharlal Nehru Memorial Fund, p. 148 fn.

2. *Ibid.*, p. 148.

3. See 1947, *Constituent Assembly of Pakistan Debates, Vol. 1, No. 2*, Karachi: Governor General's Press and Publications, 11 August, pp. 19–20.

4. *Ibid.*

5. Congress resolution moved by Nehru at the All India Congress Committee (AICC) meeting, New Delhi, 15 November 1947, File no. ED-7 (Part II) 1947–48, *AICC Papers*, Nehru Memorial Museum and Library (NMML); emphasis added.

6. *Hindustan Standard* (*HS*), 27 July 1947, p. 4. Also, see *HS* (Editorial), 15 July 1947 and letters to the editor in the *HS*, 17 July 1947, where the writers' prophesized that the condition of Hindu minorities would depend on reciprocal treatment of Muslim minorities in India.

7. Congress Resolution at AICC meeting in New Delhi, File no. ED-7 (Part II) 1947–48, *AICC Papers*, NMML; emphasis in original.

8. M.A.K Azad, 1960, *India Wins Freedom*, New York: Longmans, Green and Co., p. 232.

9. Pravash Chandra Lahiry, 1968, *Pak Bharater Ruparekha* (An Outline of India and Pakistan), Chakdah, Nadia: Shyama Prakashani, pp. 51–2.

10. *Ibid.*

11. Azad, *India Wins Freedom*, pp. 243–4.

12. Lahiry, *Pak Bharater Ruparekha*, pp. 36–7.

13. Samar Guha, 1951, *Non-Muslims behind the Curtain of East Pakistan*, Dacca: East Bengal Minorities Association, p. 37.

14. *HS*, 19 November 1947, p. 4.

15. Gopal (ed.), *Selected Works of Jawaharlal Nehru, Vol. 4*, p. 214.

16. See *HS*, 1947, 'Task before Hindus in East Pakistan', 21 June, p. 4; *HS*, 1947, 'The Fate of East Bengal Hindus', 26 June, p. 4; *HS*, 1947, 'Future of

East Bengal Hindus in Government Services', 1 July, p. 4; *HS*, 1947, 'Minorities in East Bengal', 15 July, p. 4; and *HS*, 1947, 'What the East Bengal Hindus Feel', 15 July, p. 4; and see similar letters and articles in *HS*, 17 July 1947, p. 4; *HS*, 20 July 1947, p. 7; *HS*, 23 July 1947, p. 4; *HS*, 25 July 1947, p. 4; *HS*, 5 August 1947, p. 3; *HS*, 8 August 1947, p. 4; *HS*, 28 August 1947, p. 4.

17. *HS*, 15 June 1947, p. 4.

18. Resolution, 30 June 1947, File no. G-30/1947–48, *AICC Papers*, NMML, New Delhi.

19. A.N. Mukherjee, 1947, 'Nationality in the Indian Union', *Modern Review*, vol. 82, September, pp. 203–4.

20. *Ibid.*, p. 204.

21. *Ibid.*

22. *Ibid.*

23. *Amrita Bazar Patrika*, 8 April 1948, p. 4.

24. Jawaharlal Nehru, 'Towards Amity between India and Pakistan', Speech at the plenary session of the Indian National Congress, Jaipur, 19 December 1948, *Hindustan Times*, 20 December 1948, p.1..

25. For an elaboration of the condition of minority Muslims in West Bengal after the Partition, see Joya Chatterji, 2005, 'Of Graveyards and Ghettos: Muslims in Partitioned West Bengal 1947–67', in Mushirul Hasan and Asim Roy (eds), *Living Together Separately: Cultural India in History and Politics*, New Delhi: Oxford University Press, pp. 222–49; Gyanendra Pandey, 2001, *Remembering Partition: Violence, Nationalism, and History in India*. New York: Cambridge University Press; and Vazira Zamindar, 2007, *Divided Families and the Making of Modern South Asia: Refugees, Boundaries, Histories*, New York: Columbia University Press. All have made similar arguments on the western side.

26. S.C. Chatterjee, Letter to the Editor, *Amrita Bazar Patrika*, 13 March 1950, p. 4; emphasis added.

27. *Constituent Assembly Debates, Vol. 8*, New Delhi: Government of India, 16 May–16 June 1949, p. 271.

28. Interview to the Press, Delhi, 12 October 1947. Based on reports from *The Hindu*, 12 October 1947 and *Indian Information*, 1 November 1947, in Gopal (ed.), *Selected Works of Jawaharlal Nehru, Vol. 4*, p. 148.

29. *Ibid.*

30. *Ibid.*, p. 147.

31. *Morning News*, 14 February 1948.

32. Lungi is a piece of coloured or checkered cloth wrapped around the lower part of the body. In the communal climate of the Partition, the lungi signified both class and religion as it became associated with lower-class Muslim attire. In contrast, the dhoti, mainly white, became symbolic of upper-class Hindu elite. For the semiotic significance of clothing in the colonial

period, see Emma Tarlo, 1996, *Clothing Matters: Dress and Identity in India*, Chicago: University of Chicago Press.

33. Fazlur Rahman, Letter, 1 April 1948, File PM 119-48, West Bengal Police, Special Branch (henceforth WBPSB), 1948.

34. Anonymous letter, 10 March 1948 (*ibid.*).

35. *Amrita Bazar Patrika*, 15 July 1948, p. 4.

36. Not everybody supported this division of the civil services on a communal basis. Maulana Abul Kalam Azad suggested that 'officials from West Punjab, Sind, or East Bengal, whatever their community, should remain in Pakistan. Similarly service men who belonged to the Indian provinces should serve India regardless of whether they were Hindus or Moslems ... Administration would thus be free of communal poison and the minorities in each state would feel a greater sense of security.' See M.A.K Azad, *Indian Wins Freedom*, p. 237.

37. Chatterji alludes to 'a systematic campaign of intimidation launched to "persuade" Muslims in government service to quit West Bengal and go to Pakistan', in 'Of Graveyards and Ghettos', p. 230.

38. Saroj Chakrabarty, 1974, *With Dr. B.C. Roy and Other Chief Ministers: A Record upto 1962*, Calcutta: Benson's, p. 45.

39. *HS*, 27 July 1947, p. 4.

40. *Ibid.*

41. 'East and North Bengal Hindus', Pamphlet, 15 August 1947, File no. G-30/1947–48, *AICC Papers*, NMML, New Delhi.

42. Note, 30 September 1947, in Durga Das (ed.), 1972, *Sardar Patel's Correspondence, 1945-50*. Vol. 1–8, Ahmedabad: Navajivan Publishing House. p. 433.

43. Govind Malaviya to Sardar Patel, 4 July 1947 (*ibid.*, p. 411; emphasis added).

44. Patel to Malaviya, 7 July 1947 (*ibid.*, p. 413; emphasis added).

45. Nasir Hussain Rizvi to Patel, 15 October 1947 (*ibid.*, pp. 437–8).

46. *Ibid.*

47. Government of India (GoI), 1950, *The Constitution of India*, available at http://www.constitution.org/cons/india/const.html (accessed 14 March 2009).

48. As per Article 7 of the Indian constitution, entitled 'Rights of Citizenship of Certain Migrants to Pakistan', the rules note, 'Notwithstanding anything in articles 5 and 6, a person who has after the first day of March, 1947, migrated from the territory of India to the territory now included in Pakistan shall not be deemed to be a citizen of India: Provided that nothing in this article shall apply to a person who, after having so migrated to the territory now included in Pakistan, has returned to the territory of India under a permit

for resettlement or permanent return issued by or under the authority of any law and every such person shall for the purposes of clause (b) of article 6 be deemed to have migrated to the territory of India after the nineteenth day of July, 1948' (*ibid.*).

49. As per Article 9 of the Indian constitution, entitled 'Persons Voluntarily Acquiring Citizenship of a Foreign State not to be Citizens', the rules note, 'No person shall be a citizen of India by virtue of article 5, or be deemed to be a citizen of India by virtue of article 6 or article 8, if he has voluntarily acquired the citizenship of any foreign State' (*ibid.*).

50. This date was initially fixed at July 1948, less than a year after the Partition.

51. Proceedings of the CAI (legislative) v. II no.1, cited in Nilanjana Chatterjee, Midnight's Unwanted Children, 72.

52. *Ibid.*

53. *Ibid.*

54. *HS*, 28 July 1948, p. 4.

55. *Ibid.*

56. *Ibid.* Emphasis added.

57. *Amrita Bazar Patrika*, 4 July 1948, p. 3.

58. *Amrita Bazar Patrika*, 21 July 1948, p. 4.

59. Voice of India. 1966, *A Tale of Woes of East Pakistan Minorities*, 1st edition, Calcutta: D.R. Sen, p. 15.

60. Letter to B.C. Roy, 22 August 1950, *Shyama Prasad Mukherjee Papers* (*SPM Papers*), *Refugees and Minorities, 1950–1951*, File no. 39, Index vol. 1, NMML, New Delhi.

61. Article 6 of the Indian Constitution charts the rights of citizenship of 'certain persons' who have migrated to India from Pakistan. According to the Indian constitution, 'a person who has migrated to the territory of India from the territory now included in Pakistan shall be deemed to be a citizen of India at the commencement of this Constitution if (a) he or either of his parents or any of his grandparents was born in India as defined in the Government of India Act, 1935 (as originally enacted) and (b) (i) in the case where such person has so migrated before the nineteenth day of July, 1948, he has been ordinarily resident in the territory of India since the date of his migration, or (ii) in the case where such person has so migrated on or after the nineteenth day of July, 1948, he has been registered as a citizen of India by an officer appointed in that behalf by the Government of the Dominion of India on an application made by him therefore to such officer before the commencement of this Constitution in the form and manner prescribed by that Government: Provided that no person shall be so registered unless he has been resident in the territory of India for at least six months immediately

preceding the date of his application.' The Constitution of India, Government of India, 1950, http://www.constitution.org/cons/india/const.html; Internet; accessed 15 April 2005.

62. The three main axes of the debates revolved around: citizenship of Indians within the Commonwealth; whether a corporation was to be given the recognition of a person; and the rules for acquisition and termination of citizenship.

63. Citizenship Bill, *Parliamentary Debates*, New Delhi, 3 December 1955, p. 1176.

64. *Ibid.*, 2 December 1955, p. 1089.

65. *Ibid.*, 3 December 1955, p. 1177.

66. A memo from the Ministry of External Affairs to the Ministry of Home Affairs noted that 'To some extent these persons may be treated as potential citizens of India'. Memo, 8 December 1957, File no. 1/34/58-FIII, Ministry of Home Affairs, GoI, 1958, National Archives of India (NAI).

67. An internal memo concluded that Indian authorities would take up the matter with their Pakistani counterpart and in the meantime, 'the only remedy was to let these persons stay on in India with expired Pakistani passports...In most of the cases the members of the minority community from Pakistan their applications for permanent resettlement would ultimately be granted. If it is found at a later stage that a particular individual cannot be allowed to remain in India, he can be deported in accordance with the powers delegated to the State Governments under the Foreigners Act.' Memo, 10 April 1958 (*ibid.*).

68. The permit system was mainly in operation between West Pakistan and India. In the east, the first documentary regulation came in the form of the passport and visa system in 1952. Zamindar argues that Indian Muslims who migrated to Pakistan in the aftermath of the Partition violence were denied return entry by the Indian state who instituted a permit system especially for this purpose. See Zamindar, *The Long Partition*, pp. 79–119.

69. The domicile requirement was initially for one year and then changed to six months after the Citizenship Act came into place.

70. *All India Reporter*, Calcutta, 1950, p. 193.

71. The Revolutionary Socialist Party member from Behrampore, Tridip Kumar Chaudhuri, took up the case of these Muslim optees in the Lok Sabha debates. *Parliamentary Debates, House of the People, Official Report*, Part II (Proceedings other than Questions and Answers), Vol. VI, No. 8, Friday, 12 December 1952, pp. 2142–3.

72. As per Indian government rules, there was to be no contradiction between being Indian nationals and serving a foreign government. Further, the Pakistan government had also publicly declared that the adoption of Indian

nationality by such public servants would in no way affect the tenure of service of these people (*ibid.*, p. 2143).

73. Government of Bihar, Political Department, General Branch, Secret, Letter from M.S. Rao, ICS, Chief Secretary to Government, to the Secretary of Ministry of Home affairs, 17 May 1958, File no. 1/36/58-FIII, Ministry of Home Affairs, GoI, 1958, NAI.

74. *Ibid.*

75. *Ibid.*

76. Letter from C.B. Lal, Under Secretary, Ministry of Home Affairs, 10 September 1958 (*ibid.*).

III

Identities

5

The Routine of Violence

In August of 1947, the majority Muslim population of a village in Noagaon in Sylhet district, which was now part of East Bengal, attacked the section of their village where Scheduled Caste Kaibartas lived. The official report noted that this attack was foiled as the villagers had been at home and had thus 'been able to give a heroic defense which had baffled the Muslim mob who had been waiting for an opportunity ever since'.[1] Such an opportunity presented itself six months later, on the midnight of 11 February 1948, when 'a mob of a thousand or twelve hundred Muslims attacked *Kaibarta Hati* ... and burnt down the whole village ... the mob used slogans of Allah ho Akbar, and used crackers to scare away people'.[2] The success of the second attack was greatly facilitated by the fact that most of the male members of the Kaibarta community were away on a fishing trip. Official investigation of this incident found substantial economic damage but no loss of human lives. Their report concluded that the last attack had been well planned and preceded by sporadic incidents of dacoity. The removal, in January 1948, of official armed guards who patrolled the locality after the first attack suggested the complicity of local authorities. Purnendu Kishore Sengupta, a member of the East Bengal Legislative Assembly, who investigated the incident, indicated that such riots had produced a sense of insecurity among the Hindus of the area and some had already migrated to India. He concluded that the only way to restore confidence among the minorities was for the East Bengal government to take prompt action against the miscreants.[3]

Such incidents and their records within official correspondence were routine in post-Partition Bengal. Although the region had witnessed major rioting in 1946, after Partition, it had remained relatively riot free until 1950.[4] Such peace, however, was punctuated by small-scale incidents of stabbing, looting, random cases of abduction of women, and murder. They were distinctive in that they were well planned with the appearance of spontaneity, perpetrated by members of majority community on members of minority community, and raised issues of national and community belonging for those caught on the 'wrong' side of the border. For instance, the Kaibarta, who had traditionally been a Scheduled Caste fishing community outside the Hindu community, were now perceived as part of a homogenous minority Hindu community in East Bengal. Class-based politics in Bengal during the 1930s and the 1940s had ensured that their identities align closely with the dominant Hindu one.[5] Further, the official report indicated that the villagers themselves believed that they belonged within the minority Hindu community as they highlighted the use of religious terms such as, *Allah ho Akbar* by the perpetrators. They clearly embellished the number of perpetrators and regarded official complicity a certainty in encouraging the occurrence of such violence. More importantly, violence had occurred when the men were away, and had been limited to damage and theft of property rather than loss of life, indicating careful planning ahead of time.

Scholarship on Partition violence has focused primarily on Punjab and on pre-Partition riots leading up to the Partition in Bengal. These invariably focus on large-scale violent riots and privilege physical violence that marks the body as well as differentiates between perpetrators and victims. This chapter attempts to place a different kind of Partition violence on the centre stage: small scale, sporadic, and threatening psyche rather than the body. Such *routine* violence was mediated by: actual singular incidents of petty theft, loot, kidnapping of women, and murders; destruction and/or defacement of religious icons; by verbal threats, rumours aimed at maximizing minority insecurities; and through embellished representation of communal incidents in the public media, political speeches, and thinly veiled state propaganda. Together they created a continuous ecology of fear and acted as catalysts for minorities to abandon their homes and cross the border. This chapter shows that the communist-inspired peasant riots of 1950, which engulfed both side of Bengal, could easily transform into a communal riot because of the persistence of such violence in the region.

Routine violence in post-Partition Bengal needs to be examined for another reason. As an important corollary to any articulation of minority rights, demands of refugee rehabilitation, and citizenship, representations of violence were a necessary component in the narratives of victimhood. Refugees, especially the Hindus from East Bengal, tended to identify as incidents of violence those instances of transgression which not only targeted their physical bodies, but some thing even greater—their religion, culture, honour, and the embodiment of all these, their women. Some of these incidents were reported to the local thana (police station), while others became key to inter-dominion dialogues between India and East Bengal. Still others were not reported to officials and were reiterated in refugee narratives of exile. This chapter uses both 'low level' but often classified police reports as well as 'high-level' records of the Indian and East Bengali state. In addition, propaganda leaflets and newspaper reports which emphasized the ubiquity of such violence in minority lives are also used. I use these sources with the understanding that however far one reads 'against the grain', such documents have their own epistemological problems: they are, first and foremost, documents generated by states and by people who had specific agendas in mind. However, used in conjunction with contemporary letters and petitions from the minorities themselves, such sources offer us a different way of historically contextualizing the representations of violence. What is important is not the actuality of physical violence but the potential for it, and how the lives and identities of post-Partition minorities where shaped by such representations of violence.

THE ECOLOGY OF FEAR

After 1947, the minority Hindu elite in East Bengal began receiving threatening letters asking them to leave their home immediately. One such letter, addressed to a prominent Hindu of Rajshahi, began with the premise that hitherto Hindus had oppressed the Muslims and had 'torpedoed' Muslim initiatives at bridging the social gap. Now that Partition had become a fact, the letter warned that if the Hindus did not leave, then, 'your dispensary [sic], properties will be ruthlessly massacred, the prestige and honor of your womenfolk must be at stake'.[6] The letter then goes onto describe the act of intercourse between the writer of the letter and the women in Hindu household, an act which threatened to physically 'mark' their conquest by making them pregnant. Although there were no reported cases of such incidents actually happening, such letters acted as a catalyst for migration of the Hindus from the area.

In addition to such letters, in early 1951, a number of posters depicting Hindus as fifth columnists began to appear at various railway stations in East Bengal. Captioned in English, Bengali, and Urdu and bearing certificates of issue under Pakistan government, these posters clearly identified the 'enemies' of the state.[7] One set showed a man dressed as a Hindu and another as a Muslim engaged in conversation and the caption was, 'Beware! He maybe an agent of our enemy. Watch your words' (Figure 5.1). In another set of posters, a Hindu

Figure 5.1: Enemy Agent

is shown to be trying to overhear what a Muslim is saying, with the subtitle 'Speak Carefully. The enemy is listening' (Figure 5.2). The West Bengal government immediately petitioned for the withdrawal of such posters in East Bengal, but could not do so before some damage had been done.[8]

On the other side of the border in Calcutta, Muslim minorities were the objects of threats from certain Right-wing Hindu groups. Barkat Ali Brothers, a well-known tailoring concern in central Calcutta, received a number of anonymous threatening letters around March 1948. Written by a group claiming to represent the 'Indian Terrorist Party', one letter warned the Muslim proprietors of Barkat Ali Brothers to stop 'their anti-Indian and anti-Hindu activities'.[9] Though Barkat Ali did not close their shop, such an atmosphere of distrust stimulated other minority citizens to rethink their continued residence in West Bengal. Often, a rumour of violence would trigger panic among the minorities. A West Bengal police memo of 28 May 1948 noted that there was general panic amongst the Muslims of Blockman Street, Wellesley Street, and Elliot Road in Calcutta because of a rumour of an imminent riot. Accordingly, 'many Muslims had sent out their wives and children out of Calcutta. They are disposing of their valuable furniture and also ornaments.'[10]

The police in West Bengal reported that in the wake of the post-Partition peace drive in Calcutta, 'a campaign of vendetta against Muslims vis-à-vis the West Bengal ministry is being carried on secretly'.[11]

Figure 5.2: Speak Carefully

To substantiate their claim, the police had seized the circulation of a 'highly objectionable and inciting'[12] leaflet, which had been in circulation around end of August 1947 in various congregation points in the city. The leaflet printed in Bengali under the caption 'A Word of Warning to the West Bengal Ministry', claimed to have been issued by the Revolutionary Party of Bengal. It claimed that the notorious Muslim officers such as Doha and Hafizuddin who had subjected the Hindus to various tortures during the 1946 riots had gone to East Bengal where the Hindus were being oppressed, and urged the West Bengal ministers to prevent such oppression of Hindus and take steps to rescue the kidnapped Hindu women. The leaflet concluded with a threat that not a single Muslim will be left alive in West Bengal. Intelligence officials were unable to pinpoint exactly who was behind the circulation of such malicious propaganda but conjectured it to be the work of an extreme and communal organization known as the 'Muchipara' group who had taken an active part in the violence during the 1946 riots.[13]

Those seeking redress for such routine violence found the East Bengali authorities understaffed and, at times, unwilling to pursue matters. In a memorandum to the provincial minority board, describing the kinds of violence he and his family had to suffer, a resident of Medinimandal in Munishiganj subdivision of Dacca district cited several incidents of molestations of women and theft of household items. When his brother had been fishing in their own tank, the writer alleged that four or five local Muslims abused him and forcefully pointed out that 'this is now Pakistan and all these belong to us. Who are you "sala"[14] to catch fish here, stop it at once.'[15] Although the writer had identified the perpetrators, the police and local authorities were of little use since the nearest police station was 5 miles away and the perpetrators enjoyed the 'full support' of the local union board president. He concluded that such incidents were not 'occasional happenings, [but] I should say of everyday'.[16] For him and for other Hindu minorities who became East Bengal citizens after 1947, such forms of violence had become regular occurrence. The East Bengal authorities however pointed out that while such petty thefts and intimidation of non-Muslims had become routine, 'there is nothing extraordinary in these as the victims are both Hindus and Muslims'.[17] Such an explanation was to diminish the idea that minorities in East

Bengal were being persecuted, and simultaneously assert that the political situation in East Bengal was normal.

Provincial and district minority boards were established in India and East Bengal after the Inter-dominion Conference of April 1948, to address minority grievances in each state. Each board had a chairman and five members, three of who would belong to the minority community of that state.[18] However, such boards functioned erratically, and a significant number of Hindu members of these boards in East Bengal had already migrated to India.[19]

At times, these minorities used such reports of petty violence to legitimate their demand for rehabilitation from the neighbouring Indian states of West Bengal and Assam. Thus, instead of writing to the East Bengal authorities, the non-Muslim representatives from the villages within Jaintiapur, Goainghat, and Kanaighat thanas of Sylhet district, East Bengal, wrote to the Chief Minister of Assam reporting violence and seeking protection from the Assam government. Representing mostly the Scheduled Caste and tribals such as the Khasis and Mikirs, Jogendra Chandra Nandi, Dhansing Khasia, Nanigopal Dey, and others pleaded, 'We are mostly poor and illiterate and as such many of us lack in courage to stand the oppressions of the Majority Muslim community of our localities. Our life and property and above all our womenfolk and even children are not at all safe in their hands.'[20] Moreover, the writers alleged that there were 'several cases of kidnapping, abduction and rape. Loot has almost become *the order of the day*. Only arson is not taking place on the ground as given by the perpetrators of all other misdeeds, that after the non-Muslims will have been turned out their houses will go to them.'[21] Violence was thus represented as communal as well as being carefully planned by the Muslim majority who sought economic gains.

Although this letter is similar to the written complaints sent to the provincial minority board and to East Bengali and Indian leaders, it is also representative in its demand for rehabilitation within India. The only way for these villagers 'of saving our life and property and our womenfolk and children' was 'by migrating altogether from our homes in Pakistan and settling in the nearest available place in Assam within the dominion of India.'[22] In support of their request for rehabilitation in Assam, they claimed that if they were not allowed residence within India, then they would be converted to Islam en masse, and most likely would be 'exterminated by the neighboring Muslim population of our localities who are gathering much arms etc. for launching an attack on us on a large scale'.[23] If their continuing victimhood failed to convince the Assam authorities to facilitate their migration and rehabilitation, they attempted to establish historical claims by noting that the Jaintia Hills and Assam had been one unit before the British, in 1835, separated and annexed their particular region to Sylhet for administrative purposes. In addition to evoking historical ties, the writers asserted that the Assam government would accrue economic benefits of labour and revenue from the settlers. Thus, it was not their intention to migrate to Assam as refugees but as legitimate and productive citizens.[24]

However, for the Government of Assam, such migration was 'not desirable' and Assam authorities urged the East Bengali officials to ensure that these people 'may be set free from apprehension and may rest contented without approaching a Government who have no jurisdiction over them'.[25] After an investigation, the East Bengali Inspector General (IG) of Sylhet found that the allegations were 'maliciously false'. He also noted that people who were, in general, migrating to India were not doing so as a result of torture by the majority community. Rather, they left because 'they are at heart deadly against Pakistan'.[26] According to the Pakistani IG, the petitioners had painted such a false picture with the motive of getting reserve land and rehabilitation in Assam. Thus, economic benefits on the other side rather than minority persecution in East Bengal was represented as the primary basis for migration and new citizenship.

Nowhere was the confluence of violence and identity formation more crucial than for abducted women and their forcible recovery by the Indian and Pakistani states.[27] In Bengal, the intertwining of violence and women's sexuality was manifested through abduction, conversion, and physical molestation during the riots of 1946, 1950, and 1964. In addition, sporadic incidents of verbal and physical abuse targeting women during relatively peaceful times became ways in which men, both Hindus and Muslims, communicated their threats to each other.

Unlike Punjab, where women were subject to horrific acts of physical disfigurement targeting their reproductive functions, Bengal, during the 1946 riots, did not report many such cases.[28] In a secret note to Secretary of State, Pethwick–Lawrence, reporting on the 1946 Noakhali riots, the then Governor of Bengal, F.J. Burrows, wrote that one of the specific features of the disturbances at Noakhali had been that 'mobs seldom seriously injured or killed women'.[29] Rather, women were generally subject to conversion through the 'removal of caste marks from the foreheads of girls and women, breaking the conch bracelet on the wrists of married women, and making them recite prayers and forcing them to eat beef.[30] Conversion was taken to have dissolved all marriage bonds, as 'for maidens it was but proper that they should be wedded to the valorous warriors of Pakistan'.[31] Women in such violence became symbols of elite Hindu culture that had traditionally banned interpersonal and social relations with non-Hindus. Conversion and marriage signalled a greater dissolution of such traditions than mere decimation of the male members of the community. Women often committed suicide to escape molestations and preserve family honour.[32]

In post-Partition Bengal, although reported cases of abduction of women were few,[33] fear of such a catastrophe was always at the forefront in the minds of the Hindu minorities, perpetuated by intermittent but consistent media reports on incidents of abduction and molestation of Hindu women. In addition, reports of the Indian state's recovery operations carried out under the leadership of Mridula Sarabhai also received wide publicity and ensured that violence against women continued to be a key theme within public discourse after 1947.

Bengali literature is replete with depictions of the plight of women in situations of violence arising out of the riots during and in the post-Partition period. Jyotirmayee Devi's *The River Churning* describes a Hindu family in an East Bengal village who become victims of communal frenzy.[34] When the father is killed and the mother jumps into a pond to preserve her honour, their two daughters face abduction and physical molestation. For Sutara, the younger daughter, who regains consciousness in her Muslim neighbours' home, this one night of violence changes her identity. In addition to being a victim, her rescue by a Muslim family ensures that she becomes an outcaste in her brother's family. Her encounters force her to become independent of her family, but her experiences of violence continue to colour her interactions with other people. Violence for Sutara comes not only from the 'other' community but also from members of her own community who refuse to include her within their fold of respectability. Similarly, in 'Karun Kanya' (Daughter of Sadness), a short story, Ramapada Chaudhury portrays the fate of the women who had the misfortune of being caught in between the crossfire of communal violence.[35] State machinery in the form of the recovery programme 'rescues' Arundhuti, the main protagonist, from her life as a wife of her abductor and returns her to family. However, her family welcomes her only so long as the physical sign of her abduction, her child, was kept a secret. Violence for these women did not end with the physical act of molestation and rape. It began a cycle of exclusion and cultural censorship that hindered their assimilation as citizens of the new nations and fractured their identities within their own families and communities.

Women faced abduction not only from men of the other community but also from men of their own community. J.M. Chatterjee, who was connected with the recovery programme in West Bengal, reported to Mridula Sarabhai that refugee women from East Bengal, who had camped out in Sealdah Station in Calcutta and other refugee transit centres after the riots of 1950, often fell prey to enticement from traffickers in younger women.[36] Newspapers intermittently reported on cases where Hindu men posing as Congress workers kidnapped Hindu refugee women to sell them.[37]

Recovery operations were implicitly paternalistic in their aim to recover women. They were essentially disruptive for the women whom they wanted to save in order to preserve the honour of the community. A police report on the 'rescue' of a Hindu woman from a Muslim bustee (slum) in Calcutta reveals the dispossession of the rights of the women during the process of preserving community and national honour. Some Muslims had killed Sarajbala Dey's husband during the 1946 riots. She had moved from Howrah to Calcutta with her 6 year old son and began living with a man named Chatua. After seven months, she came to know that he was actually a Muslim and his real name was Sadhu Mia. Recently, they had again moved to a Muslim bustee where he died of natural causes. On the day of her rescue, she had gone to take water from a roadside tap and 'came to the notice of neighboring Hindus who rescued her and her son' and informed the local police station.[38] Although this was not a case of abduction, the Hindu neighbours decided that Sarajbala Dey should be rescued once her male protector had passed away and restored to her community.

In another incident, tension prevailed among Hindus at Sealdah station over three Muslim men escorting an unidentified woman to East Bengal.[39] Even though the police officer in charge intervened and discovered that the woman was a Muslim, he failed to convince the members of Hindustan National Guards who were on duty at Sealdah refugee centre. Although the three men and the woman were allowed to leave the next day, the Hindu public continued to insist that she had been a Hindu and should have been sent to a rescue home. This episode not only questioned the effectiveness of the state police but also demonstrated that the predominantly Hindu public of Calcutta felt responsibility for protecting what they considered to be the embodiment of their honour.

DELINEATING VIOLENCE

During the countdown to Partition, civic space remained communalized in both Bengals. Small-scale incidents of violence, which most often resulted due to a temporary breakdown in the law and order functions of the state, were swiftly translated into communal terms. Occurrence of petty incidents of theft and murder, and their intensive and continuous coverage in Indian newspapers, ensured that the spectre of the Calcutta–Noakhali riots of 1946 persisted in public memory.

In July 1947, when some members of the Muslim League National Guard demanded free mangoes from a local shopkeeper in Akhaura, on the border of Comilla and Tripura state, trouble erupted when the shopkeeper refused. A fight ensued and the shopkeeper was severely beaten.[40] The next day, rumours circulated that the Hindus had killed some National Guards, and retaliatory violence included the burning of local houses belonging mostly to Scheduled Castes and coolies. The *Hindustan Standard* carried an editorial on this incident that was symptomatic of the prevailing communal environment. The editorial identified the Muslim National Guards as 'minions of a theocratic state' out to 'exact levies' from the Hindu minority, of which the shopkeeper was a member. While reporting on a familiar incident of abuse within the traditional state–proletariat power structure, which had swiftly become communalized, the editorial also contributed to

Hindu elite's fear of living in a 'theocratic state' and being swamped by the Muslim majority in Bengal.

By 1901, the enumeration process of the Census of India had established the numerical predominance of Muslims in the Bengal delta. In addition, the Bengal Partition of 1905, which aimed to divide the Muslim-dominated eastern region from the Hindu-dominated western Bengal, and the Communal Award of 1932 for the Muslims in provincial governments, had undermined the traditional Hindu hegemony within the political structure in Bengal. Thus, when this particular editorial reported that 'nearly 8,000 hooligans immediately made an attack on the station ... and then set fire to a number of adjacent houses,'[41] it played on the existing apprehensions of the Hindu *bhadralok* of losing power in the public sphere. News of incidents of violence where the Muslims were the perpetrators usually emphasized their numerical advantage over their 'victims'.

Another key theme in newspaper reports describing aggression against Hindus was the implicit and sometimes explicit allusion to the utter mindlessness of the violence. Rather, the baser instincts usually drove the Muslim mob to attack innocent people. Thus, the editorial prefaced the report of the above-mentioned incident with the following insight of the conditions prevailing in East Bengal,

... these Muslim masses have been in many places charged with a fanatical desire to exterminate the Hindus if they cannot be brought to a state of abject subjection. All the baser propensities of their nature have been stirred up by this anti Hindu passion. No wonder that in many a place in Pakistan the Hindus feel as if they are lying in a powder dump. For they know that even the resistance to ordinary crimes like theft and dacoity, may well prove the fatal spark to set ablaze the base below.[42]

A corollary to such representations was the identification of the Hindu minority as passive victims not as a sign of their emasculation but as juxtaposed with the stereotype of the 'fanatical' Muslim whose sole goal had traditionally been the decimation of their Hindu brethren.

The same newspaper reported an incident of trespassing and abuse occurring in the eastern sector of Dacca in the following terms: 'On June 20th, 1947, some miscreants belonging to the majority community along with a mob numbering *three to four hundred* forcibly entered the house of Narayan Bose and molested some young men of the house and abused some other members in the filthiest terms.'[43] Superficially, such an incident was yet another example of the powerlessness of the minority Hindu elite in eastern Bengal. However, what is more interesting is the immediate background to this incident of forcible entry. A crowd had gathered near the house to watch a game of *kabadi* (a game of tag) between two teams when,

Suddenly a section of the Muslims pounced upon a Hindu boy. The boy was then chased by the mob, who in spite of protest from the inmates entered the house of Narayan babu shouting that Muslims were entitled to enter anywhere in Pakistan. Coming out of this house the mob in pursuit of the boy attempted to enter other houses also and on the way the mob caught hold of a young passerby named Kamal Bose, and severely manhandled him.[44]

The editorial, thus, indicates that the Muslim mob had randomly pounced upon a young boy, and later, for no reason again, had harassed Kamal Bose. Not only had the mob violated the private and now communalized space of a Hindu elite household but had dared to threaten it by espousing their 'rights of entry' in a place yet to become Pakistan.

The Indian newspapers, in the post-Partition period, continued to report cases of arson, murder, and harassment of Hindu minorities related to the requisition of property and gun control. These reports emphasized the quotidian nature of these crimes that sought to leave no doubt in the readers' minds that such harassment and violence had become a regular feature of daily life in East Bengal and that the Hindu minority were usually the target victims of such violence.[45] Moreover, the requisitioning of houses in East Bengal was portrayed in Indian newspapers as a method of forced evictions targeting Hindu minorities even though houses of both Hindus and Muslims were requisitioned for these purposes.[46]

Newspapers in West Bengal were significant conduits in the repeated portrayal of small incidents of crime as challenges to pre-Partition social norms between elite but minority Hindus and the majority Muslim underclass. Like many educational institutions funded by elite Hindu groups in eastern Bengal, Daulatpur College, situated 5 miles from the district town of Khulna, was also a religious institution with a temple within its premises. It did not hire non-Hindu staff and segregated its Muslim students in residences outside the college campus. In September 1948, when some Muslim students demanded accommodations within the college compound after the migration of a majority of the Hindu students of the college, their action was construed as rebellion and 'which threatens the very existence of the College'.[47] The *Hindustan Standard* reported the incident as another notch in the ongoing persecution of the minority Hindus.[48] Such cultural trespassing was a key theme in the narrative of persecution that circulated in the media and in the minority grievances lodged with the East Bengal government. For example, when the East Bengal state proposed to reduce the annual Durga Puja holidays from twelve days to four days, there was widespread protest. The Chittagong Bar Association sent a memorandum of protest to the East Bengal Minority Commission, arguing that such an action was a 'denial and deprivation of the right of the Hindus to worship the goddess in a proper manner'.[49]

Newspapers published in West Bengal continued their circulation in East Bengal for the next decade with intermittent bans on them by the East Bengal government.[50] Although newspapers published from East and West Pakistan such as *Azad, Insaaf,* and *Dawn* claimed to report incidents in the region, they also implicitly blacked out any communal incidents where the Hindu minorities might have been the victims. Newspapers in India, and in particular in West Bengal, also followed a similar policy with minimum coverage given to incidents where Muslim minorities in the state might have been legitimate victims. However, newspapers in both countries reported substantially on the alleged incidents of minority persecution in the neighbouring country. Most widely read Indian newspapers like *Amrita Bazar Patrika, Ananda Bazar Patrika, The Statesman,* and *Hindustan Standard* had daily special sections devoted to news from East Bengal and were the principal conduits of information for both the public in West Bengal and in East Bengal. These columns usually concentrated on small-scale, alleged incidents of violence which continued the portrayal of that region as unstable and a place where the lives of minorities were under constant threat from the majority community. Similarly, East Bengali newspapers highlighted incidents such as conflicts in Kashmir and Hyderabad and reported minor incidents of desecration of mosques and bans on cow slaughter in India.[51]

Jai Hind, published from India, summed up the situation in East Bengal as:

There is economic boycott. There are more and more thefts and dacoities. There are occasional indignities and insults. There are the general superior airs of the Muslims. There is the extortion for the Jinnah Fund ... The air in East Bengal has in fact become too poisonous for the Hindus to breathe. They feel that they are aliens in their own land, and hateful unwanted aliens in the bargain.[52]

Such depictions of the conditions prevalent in East Bengal, while providing legitimacy for Hindus to migrate, tended to question the very basis of East Bengal as a nation that was unable to guarantee the safety and security of its minority citizens. By identifying religion as the primary issue for minorities, such reports continued the communal rhetoric of Partition days. The *Ananda Bazar Patrika*, a widely read Bengali newspaper in West Bengal, reported several incidents of violence that allegedly showed how the religion and culture of the Hindus were under attack. Published in the form of letters from victims to provide authenticity, one article noted that in Barisal, a Muslim youth had snatched the *Narayan Shila* (a symbolic representation of Vishnu in stone) from a Hindu gathering and had spat on it. Again, in East Dinajpur, where some 'miscreants' had defecated within the local temple and the traditional weekly meeting to sing *kirtan* (devotional songs) had stopped under threat.[53] In addition to such symbolic transgressions, the article also reported on physical beatings meted out to hapless minorities in Pirijkandi. The *Dainik Basumati*, another Bengali newspaper, compared the conditions in Jessore as *Mager Mulluk*[54] (slang for land of the Muslims) and pointed out that the practice of abducting minority women had become a normal affair in the region.[55] In addition, it detailed several dacoities that had targeted Hindu households. Redress to the higher authorities had been ineffective. In printing these stories, the newspapers urged the majority Hindu community to respond to such attacks on their religion and honour in East Bengal by taking up the cause of Hindu minorities with Indian authorities.

In Bengal, incidents of communal violence against women continued to be one of the major themes of public discourse. Even during times of relative peace between communities, Indian newspapers continued to highlight the latest cases of abduction and molestation of women, especially those belonging to the minority Hindu community in East Bengal.[56] In addition, reports of the Indian state's recovery operations, carried out under the leadership of Mridula Sarabhai, also received wide publicity, ensuring that women continued to symbolize the honour of the community. In a letter to the editor of *Amrita Bazar Patrika*, one Rabindranath Biswas of Calcutta expressed concern over the reports of missing Hindu girls and minor boys. He asserted that most often, these abducted persons were recovered from Muslim houses, and thereby demanded that the public be allowed to 'search the suspected Muslim areas of Calcutta which would lead to the recovery of many abducted Hindu girls'.[57]

The association of abducted Hindu women with Muslim communal places achieved more prominence when the newspapers reported the recovery of a minor girl from the Gutihara Sharif mosque in Calcutta. Although the information of a 'devout' Muslim enabled the police to crack the case, the media's association of the kidnapping and the retrieval from an Islamic religious place added to the existing view that all Muslim spaces, including places of worship, harboured Hindu women and girls.[58] When the Indian government announced the week starting 16 February 1948 as the 'Restoration Week' that would be symbolic of the recovery of abducted women and children, several citizens expected immediate recovery of abducted women from eastern Pakistan. Claiming that it was a well-known fact that many women remained behind the 'iron curtain' of East Bengal, these citizens argued that the failure to recover and return the abducted women was yet another entry in the long list of false promises that the East Bengal government was becoming well known for.[59] If a state could not keep its promises with regard to women, especially women suffering in such bleak circumstances, how would it be able to protect its minorities?

In the communalized atmosphere of the post-Partition period, violence against women was seen as a violation of the perceived sanctity of the boundaries of the community. In November 1948, Suresh Chandra Bannerji, the President of the West Bengal Congress Committee, submitted a report to the major newspapers that cited the oppression of Hindu women in East Bengal as the single most significant reason for the continuing migration of refugees to India.[60] To substantiate his claim, he cited numerous reports that his East Bengal colleagues had forwarded to him. One report described how some Muslims of a village in Faridpur district had forcibly kidnapped a local fisherwoman and how the police had arrested those who had come to the defence of the woman. Such an incident had resulted in the mass migration of fisherfolk from that locality. Bannerji went on to clearly identify the nature of oppression on women under three headings: (a) ugly gestures made by the majority community, which 'was responsible [sic] sending away women, specially young girls to safe places outside Pakistan';[61] (b) ugly proposals made towards Hindu women in the absence of their male family members; and (c) threatening letters made to rich Hindus demanding either their women or money in exchange for the safety of the women. To bolster his argument, he pointed out that although the Muslim minority in West Bengal also bore the brunt of occasional, localized communal clashes, they did not migrate because 'their religion, their person, their property and honor were safe here'.[62] Thus, it was not merely the threat of physical violence, but the threat to something larger—religion and honour as embodied in their women—that propelled the minority exodus from East Bengal.

In a booklet published after the 1950 riots, Samar Guha, the Secretary of the East Bengal Minorities Association and a veteran Congressman, identified crimes against Hindu women and the lack of authoritative response from the government as the key reason why East Bengal had ceased to be an 'honorable place for their (non-Muslims) peaceful living'.[63] Guha cited several reports of crimes against women, particularly in rural areas. In one instance, the daughter of a Hindu clerk in Rangpur was abducted by one of his subordinate employee. When both the abductor and the abducted were arrested and produced at court in Dacca, the woman declared that she had converted to Islam and had married her abductor. The abductor was acquitted and the court recognized the marriage. Guha noted that such cases were frequent and interpreted the court's verdict as an 'utter violation of Hindu sentiments' and were a catalyst to Hindu guardians' attempts to move their womenfolk to the other side of the border.[64] What Guha and others like him did not consider is the place of the abducted woman in Hindu society if she chose to denounce and leave her abductor, now husband.

Some members of the Hindu public in West Bengal made the connection between migration and continued harassment of minority

Hindu women in East Bengal. B.K. Nag wrote to the editor of *Hindustan Standard* that 'there has been a continued threat to the prestige and honor of women in Eastern Bengal to save which the Hindus have ever since been evacuating their womenfolk to the Indian Union'.[65] Nag's sources were mainly newspaper reports and hearsay from the refugees who had already crossed the border. He went on to conclude, 'When honor is lost, everything is lost' and urged the East Bengal government to ensure that such harassments cease and thereby also reduce the influx of refugees.[66]

THE RIOTS OF 1950

Small-scale and sporadic incidents of murder and looting, requisition of property, propaganda, rumours, and media reports on alleged incidents of violence created, at least for the minorities in India and Pakistan, a volatile and insecure psychological environment that continued as they began to identify themselves as citizens of the respective states. Narratives of persecution gained currency through rumours and newspaper reports and drew upon communal stereotypes to create a pre-history of communal animosity. The riots of 1950 that occurred in West Bengal and East Bengal seemed to corroborate the breach between communities. Even for those minorities who had continued to reside in their ancestral homes in the hope that situation after the Partition would stabilize, the 1950 riots only confirmed and sustained general apprehensions that communal violence could only be resolved with the wholescale 'population exchange' or migration of minorities.

The Khulna–Barisal riots of February 1950, which witnessed the largest cross-border migration from East Bengal and India, had little to do with communal tensions initially.[67] Two key incidents relating to the East Bengal police's attempts to control communist peasant activists acted as catalysts that triggered mimetic riots across borders. On 20 December 1949, the police carried out a raid on Kalshira village of Bagerhat subdivision in Khulna district to apprehend some communists who were active in the local peasant movement. During their search for the leaders, the police party tried to rape some women of the predominantly Namasudra village. In protest, the villagers attacked the police party and killed one constable on the spot and injured two others. Meanwhile, the local Ansars, who had managed to mobilize some Muslims from nearby villages, launched a rescue operation for the besieged policemen.[68] The situation quickly evolved into a communal conflict with battle lines clearly drawn between the police party and Ansars, who were all Muslims, and the villagers who were Scheduled Caste Hindus. Apprehending trouble, the villagers evacuated the area, taking minimal belongings, and crossed the border to India seeking temporary safety. In the next few days, local Muslims ransacked the abandoned Hindu houses and by the end of the month, twenty people had been arrested in this case.[69]

A similar incident occurred in the Nachol area of Rajshahi district, leading to large-scale migration of the local Santhal residents to India. Traditionally, the Santhals had been sharecroppers in this area and more recently, had become involved in the *tebhaga* movement.[70] From around May 1949, the police had been actively trying to quell the movement and had indiscriminately torched several villages, arrested and tortured villagers, and looted houses. Such actions had quickly identified them as agents of landlords and synonymous with peasant oppression. On 5 January 1950, when a police party of three constables and a sub-inspector arrived in Ghasura village in Nachol to seize the paddy from being transported to the local communist camp, they soon became targets of an angry Santhal mob.[71] The situation deteriorated as the mob killed all the members of the police party.

In retaliation, the East Bengal government sent in armed troops and several Ansar groups. Several villages were torched, and the skirmishes between the police and villagers continued for a week. Members of the communist party were arrested and Ila Mitra, a young communist leader, was raped and brutally tortured in custody. Fear of police brutality led the Santhals to migrate en masse to Murshidabad, where their tales of violence incited retaliatory violence on the Muslim minorities in nearby towns of Behrampore, Nimtita, and Beldanga.[72] This episode led some of these Muslim minorities to seek safety across the border in East Bengal, thereby setting off a chain of communal reactions.

What had started as anti-communist campaigns in East Bengal were swiftly translated into communal incidents through the narratives of violence of those crossing the borders and through media representations in India and Pakistan. The persistence of an ecology of fear, sporadic incidents of violence, and unsettled political and economic conditions after the Partition proved to be a fertile base on which communal antagonism rapidly escalated.

An adventitious set of circumstances in early 1950 considerably aggravated the situation. The Hindu Mahasabha, which had been temporarily banned after the assassination of Gandhi by one of its cadre members, held its first general conference in Calcutta between 24 and 26 December 1949. At this conference, N.B. Khare, its all-India President, cast aspersions on the legitimacy of East Bengal state and demanded the accession of additional territories from East Bengal to accommodate the influx of refugees.[73] He was not the first to advocate the union of the two Bengals and was certainly not alone in his demand for territory. In a series of speeches in January 1950 delivered at urban centres such as Bombay and Calcutta, Sardar Patel, the Deputy Prime Minister of India, held Pakistan responsible for India's refugee problems and threatened it with armed intervention if it did not fulfil its promises to safeguard its minorities. In his speech on 15 January 1950, delivered in Calcutta, Patel clearly evoked the terror of the Calcutta and Noakhali riots of 1946 and laid the blame squarely on the Muslim League. He argued that the borders of West Bengal and East Bengal were artificial and could not come in the way of Hindus who wanted to help their distressed brethren on the other side.[74] Such speeches provided the fuel to the already smoldering communal antagonism on both sides of the border as well as contributed to an atmosphere of imminent war.

Although newspapers had been instructed to blackout reports of communal incidents happening across the border, few adhered to such restrictions. Several editorials in popular newspapers in West Bengal painted the anti-communist campaigns in East Bengal in communal overtones.[75] In its editorial of 14 January 1950, the *Ananda Bazar Patrika* described the conditions in East Bengal as such: 'News received here regarding the condition of Barisal may be expressed in a sentence,—abduction, kidnapping, forcible conversion, forcible occupation of Hindu houses and looting—these are materials by which the Pakistanis made their history.'[76] The editorial alleged that it was symptomatic of what was happening in the whole of East Bengal and borrowed the familiar tropes of violence which had been in circulation in West Bengal's public discourse since Partition. The editorial also identified the East Bengal Hindus as separate from the

East Bengal Muslims because the latter had 'made no contribution to the freedom movement [but] have got the reins of administration in their hands. The Hindus by dint of whose sacrifice, sorrows and struggle freedom has been achieved are being driven out and ejected from their forefather's landed property.'[77] In this particular rewriting of the history of India's national movement, the Partition had clearly created a partitioned memory.

In their descriptions of the alleged atrocities happening in East Bengal, these editorials were consistent in identifying two key distinctive features. First, violence was unidirectional, aimed at minorities who were helpless, unarmed victims of a majority Muslim community. The *Jugantar*, a popular Bengali newspaper claiming to serve 55,000 households,[78] identified incidents in Khulna with 'medieval barbarity'. It described the 'official aggression of the majority against the minority' in graphic terms,

Police spread out in villages and began beating and killing menfolk and raping womenfolk. It is a repetition of that medieval barbarity of which we had so many instances in 1946. Women are raped while their men are kept under arrest. The groans of the mothers, sisters and daughters did not rouse in the Pakistani police any feeling for the sufferers. But it excited their lust even further.[79]

The nature of violence itself was thus described in familiar and existing stereotypes of Muslim aggression. The prevalent 'historical' anecdote about the Muslim conquest of Bengal in the twelfth century C.E. seemed to effectively uphold the primary associative tropes of alleged 'medievalism' and the martial nature of Muslims. The popular version of the conquest notes that a handful of cavalrymen, under Muhammad Bhaktiyar, entered the palace of the last Sena ruler of Bengal while he was at lunch and defeated him in the ensuing skirmish.[80] The small number of the soldiers highlights the martial prowess compared to the peace-loving nature of their victims, while the fact that they took the battle into the private domain indicates their total disregard for the rules of engagement.

Specific description of communal incidents continually drew and built upon such stories. As the *Jugantar* informed its readers, it was not surprising that instead of having the 'normal' reaction to sufferings of minority Hindu women, the East Bengali police only felt lust.

Another editorial in the *Amrita Bazar Patrika* identified the rioting in East Bengal as an instance of 'primeval barbarism' and the Hindu minorities as 'helots in a sacerdotal land'.[81] While Hindu 'women must sink into dishonor worse—far worse—than death', the rioting had unleashed upon 'unarmed, peace-loving people' a 'violence—such as we do not associate even with foreign conquering armies'.[82] The contrasting imagery depicted in such editorials aimed to evoke maximum sympathy from those readers whose cognizance of the sword-wielding Muslim fanatic gained an upper hand over shared culture and language as the rioting continued to mirror the violence across borders.

Even the anti-communist origin of violence was, according to newspapers in West Bengal, merely a ruse to further minority oppression. According to the *Jugantar* editorial, generally 'Hindu young men are communist because their talent is progressive and revolutionary, whereas the Muslim young men are old fashioned reactionaries'.[83] Such a depiction turned a blind eye to the anti-communist stance in India and also to the fact that the communist party in East Bengal had a substantial number of 'Muslim young men'!

The second emphasis was to question the legitimacy of the East Bengali state. Depictions of violence underscored the tacit sanction and often direct official involvement of East Bengal authorities, which meant that redress would be futile. The failure to defend and ensure the security of its minorities became the legitimate watermark of the 'moth eaten' Pakistan's viability as a new nation state. Several editorials alleged that even after the Partition, the Pakistan government 'could not abandon their role of hatred for Hindus'[84] and that the 'East Bengal government consider the Hindus to be so many outlaws'.[85] Violence in East Bengal, in their opinion, 'draws inspiration and nourishment from a theory of State which legalizes tyranny in the name of religion'.[86] With such an unreasonable attitude, for which the editorials offered no concrete reasons but left the readers to evoke a seamless history of communal antagonism, it was imperative that the Indian government take up the cause of security and honour of the East Bengal minorities.

Government press reports published in major newspapers in both countries detailed the incidents of violence but emphasized the reduced nature of communalism involved in these incidents in an attempt alley the fears of their respective minorities. However, 'real facts' only confirmed the minorities' worst fears. News also travelled with the victims of violence, was rapidly disseminated, and was embellished as it circulated by word of mouth. By the end of January 1950, as these stories and rumours of murder and violence began to circulate, the situation in both Calcutta and Dacca rapidly deteriorated. Saroj Chakarabarty, the Secretary to the Chief Minister, B.C. Roy, provides a vivid contemporary account of the days prior to the riots in Calcutta in early February 1950.

Stories of horrors and atrocities perpetrated on Hindu minority spread like wildfire with the arrival of about 1300 fleeing refugees at the border town of Bongaon ... Masses of refugees were stranded at railheads, steamer stations and at the Dacca airport waiting for transport ... Stories of butchering of Hindus during transit by train and steamer were pouring in and journey by land or river from East Bengal without armed escort was extremely risky. One evening when he returned from the Secretariat, news reached him from Sealdah Station that some bogies from border areas had reached without any passengers. They were filled with broken conchshell bangles, shreds of wearing apparels of women and men with bloodstains ... Calcutta was in flames immediately after this. The city of Howrah which contained industrial population was the scene of worst rioting.[87]

As West Bengal newspapers published reports of attacks on trains plying across borders, memories of train travel during the Punjab massacres hovered in the background. Even though such attacks concentrated on looting the passengers and were frequently foiled by the presence of armed escorts in the trains, stories of 'empty trains and broken conch shell bangles' found fertile ground on which to breed communal antagonism. In later years, memories of the 1950 riots inevitably brought up the spectre of trains which arrived without passengers but 'smeared with blood, and adorned with remnants of torn *dhoti*, blouses and saris'.[88]

As the refugees from East Bengal arrived in Calcutta, stabbings, arson, and mob attacks became daily occurrences in the city. Mridula Sarabhai, who was closely connected with the refugee relief operations in Delhi, received daily reports from Congress workers in Bengal. A typical report in the month of February talked about the 'total annihilation of the Muslims'; police incapability and occasionally, their culpability in the rioting; and refugee camps opened up in the city for Muslims displaced by the rioting.[89] In addition, relief workers strongly urged the authorities not to let refugees from East Bengal mingle with the citizens of Calcutta and spread tales of their plight. Sarabhai came to Calcutta in March 1950 to oversee relief operations and report on the situation. She concluded that although the popular cause of rioting was retaliation for events in the east, several anti-social and communal elements such as the Hindu Mahasabha and the Council for the Protection of Rights of East Bengal minorities, a self-styled semi-military outfit led by J.P. Mitter, were primarily responsible for inciting the public in the riots in West Bengal.[90]

In Calcutta, rioting occurred in pockets where Muslims were a numerically substantial presence but not the local majority. From 5 February onwards, Batanagar, Manicktolla, Ultadanga, and Baghmari areas in Calcutta succumbed to arson and looting. In the subsequent days, communal violence moved away from the city and spread rapidly into the border districts of Murshidabad, 24 Parganas, Nadia, and Cooch Behar, which had been receiving a steady stream of refugees since early January. In March 1950, Muslim members of West Bengal Legislative Assembly submitted a memorandum to Nehru detailing the various aspects of a 'reign of terror and extreme lawlessness' in the previous two months. According to their report, anti-Muslim rioting reached its peak on 12 February when 'arson, loot, plunder firings, bombings, assassinations went on in full swing till late at night. The imams of Mosques were burnt alive with the Holy Quran hung round their necks ... and other innocent Muslims burnt alive.'[91] The legislators alleged that the Indian government had been paying scant attention to the sufferings of its own minorities. Rather, 'it appears that minorities in East Bengal are the sacred trust of India and are the "blood of our blood"' if one compared the measures taken to alleviate their sufferings.[92]

The arrival of Muslim refugees in East Bengal from three different provinces, Assam, West Bengal, and Bihar, created a similar volatile situation in Dacca. Muslim minorities in Assam had long been bearing the brunt of the *Bongal Kheda* (Oust Bengalis) movement aimed at expelling Bengalis from that province. After Partition, this movement targeted Bengali Muslim peasants who had settled in that province generations earlier but were now perceived as 'alien' to Assamese identity. Intermittent riots in Bihar had evicted a significant number of Bihari Muslims who migrated to Dacca around this time. The last straw on the proverbial camel's back was the arrival of Muslim minorities from different parts of West Bengal who had faced retaliatory persecution due to the incidents in Nachol and Kalshira. Rumour, propaganda, and stories of atrocities committed on the minority community in India accompanied the recent arrivals in Dacca in early February 1950. The chief secretaries of West Bengal and East Bengal met in Dacca to discuss the various inter-dominion problems and discuss proposals to contain the current phase of communal rioting. At the same time, on 10 February, the East Bengal secretariat employees held a protest demonstration and meeting at Victoria Park, the traditional site for political rallies in Dacca. As the meeting broke up, the mob turned violent and started ransacking and looting shops and commercial enterprises belonging to minorities. On 12 February, an armed mob attacked a crowd of Hindu passengers at the Kurmitolla airport near Dacca, killing and wounding some of the passengers.[93] In accounting for the rioting in Dacca between 10 and 12 February, Tajuddin Ahmed, a prominent Awami League leader, identified the main reason behind the current riots as repercussion from the communal violence in Calcutta. Further, minority representatives of the East Bengal Legislative Assembly had further exacerbated the situation by their decision to abstain from Assembly proceedings in protest against the earlier atrocities against minorities. Thus, when the clerks of the secretariat, some of who were muhajirs from Bihar, decided to protest on 10 February, 'their action was like setting a spark to a gunpowder pile'.[94] As the mob violence spiralled out of control, curfew was imposed on Dacca and the army patrolled the main roads and thoroughfares.

Amy Geraldine Stock, who was a visiting English professor at the Dacca University, provides some vivid impressions of the situation in Dacca in 1950. Her first warning of any trouble came from her *Hindu chaprashi* (peon), Kalipada, who had enquired whether it would be wise for him and his family to leave East Bengal for India. On 10 February, Stock received news of trouble in parts of the city. Her acquaintances in Dacca reported the circulation of a number of rumours: 3,000 women refugees whose husbands had been killed in Bihar had just arrived in Dacca bringing with them their tales of violence; or that reinforcements in the form of firebrands from Mymensingh had arrived to participate in the day's rioting which continued to fuel communal violence in the city. The primary rumour which may have been the catalyst to rioting was, however, the news that

Fazlul Huq's nephew, a government official in West Bengal, had been stabbed and killed by way of reprisal for events in Barisal. Troops had been called out in Calcutta to check riots, a curfew proclaimed. Angry processions were going round Dacca, police and military were on guard, and Nawabpur Road (the main road through the city from the university side) looked ugly.[95]

One of Stock's students, Khorshed, reported to her that the news of the Calcutta troubles and assassination had led the clerks at the secretariat to march in a protest demonstration. The situation had deteriorated when some Hindu shops were looted and the owners fired in self-defence killing four Muslims. 'That Muslims could be shot in Dacca was too much for the goonda's public spirit—besides they were ready for some looting.'[96] Later in the day, Stock herself witnessed two policemen beating up some miscreants who had assaulted some women and a fire in a Hindu-owned chemical factory.

While Dacca remained in the eye of the storm, communal rioting spread rapidly to other parts of East Bengal such as Noakhali, Faridpur, Madaripur, Khulna, Jessore, Bogra, and Mymensingh. In Chittagong, local mobs attacked Buddhist monasteries and a number of Buddhist minorities were killed. Non-Muslims of that area crossed the border and took shelter in the Lushai Hills. Barisal, the home district of the Krishak Praja Party leader, Fazlul Haq, was one of the worst hit districts in East Bengal. Rioting here began on 13 February as rumours circulated of the death of Fazlul Haq and/or his nephew in the communal riots in Calcutta. Haq, who had been at that time visiting Calcutta, hastened back to East Bengal but rioting in several villages preceded his arrival.

Although the main phase of rioting petered out by the third week of February 1950, intermittent incidents of violence continued to persist in the subsequent months. On the one hand, Liaquat Ali Khan and Nehru exchanged telegrams proclaiming their readiness to go to war if needed. On the other hand, both assured each other of their efforts to protect the security of their respective minorities. Meanwhile, panicky refugees from East Bengal continued to arrive in West Bengal in a steady stream via steamers, planes, and trains. In a letter to B.C. Roy, Nehru noted, 'From 1950–52, 9.32 lakhs of Hindus have come to West Bengal and 3.84 lakhs Muslims have gone to East Bengal.'[97]

East Bengali authorities were not keen for Hindu minorities to cross the border, and sometimes were overzealous in their attempts to curb their movement. In an urgent telegram to Liaquat Ali Khan, Jawaharlal Nehru pointed out two instances of attacks on trains carrying Hindu refugees to West Bengal. On 26 February 1950, some unknown 'miscreants' stopped the Dacca Mail and forcibly detrained the passengers. Nehru's telegram cited another incident where on '27th morning the steamer bound to Goalondo from Narayanganj carrying 1500 evacuee passengers was forced by some Muslim volunteers to disembark on a char named Kazirkhila in district Faridpur. This was not deemed a halting station and steamer left for Goalondo leaving passengers stranded but carrying part of their luggage. After some time they were attacked by local hooligans.'[98] News of such train and steamer de-boardings were reported in the Indian newspapers depicting yet more instances of persecution of Hindu minorities in East Bengal.

In the months following the riots in West Bengal and East Bengal, public opinion in the former began to advocate a 'population exchange' and long-term rehabilitation of the East Bengali Hindus. The prevailing public discourse on violence and victimhood of the East Bengali Hindus now reached an all-time high as tangible victims bearing the marks of violence crossed the borders. The *Amrita Bazar Patrika* decided to use its pages to elicit the help of its readers in finding a solution to the crisis and requested them to provide opinions.[99] The text of the appeal referred to the earlier Gallup poll of April 1947 which had requested public opinion on the issue of partitioning Bengal. With similar intentions of gauging the public mind in 1950, the newspaper urged,

Today, in the face of a much bigger peril when the very existence of the 12 million of East Bengal Hindus is at stake, the Government in all seriousness is searching for a way out. We appeal to all our countrymen to give their considered opinion as to what may be the permanent solution to this vital problem, so that our government might know the voice of the people and act accordingly, once more. We shall send this national verdict to the proper authorities and duly interpret them through our columns. Let our countrymen help us in crystalizing public opinion on this most momentous problem of the hour.[100]

The appeal reappeared several times in subsequent editions of the newspaper as it published the letters in response as a full page feature.

Several readers urged the evacuation of the minorities as 'the only solution'.[101] Nalinakshya Sanyal, a veteran Congress worker, urged that 'India should unequivocally declare her doors open for the reception of the minority community of East Bengal and their re-settlement in suitable areas throughout India'.[102] Further, the 'protection of the person, property and honor of East Bengal Hindus will be a concern for the Government of India'[103] and the minorities should be declared Indian nationals even when they continued to reside in East Bengal.

For another section of the *Amrita Bazar Patrika*'s readers, evacuation was 'cowardly and not manly' and the East Bengali minorities had as many rights of citizenship to their homeland as their Muslim brethrens. Thus, the Indian state should do everything to ensure the minority's safety and security in East Bengal even if it meant going to war or the direct annexation of East Bengal to the Indian Union.[104] Another letter described the events in East Bengal in gendered terms depicting the incidents as instances when the 'very soul of India is being molested'.[105] Arguing that the question of evacuation of the minorities was no longer viable, the letter urged all West Bengalis 'to do or die for protecting the honor of their mothers and sisters' and save 'all that which makes a man a man'.[106] Identifying the Muslims in East Bengal with Nazis and Japanese, Nirmal Sinha, a professor based in Burdwan, urged the Indian authorities, 'Let us therefore, with all our moral courage and unflinching devotion to the right cause tackle the Pakistan danger rather than shrink from it and be dubbed moral cowards and defeatists. Moral courage must be shown not only through words but also through action, when necessary.'[107]

In an atmosphere where both public and political rhetoric increasingly adopted a bellicose attitude, Nehru and Liaquat Ali entered into high-level talks and concluded a pact that promised to ensure safety and security of minorities in each country. Known popularly as the Delhi Pact or the Nehru–Liaquat Pact of April 1950, it urged minorities to return to their homeland where their property would be returned and their personal safety assured by the respective governments. In an effort to provide a sense of security to the minorities, the Pact incorporated provisions that guaranteed equality of citizenship, job opportunities, and safeguards for minority interests. Although the Pact initially helped to check the exodus, conditions remained unstable in East Bengal and the migration continued unabated. Some groups like the Hindu Mahasabha launched a strong public campaign to highlight the atrocities committed on the Hindu minorities in East Bengal. Even the more secular Bengal Rehabilitation Organization, comprising eminent public figures in Calcutta, criticized the Pact as not having 'at all helped to create confidence or a sense of security in the minds of the Hindus'.[108]

The Nehru–Liaquat Pact was arguably a band-aid solution to curb minority migration and reduce the risk of an international war. Although both India and Pakistan promised to protect the rights of their minority citizens, provisions to implement such promises remained, at best, rudimentary. For the refugees, the Pact represented a Hobson's choice; they could either go back to their hometowns which continued to reverberate with communal tensions, or the could remain in an alien environment in West Bengal or East Bengal as the case may be and hope to be rehabilitated by the respective governments. A number of East Bengali Hindus returned but the deteriorating economic conditions, the continuation of sporadic communal violence, and the imposition of the passport regulations at the border forced them to cross the border continually. Amy Stock writes poignantly of the situation facing the minority Hindus in East Bengal,

Kalipada decided not to emigrate for the present. But the crisis brought him to one momentous step: he sold his remaining cow, his favorite a beautiful dark brown creature with a newborn calf, to Abdul. He could hardly bear to part with her but the responsibility of caring for a sacred animal in this troubled world was more than he could face, for if any Muslim tried to steal or kill her it would be his religious duty to defend her life with his own. Abdul promised not to slaughter her, and Kalipada put her under my protection in committing her to Abdul and calling me to witness. The transaction took place in my office, ceremoniously, as if it symbolized the ordeal of the Hindus and the irretrievable decline of their security under the apparent restoration of goodwill. Kalipada shed tears of emotion, and Abdul, who had made an excellent bargain, stood triumphantly erect … he (Abdul) was a man of his word: cow and calf lived in safety, and if she ceased to be a goddess the quality of her morning milk was not impaired.[109]

After the 1950 riots, like Kalipada, Hindu minorities in East Bengal and Muslim minorities in India came one step closer to migration. Psychological violence informed minority insecurities. The public discourse on violence focused on validating hearsay and highlighting victimhood of the minorities while emphasizing the wanton destruction of religious places such as temples and mosques. Rumours and tales of atrocities across the border reported in the media continued to circulate even during times of peace, feeding on existing paranoiac stereotypes of the 'Other'. Local propaganda of Right-wing groups like the Hindu Mahasabha underscored the cultural ties of the East Bengali minority Hindus with the West Bengali Hindus but, in the same breath, denied ties of common language and cultural tradition to the Bengali Muslims.

Violence in divided Bengal continued to operate as part of everyday life, targeting minorities and making them question their decision to remain in their ancestral homes. All those who opted to migrate, had to face indifference, lack of resources, and faulty relief and rehabilitation mechanisms that reconstituted them as economic migrants rather than victims of violence. The perception that Bengal had not witnessed large-scale violence persisted even after the 1950 riots, and this is what led India to frame ad hoc policies towards refugees from East Bengal rather than provide them permanent rehabilitation.

NOTES

1. File no. 27C-4 of 1948, B Proceedings 207–34, Home Political, October 1950, Bangladesh National Archives (BNA).

2. *Ibid.*

3. *Ibid.*

4. Max Jean Zins has argued that the Calcutta killings of 1946, in which brutal violence on women was first perpetrated on a large scale, provided the impetus and emulatory model to the later Punjab Partition riots. Max Jean Zins, 2001, 'The 1947 Vivisection of India: The Political Usage of a Carnage in the Era of Citizen-massacres', in Mushirul Hasan and Nariaki Nakazato (eds), *The Unfinished Agenda, National Building in South Asia*, New Delhi: Manohar, pp. 49–77.

5. Sekhar Bandyopadhyay, 1994, 'Development, Differentiation and Caste: The Namasudra Movement in Bengal, 1872–1947', in Sekhar Bandyopadhyay, Abhijit Dasgupta, and Willem Van Schendel (eds), *Bengal: Communities, Development and States*, New Delhi: Manohar, pp. 90–119.

6. File no. 972/47, West Bengal Police, Special Branch (WBPSB), 1948.

7. File no. 11P–22/1951, B Proceedings 585–91, Public Relations, August 1953, BNA.

8. File no. 4L-B/1950, B Proceedings 142–5, Home Political, September 1951, BNA.

9. File no. PM 816/48, WBPSB, 1948.

10. File no. PM 1019/48, WBPSB, 1948.

11. File no. PM 506/47, WBPSB, 1947.

12. *Ibid*

13. *Ibid.*

14. A pejorative term that literally means brother-in-law but suggests an intimate relationship with someone's sister.

15. Unsigned Memorandum to the Provincial Minority Board, File no. CR 7M-1, B Proceedings 277–303, Home Political, September 1949, BNA.

16. *Ibid.*

17. Intra-dominion telegram between Dacca and Karachi, 4 March 1948, File no. 12C-4, B Proceedings 371–5, Home Political, August 1949, BNA.

18. *Ibid.*

19. With the departure of such leaders and upper and middle-class Hindus from the official administration, the political and social life of eastern Bengal witnessed the splintering of traditional Hindu dominance in these spheres.

20. Letter, 10 November 1947, File 4P-7/48, B Proceedings, Home Political, July 1948, BNA.

21. *Ibid.*; emphasis added.

22. *Ibid.*

23. Report, 17 March 1948 (*ibid.*).

24. See Chapter 6.

25. Letter from Sir Harold Dennehy, Chief Secretary, Assam, to Chief Secretary, Government of East Bengal, 12 January 1948, File no. 4P-7/48, B Proceedings, Home Political, July 1948, BNA.

26. *Ibid.*

27. Ritu Menon and Kamala Bhasin have argued that 'Dramatic episodes of violence against women during communal riots bring to the surface, savagely and explicitly, familiar forms of sexual violence—now charged with a symbolic meaning that serves as an indicator of the place that women's sexuality occupies in an all male patriarchal arrangement of gender relations between and within religious or ethnic communities.' Ritu Menon and Kamala Bhasin, 1998, *Borders and Boundaries: Women in India's Partition*, New Delhi: Kali, p. 41.

28. Although reported cases of abduction of women were few, some leading intellectuals in Bengal felt the need to form an organization which would prevent crimes against women and 'rescue, protest [*sic*] and rehabilitate abducted women'. Known as the Bangiya Nari Raksha Samity, Sucheta Kripalani was its President and Radha Kumud Mukherjee was the President of its working committee. See *Hindustan Standard* (*HS*), 5 August 1947, p. 3.

29. But he also pointed out the reluctance of the victims to admit to being raped, abducted, or converted. F.J. Burrows, Letter, 18 November 1946, File no.

L/PJ/8/575 coll.117/B5 Pt.4, Oct. 1946–July 1947, Oriental and India Office Collections (OIOC), London.

30. *Ibid.*

31. Cited in Suranjan Das, 1991, *Communal Riots in Bengal, 1905–1947,* New Delhi: Oxford University Press, p. 198.

32. *Ibid.*

33. The numbers are few only in comparison to the cases in the Punjab. East Bengal records provide intermittent evidence of abductions of Hindu women beyond 1947. For example, see Home Political (CR) Proceedings 218–19, March 1950, BNA.

34. Jyotirmayee Devi, 1995, *Epar Ganga–Opar Ganga* (The River Churning), translated by Enakshi Chatterjee, New Delhi: Kali.

35. Ramapada Chaudhury,1992, 'Karun Kanya', in Manabendra Bandyapadhya (ed.), *Bhed–Bhibed, Vol. 1–2,* Calcutta: Dey's, pp. 292–306.

36. J.M. Chatterjee to Mridula Sarabhai, April 1950, File no. R/ Bengal/15-1950-54, *Mridula Sarabhai Papers,* Nehru Memorial Museum and Library (NMML). Such incidents were also reported in *HS*, 7 July 1948, p. 6.

37. *HS*, 26 June 1948, p. 8.

38. Note by Sub-Inspector J.L. Sen, 10 July 1948, File no. PM 506, WBPSB, 1948. Some vernacular newspapers, like the *Dainik Basumati,* also reported the story.

39. Official Memo, 22 July 1948 (*ibid.*).

40. Editorial, *HS*, 15 July 1947, p. 4.

41. *Ibid.*

42. *Ibid.*

43. *HS*, 25 June 1948, p. 4; emphasis added.

44. *Ibid.*

45. For news reports on violence and harassment of Hindu minorities in East Bengal, see *Amrita Bazar Patrika,* 22 February 1948, p. 8; *Amrita Bazar Patrika,* 21 March 1948, pp. 1, 5; Editorial, *Amrita Bazar Patrika,* 24 March 1948, p. 4; *Amrita Bazar Patrika,* 25 March 1948, p. 8; *Amrita Bazar Patrika,* 14 April 1948, p. 8; *HS*, 1 June 1948, p. 6; *HS*, 16 June 1948, p. 6; *HS*, 25 June 1948, p. 6; *HS*, 4 August 1948, p. 6; *HS*, 24 August 1948, p. 6; *HS*, 28 September 1948, p. 8; *HS*, 19 October 1948, p. 4; *HS*, 6 November 1948, p. 6; *HS*, 7 November 1948, p. 10; *HS*, 10 December 1948, p. 1; *HS*, 23 December 1948, p. 5; *HS*, 1 January 1949, p. 6; *HS*, 2 January 1949, p. 6; *HS*, 3 April 1949, p. 9.

46. See Chapter 4.

47. *HS*, 28 September 1948, p. 8.

48. *Ibid.*

49. Chittagong Bar Association to Manoranjan Dhar, Member of the East Bengal Minority Commission, 30 August 1950, File no. 2p-69, B Proceedings 51–2, Home Political, January 1952, BNA.

50. When certain Indian newspapers were banned on a temporary basis in 1951, the East Bengal government prohibited the correspondents of key Indian newspapers from operating in East Bengal. Among those targeted were reporters of *Ananda Bazar Patrika, HS, Swaraj, Jugantar, Dainik Basumati, Ittehad, The Nation, Roshni,* and *Mandira*.

51. Editorial, *Pakistan Observer*, 3 December 1949, p. 2.

52. *Jai Hind*, 12 March 1948.

53. *Ananda Bazar Patrika* (Bengali), 16 March 1948, p.5.

54. Although 'Mag' refers to the Maratha marauders who in the sixteenth and the seventeenth century periodically attacked Bengal and are incorporated into lullabies, recent usage of the term refers to Muslims.

55. *Dainik Basumati* (Bengali), 12 March 1948, p. 3.

56. For reports on abduction and molestation of Hindu women in East Bengal and failure of East Bengal authorities, see *Amrita Bazar Patrika*, 9 February 1948, p. 8; *Amrita Bazar Patrika*, 10 February 1948, p. 5; *Amrita Bazar Patrika*, 15 March 1948, p. 5; *HS*, 1 May 1948, p. 5; *HS*, 16 June 1948, p. 6; *HS*, 25 June 1948, p. 6; *HS*, 10 December 1948, p. 1; *HS*, 18 April 1949, p. 8; *HS*, 2 May 1949, p.3.

57. *Amrita Bazar Patrika*, 2 July 1948, p. 4.

58. *HS*, 25 November 1948, p. 3.

59. Letters to the editor, *Amrita Bazar Patrika*, by Rajoni Kanta Mojumder, 26 February 1948, p. 4; by Ruby Chakravarty, 13 March 1948, p. 4; by Mrs Amita Sen and Krishna Sarker, 22 March 1948, p. 4; *HS*, 28 November 1948, p. 4.

60. *The Nation*, 28 October 1948, p. 3; also published in *HS*, 28 October 1948, p. 3.

61. *Ibid.*

62. *Ibid.*

63. Samar Guha, 1951, *Non-Muslims behind the Curtain of East Bengal*, Dacca: East Bengal Minorities Association.

64. *Ibid.*, pp. 73–4.

65. *HS*, 28 November 1948, p. 4

66. *Ibid.*

67. In the year 1950, the influx of refugees from East Bengal reached an all-time high of 15,75,000 recorded persons. See Government of West Bengal (GoWB), 1980, *Report of the Refugee Rehabilitation Committee*, Calcutta: Saraswati Press, cited in Nilanjana Chatterjee, 1992, 'Midnight's Unwanted Children: East Bengali Refugees and the Politics of Rehabilitation', Unpublished PhD thesis, Brown University, p. 27.

68. Press Note issued by the Government of East Bengal on 3 February 1950. See East Bengal Home Department, 1950, *Note on the Genesis of Communal Disturbances in West Bengal*, Dacca: East Bengal Government Press, p. 38.

69. Badruddin Umar, 1970, *Pūrbabāalāra Bhāshā Āndolana o Tatkālīna Rājanīti* (The Language Movement in East Bengal and Contemporary Politics), Dhaka: Moula Brothers, p. 228.

70. The demand for tebhaga was a movement of sharecroppers to reduce their rent from two-thirds to one-third of their crop.

71. Mesbah Kamal and Eshani Chakraborty, 2001, *Nacholer Krishak Bidroho: Shamokalin Rajniti O Ila Mitra*, Dhaka: Institute of Liberation Bangabandhu and Bangladesh Studies, National University, pp. 126–64.

72. Press Note issued by GoWB, 6 February 1950, East Bengal Home Department, *Note on the Genesis of Communal Disturbances in West Bengal*, p. 40.

73. In the course of his speech, N.B. Khare noted, 'In East Bengal also the Hindus are being persecuted and their property and honor are not safe. As a solution for the sufferings of Hindus in East Bengal, in view of the common factors between West and East Bengal, it is clearly in the interest of East Bengal to align with India. Failing this, India should demand cession of two or three border districts from East Bengal to rehabilitated their refugees there' (*ibid.*, appendix, pp. 2, 20).

74. *Ibid.*, pp. 3–4.

75. See editorials in *HS*, 2 February 1950; *Amrita Bazar Patrika*, 25 February 1950, p. 4; the major newspapers printed reports on the Khulna and Nachol incidents from 15 January 1950 onwards.

76. *Ananda Bazar Patrika* (Bengali), 1950, 'Unbearable Conditions', Editorial, 14 January, p. 4.

77. *Ibid.*

78. Advertisement, Independence Number, *Amrita Bazar Patrika* (Calcutta), 1947, p. 2.

79. Editorial, *Jugantar*, 18 January 1950, p. 4.

80. A variation of the story of the conquest describes Bhaktiyar Khilji as a merchant in disguise who visited Nadia with the pre-planned motive of conquering the province. When Lakshman Sena, on the pretext of buying merchandise, came out of his palace, the Khilji soldiers, numbering only a few, attacked him. Although the king's bodyguards put up a good fight at the sudden unexpected attack, they were defeated and brutally killed. The king was captured and Bhaktiyar Khilji became the lord of Bengal. Ramesh C. Mazumdar, 1957, *Bangla Desher Itihash*, Calcutta: General Printers and Publishers, pp. 91–7. The book was first published in 1943, as the first volume of a comprehensive trilogy of Bengal's history. Jadunath Sarkar wrote the second and third volumes. Mazumdar, who was earlier the Vice Chancellor of Dacca University and migrated to West Bengal in the wake of the Partition, provides detailed accounts of the popular stories of the Muslim conquest of Bengal but casts doubt on the veracity of the contemporary historical accounts such

as those of Minhajuddin and Ishami. Also, see Richard Eaton, 1993, *The Rise of Islam and the Bengal Frontier, 1204–1760*, Berkeley: University of California Press, pp. 1–2.

81. *Amrita Bazar Patrika*, 1950, 'A Grim Moment', Editorial, 26 February 1950, p. 4.

82. *Ibid*.

83. Editorial, *Jugantar*, 18 January 1950, p. 4.

84. *Ibid*.

85. *Ananda Bazar Patrika*, 18 January 1950, p. 4.

86. *Amrita Bazar Patrika*, 'A Grim Moment', p. 4.

87. Saroj Chakrabarty, 1974, *With Dr. B. C. Roy and Other Chief Ministers: A Record up to 1962*, Calcutta: Benson's, pp. 154–5.

88. For example, see Durgadas Acarya, 1978, *Udvastu, Dandyakaranya o Andamana*, Calcutta: Indian Progressive Publishing Company, p. 7; Pravash Chandra Lahiry, 1968, *Pak Bharater Ruparekha* (An Outline of India and Pakistan), Chakdah, Nadia: Shyama Prakashani, pp. 201–3.

89. Statement of Mridula Sarabhai, 1950, Home Political (Confidential), No File no., West Bengal State Archives (WBSA).

90. *Ibid*.

91. Memorandum presented by the Muslim Members of the West Bengal Legislative Assembly to the Prime Minister of Bharat, 1950, *Tragedy of Calcutta, January–March 1950*, 7 March, Dacca: West Bengal Refugees Association, pp. 4–6.

92. *Ibid.*, p. 3.

93. Nehru's statement on the Bengal situation in Indian Parliament on 23 February 1950, reported in *Amrita Bazar Patrika*, 24 February 1950, p. 1.

94. Excerpts from Tajuddin Ahmed's Diary, reproduced in Badruddin Umar, *Purba Banglara Bhasha Andolana*, pp. 235–6.

95. A.G. Stock, 1973, *Memoirs of Dacca University, 1947–51*, Dacca: Green Book House Ltd, p. 162.

96. *Ibid.*, p. 165.

97. Jawaharlal Nehru, Letter, 2 December 1952, in G. Parthasarathy (ed.), 1985, *Letters to the Chief Ministers 1947–64, Vol. III*, New Delhi: Oxford University Press.

98. Telegram no. 30592, 2 March 1950, File no. 214/50, Home Political CR, 1950, WBSA.

99. *Amrita Bazar Patrika*, 1950, 'What is the Solution?', 28 February, p. 1.

100. *Ibid*.

101. *Amrita Bazar Patrika*, 25 February 1950, p. 4; *Amrita Bazar Patrika*, 7 March 1950, p. 7; *Amrita Bazar Patrika*, 13 March 1950, p. 4; *Amrita Bazar Patrika*, 16 March 1950, p. 7.

102. *Ibid.*

103. *Amrita Bazar Patrika*, 9 March 1950, p. 4.

104. *Amrita Bazar Patrika*, 27 February 1950, p. 4; *Amrita Bazar Patrika*, 7 March 1950, p. 7; *Amrita Bazar Patrika*, 16 March 1950, p. 7.

105. *Ibid.*

106. *Amrita Bazar Patrika*, 28 February 1950, p. 4.

107. Letters to the Editor, *Amrita Bazar Patrika*, 15 March 1950, p. 4.

108. Cited in Gyanesh Kudaisya, 1998, 'Divided Landscapes, Fragmented Identities: East Bengal Refugees and their Rehabilitation in India, 1947–79', in D.A. Low and Howard Brasted (eds), *Freedom, Trauma, Continuities: Northern India and Independence*, New Delhi: Sage, p. 110.

109. Stock, *Memoirs of Dacca University*, p. 178.

6

Refugees and the Indian State

The Partition generated large-scale movements between India and West and *East Bengal* as both minority Hindus and Muslims sought the safety of numerical majorities across the new borders. While the migration in Punjab was nearly over by 1949 and entailed both communities, in Bengal, the migration continued chronically over the next two decades, its peaks coinciding with the passage of legislations aimed at restricting border travel. The national leadership was ambivalent about the chronic refugee migration in the eastern sector. While some viewed it as a threat to the fragile economy of India, others argued that the migration of Bengali Hindus undermined India's foundational principle of secularism. Were these border crossers refugees, migrants, or citizens of new India? If they were indeed refugees, then should they be provided with temporary relief or permanent rehabilitation? These were the central questions that plagued Indian policymakers as they grappled with the eastern 'problem'. Anticipating such dilemmas, the representative at the constituent assembly thus hoped to stake the claims of Indian citizenship for East Bengali Hindus as early as possible.

The figure of the 'refugee' and the violence that they faced, consequent uprooting and 'exile', and the search for a home in a country which was no longer their own have been the core of many representations and discussion of the human tragedy of the Partition. In the case of Bengal, the lack of large-scale violence and the chronic migration over two decades shifted scholarly focus towards their relief and rehabilitation. Such scholarship, which began from the early 1950s, included sociological explorations of their caste and class structures[1] and attempts to connect this migration to the rise of the Left in West Bengal in the 1970s to the preceding migration and rehabilitation.[2] Studies of refugee rehabilitation also focused on both the spatial development of the Calcutta metropolitan region[3] and the development of official policies in the face of continuing migration in the succeeding decades after 1947.[4] In recent years, focus on Bengali refugees has highlighted the ways in which these refugees initiated, contested, and negotiated their rights of relief with authorities, who conceptualized rehabilitation as a form of charity.[5] It has also emphasized the modalities of reconstitution of the refugee self within the new nation states.[6] However, such scholarship remains limited in their continued use of a single refugee experience to represent the experiences of different classes and castes of refugees that came across the border.[7] Further, the central figure of the Bengali refugee is the 'Hindu' refugee and very little focus has been on to those Muslims who migrated from eastern India to *East Bengal*.[8] Also, the focus on faulty rehabilitation policies as the primary reason for failure or success of refugee rehabilitation has continued to stress the responsibility of the Indian State. Scholars have focused on the differential disbursement of resources vis-à-vis Punjab and Bengal refugees[9] arguing that such difference stemmed from a refusal to accept that in Bengal, the migration was permanent.[10] Further, refugee rehabilitation policies were framed in conjunction with the projects of economic development and national security.[11]

What has yet to be stated explicitly is that the Indian State formulated such rehabilitation measures with expectation of 'self-rehabilitation', that is, the refugees would be able to help themselves with some aid of the Indian State.[12] In the face of limited and faulty rehabilitation, it was thus very easy to perceive the Bengali Hindu refugee as the primary cause for any failure.

This chapter shifts focus back on the Indian State's relief and rehabilitation policies in West Bengal to argue that, in addition to being a patchwork of contingent and ad hoc solutions, such policies and the public discourse surrounding them constructed a paradoxical figure of the Bengali refugee: heroic but lazy, able to abandon their homeland but parochial about rehabilitation outside the boundaries of West Bengal, an economic migrant under the cloak of a refugee, and shorn of agency yet subversive. In the eyes of the Indian State, the refugees from *East Bengal* remained a 'problem child' whose path to self-reliant citizenship was handicapped not because of faulty policies but partly due to the illegitimacy of such claims and partly due to the very 'nature' of the Bengali refugee. Such constructions stemmed partly from the official perception that the Bengal Partition had not entailed large-scale violence and consequently, did not warrant permanent migration of refugees who could claim victimhood. The debates on whether to provide temporary relief or permanent rehabilitation to these Bengali Hindu refugees were rooted in an understanding which privileged large-scale violence, such as in Punjab, as paradigmatic of any partition experience.

Migration across the Bengal border began as early as the autumn of 1946, right after the pre-Partition riots which engulfed undivided Bengal and parts of Bihar, and continued well into the late 1960s.[13] The riots of 1950 witnessed the highest peak in post-Partition migration and involved the movement of minority Hindus from *East Bengal* into India, and of minority Muslims from Bihar and West Bengal into *East Bengal*.[14] In the initial years, migrants consisted primarily of those who had the financial resources to move and bank on social networks to re-establish homes across the border. Upper and middle-class Hindus followed traditional migratory linkages and moved from East Bengal to Calcutta and other major town–cities in West Bengal, Assam, and Tripura. Along with these migrants were those who did not have access to similar avenues of social capital. The latter were the main 'beneficiaries' of the Indian and West Bengal states' relief and rehabilitation measures and acquired the term 'refugee'. The riots of 1950 changed the class and caste demographics of the migrants as the majority of the 'displaced'[15] changed as those belonging to lower socio-economic strata began to move across the border. A cash-strapped Indian State, beleaguered by its own post-colonial predicaments, tended to view such migration as induced due to economic reasons. Thus, it hoped to disassociate itself from its self-proclaimed responsibility towards Partition refugees.

THE DISCOURSE OF UNWARRANTED MIGRATION

Although Nehru had designated refugee rehabilitation as a national responsibility by the end of 1947, describing it as a humanitarian act and a realistic one that would define the future welfare of India,[16] the national leadership remained ambivalent and conflicted over the fate of the refugees streaming across its eastern border. Most viewed such migration as temporary, unwarranted, and partly due to the lure of rehabilitation measures in India. Nehru's letter to B.C. Roy, the Chief Minister of West Bengal, reflected the general attitude. In 1948, he wrote:

It is wrong to encourage any large scale migration from East Bengal to the West. Indeed, if such a migration takes place, West Bengal and to some extent the Indian Union would be overwhelmed. The problem therefore, before us is how to keep up the spirits of the Hindus in East Bengal and how to help them in so far as we can. If they come over to West Bengal, we must look after them. But it is no service to them to ask them or encourage them to join the vast mass of refugees who can at best be poorly cared for.[17]

Nehru's letter evinced the belief that the migration of Hindus was unwarranted, temporary, and could be reversed. Rehabilitation policies thus aimed to provide temporary relief in combination with high-level inter-dominion talks between India and East Bengal that hoped to stabilize the volatile political and economic climate in East Bengal and encourage Hindu minorities to remain in their homes. Indian authorities consistently declared in their press reports that conditions in East Bengal were stable and that the Pakistani government had promised to protect its minorities and guarantee them citizenship rights. Addressing a press conference in July 1948, ten months after the Partition, B.C. Roy noted, 'I still maintain that every attempt should be made not only to prevent exodus from East to West Bengal but to induce people to return to East Bengal.'[18]

In the Inter-dominion Conference held in Calcutta in April 1948, the two rehabilitation ministers of East Bengal and West Bengal, Ghulam Mohammed and K.C. Neogy respectively, made a joint declaration 'that they are determined to take every possible step to discourage such exodus in either direction'.[19] In addition, they established minority boards at the provincial and local levels in both countries, and appointed a Deputy High Commissioner in Dhaka and one in Calcutta who would be responsible not only of citizens of their own country in a foreign land but also be open to hear minority grievances in that country. Temporary relief measures in the form of subsistence doles and the establishment of relief camps along the border were a kind of piecemeal efforts to assuage fear and provide succor to those crossing the border.

Other officials also suggested that migration of the East Bengal Hindus was unwarranted, temporary, and should be reversed. In January 1951, Charu Chandra Biswas, the Central Minister for Minority Affairs, claimed at a public meeting in Bhatpara, West Bengal, 'There could be no question that the best solution of the whole problem [of refugee influx] today would be for everyone to return to his home if he could do so. It was for the refugees to find out for themselves whether conditions were such as would enable them to go back.'[20] Thus, the onus of return was also placed squarely on the shoulder of the refugee. Others, such as Gobinda Lal Banerjee, the chief whip of the Congress Party, based in East Bengal, urged Hindu minorities to stick to their 'hearth and home', rather than to become a burden on the Indian State as refugees. Banerjee exhorted,

Those who have left their home and hearth in east Bengal in search of food and shelter I have nothing to say to them. But those who have gone to West Bengal out of fear, I would appeal to them to come back—let us assert our rights in the land of our forefathers and die in the act of doing so ... It is a fight between progress versus regress and the ruling people must have something progressive to give to the society if they want to rule. Are you going to form a sect of refugees in west Bengal or become a charity citizen? Is it not more honorable to stand on and fight for your rights and obligations as citizens of your homeland in East Bengal?[21]

Significantly, Banerjee's argument deliberately made no causal connection between violence and the migration of refugees. Rather a lack of patriotism prompted by fear was implied to be the root cause of refugee migration. Others such as Nalini Ranjan Sarkar in West Bengal urged the wandering refugees from East Bengal 'not to create a sort of minority problem' within West Bengal.[22] Rather, he urged them to bear with good grace the consequences of historical change such as the Partition which he asserted was 'vitally necessary'. In a public meeting, on 5 February 1949, a minister of the West Bengal government reportedly described the East Bengal refugees as 'brother foreigners' from 'another country' and claimed that 'the question of rehabilitating the refugees in west Bengal was not as important as the question of sending them back to their own country'.[23]

Containment of the 'problem' in the east rather than full-fledged rehabilitation framed refugee policies towards Bengali Hindu refugees. Even after the riots of 1950, which engendered the highest level of migration in this region, the Indian government continued to pursue and promote its policy of providing relief (trankarya) instead of rehabilitation (punarbashan).[24] In his visit to Calcutta in March 1950, Mohanlal Saxena, the Government of India Minister for Rehabilitation, instructed the representatives of Tripura, Assam, Bihar, Orissa, and West Bengal to continue to restrict government work towards relief. Such a policy was consonant with the aims of the Delhi Pact in April 1950 that urged minorities to return home. Saxena also reasoned that unless and until the actual dimensions of the migration were gauged, it would not be possible for the Indian government to devise any plans for permanent rehabilitation. In 1955, Mehr Chand Khanna, the Minister for Rehabilitation after Saxena, reportedly noted,

We will try to provide for the four million here (eastern region) as we did for the million in the Punjab. The only trouble is that I am never sure that four million is the final figure. Our planning is at the mercy of the Pakistan government. We provide for five thousand refugees; instead, fifty thousand are turned out. What are we to do?[25]

While acknowledging that the number of refugees in the east were four times that of the west, Saxena indicated that the continuation of the migration was a serious impediment to government planning. More importantly, it was not that the Indian State was impervious or unwilling but any failure, according to Saxena, was surely due to the inability of the Pakistan government to guarantee citizenship rights to its minorities.

The perception that the migration of Bengali Hindus was unwarranted received additional credence due to official efforts to highlight the lack of violence in divided Bengal as compared to Punjab. Indian officials identified the cause of migration as psychological insecurities brought about by socio-economic conditions in East Bengal. Ironically, Indian authorities used incidences of small-scale violence targeting minorities as arsenal for one-upmanship during inter-dominion talks, but routinely ignored them as causal to the ongoing migration. Instead, they insisted that the Hindu minorities from East Bengal return back to their homes since not only had the Partition process been relatively violence free in Bengal, but the post-1947 political situation was also peaceful. Such reasoning and claims towards violence-free Bengal allowed the Indian State to assert that Bengali Hindus from East Bengal were economic migrants rather than refugees.

By privileging physical violence over psychological violence, the Indian State could also insist on a *return* since in the latter case, the marks of violence were imperceptible and deemed temporary. Bengali Hindus were thus routinely identified within public forums as migrants who suffered from a 'psychological' problem of insecurity and fear of violence rather than those who had *suffered* violence. In April of 1948, Satish Chandra Dasgupta, a well-known Congress member, claimed that 'if enquiries are made about those who are evacuating, generally the reply is that nothing has happened but there was fear of aggression and insult. Fear there is. But fear is a mental attitude.'[26] According to Dasgupta, the food crisis in post-Partition West Bengal had been exacerbated by the influx of the East Bengal Hindus. Consequently, such migration rendered the Hindu minorities as potential economic abusers. To prevent the exploitation of the strained economic resources in West Bengal, Dasgupta depicted the migrants as 'guests' whose presence should be temporary. He continued, 'It may be said the East Bengal Hindus would expect hospitality from West Bengal people as their guests. But guests are guests. They come and go. They do not settle down to share the house with the host for ever.'[27]

A few days earlier, Dasgupta had written to the East Bengal Prime Minister, Nazimuddin, and urged the need for official measures to contain the flight of the evacuees from East Bengal. However, rather than the usual instructions on the maintenance of law and order in East Bengal, Dasgupta noted that current migration, mainly of people belonging to the middle classes, was 'dictated by personal likes and dislikes.'[28] He feared that if the West Bengal government promised resettlement, then it would be a 'direct invitation to them [the evacuees] to come to West Bengal ... Then despite all the preaching against mass evacuation more and more evacuees will be encouraged to come and demand of the West Bengal government the promised amenities.'[29] He proposed that Indian government should use its resources to facilitate the return of the evacuees to East Bengal instead of rehabilitating them in West Bengal. For Dasgupta, the conditions in

East Bengal did not warrant any mass evacuation and the migration needed to be reversed with the Indian State's help.

The idea that the migration of East Bengali refugees was illegitimate was repeated by Sri Prakash, the Indian High Commissioner in Pakistan, who emphatically noted that 'the real reason [for the migration] lies in the fact that the Hindus feel spiritually hurt when they are told that they are no longer Indians'.[30] In his analysis of the causes for the migration, Sri Prakash emphasized, 'age old connections, social and political ties [which] have made the whole of India the common home of Indians living in any part of the country'.[31] Confirming the Indian government's warped logic, he privileged patriotic national identity over ties to one's regional community and locality, the very ties that, in the official view, had ensured that the Partition in the east did not experience any cataclysmic riots.

After the riots of 1950, which were cataclysmic by any standard, the Indian State continued to operate within the paradigm that there was no violence in the region. Officials believed that what was needed was public reassurance to provide 'security in the minds' of the minorities. Charu Chandra Biswas, the Minister for Minorities in the Interim Government of India and later the Union Law Minister in independent India,[32] asserted, 'Little more was happening in East Bengal than occasional incidents, many of which one could expect in the ordinary course of crime. The trouble was that in the present state of Hindu morale, every incident was felt to be communal—the theft of a chicken was taken as a warning of worse to come'.[33] At one end, Biswas concluded that there was indeed a general feeling of insecurity which only the East Bengal government could ameliorate, while on the other end, as a representative of the Indian State, he attempted to cast doubts on the refugee narratives of actual violence.

On their part, East Bengal leaders denied or minimized the migration of Hindu minorities as it called into question the credibility of the East Bengal state that seemed unable to guarantee citizenship rights to its minorities. East Bengal leaders such as Hamidul Haq Chowdhury, the Finance Minister in East Bengal, denied the existence of any large-scale migration,[34] and Nazimuddin, the Provincial Premier, contended that the agents of land development companies based in West Bengal had triggered the migration of minority Hindus. These agents 'were at work inducing feeling of insecurity among non-Muslims of East Bengal so that they would migrate to West Bengal and thereby enable such companies to make money out of their business. They have been known to manufacture stories and cause incidents the authorship of which is maliciously ascribed to Muslims.[35] For the East Bengal government, refuting incidents of violence allowed it to dissociate itself from the causes of migration and assert that there was a 'natural attraction of the Hindus for the Hindu majority Indian Union'.[36]

Coupled with the claim that the minorities had a 'natural' predilection towards India that surpassed traditional ties to their land and society, the East Bengal government also accused minorities of fabricating stories of violence against them. An intelligence report from Dacca noted that 'There are several instances in which the minority community has been known to manufacture stories and cause incidents, the authorship of which was ascribed to the majority community'.[37] The Superintendent of Police in Backerganj reported multiple incidents of breaking of Durga images in his district that, upon investigation, was found to have been undertaken by some Hindus in the area desirous of migrating to West Bengal. He claimed that all the images had remained untouched between 'Shasthi (the day of Pran Pratishtan, to infuse life) and the Dasami (the day of immersion), as it is sinful for a Hindu according to Hindu religion to break any image during the said period. But prior to that when the images are in the process of making there is no such religious bar'.[38] His report concluded that some Hindus of the area, who sought to create panic among the minorities who remained in East Bengal, had desecrated the images. Again, after the 1950 riots, Nurul Amin, the Premier of East Bengal, denied any instances of communal tension in eastern Bengal. He simultaneously accused the West Bengal government of facilitating easier cross-border movement that was inhibiting the return to normalcy in the region.[39]

The insistence on 'return' was a significant feature of the Indian government's policy towards the refugees from East Bengal. The Delhi Pact of 1950, concluded after the riots, continued to urge minorities to return home. Newspapers published reports of return migration after the Pact indicating the success of both India and East Bengal to stabilize their respective political situations and guarantee citizenship rights.[40]

CONTAINMENT OF THE 'PROBLEM'

The Indian State had early on identified the refugee migration as a 'problem' and in the later decades, Indian leaders in New Delhi projected West Bengal as a 'problem' province. For example, a cartoon in *Amrita Bazar Patrika* showed B.C. Roy, who was a physician by profession, and Vallabhbhai Patel examining an anthropomorphic West Bengal who was suffering from 'refugee-titis' (Figure 6.1).[41] Limiting refugee status became a crucial, if partial, solution to the 'refugee problem'.

Unable and unwilling to cope with the number of people claiming refugee status, the Indian State devised several methods to contain the numbers. First, the Indian State fixed the date by which a migrant could identify himself or herself as a refugee and receive government benefits. In June 1948, a West Bengal government press note, published in all major newspapers, stated that although there was a lull in migration after the recent Inter-dominion Conference, the number of refugees was again on the rise.

Figure 6.1: Refugee-itis

Government feels that whatever might have been the cause of the exodus in the past, similar situations do not now prevail. There is hardly any communal disturbance in Eastern Pakistan nor have the minority community there any great reason to entertain fear of such disturbance. Therefore the present continued exodus is due to economic causes. Accordingly the Government has decided to notify that persons arriving into this province from Eastern Pakistan after June 25, 1948 will not be entitled to registration as 'refugees', nor will they be eligible for such special assistance as may have been planned by the government for the refugees.[42]

To prove that they had arrived in India before 25 June, the refugees now had to provide either ration cards in their names or tokens from district magistrates that recorded their arrival date. B.C. Roy defended the West Bengal government's decision as a 'preventive measure against further exodus from East Bengal'.[43] Such measures did not go unchallenged as the President of the East Bengal Minority Welfare Committee in Calcutta exclaimed, 'The Press Note ... lightheartedly refers to the "economic causes" of the steadily continuing exodus. These "economic causes" are a direct consequence of Partition on a communal basis.'[44] Thus, the reason for migration, at least in the mind of the president and others like him, was firmly rooted in the Partition. In the face of public protest, the West Bengal government was constantly forced to redefine the date by which migrants from East Bengal could be eligible for refugee slips.

Second, by 1950, it was clear that the refugees from East Bengal were unlikely to return. So, the Indian State issued clear instructions to all state governments regarding the specific meaning of the term 'refugee' or 'displaced'. To obtain rehabilitation assistance granted to refugees, the Government of India identified a 'displaced person' to mean:

A person who a) was ordinarily resident of East Bengal but on account of communal disturbances occurring after the 1st day of October 1946, left East Bengal and arrived in West Bengal on or before the 31st of December 1950 and b) has no land in West Bengal which he is the owner and c) has affirmed in an affidavit filed in the office of Relief and Rehabilitation commissioner, West Bengal that he does not intend to return to East Bengal.[45]

According to this definition, in addition to migrating from East Bengal by a specific date, a person also had to declare his intentions of not returning. By becoming a refugee in order to receive the government's rehabilitation benefits, a refugee not only had to disown his or her ancestral village but also declare that his or her move had been a permanent one.[46] There was thus a shift in the view that migration of East Bengali refugees was reversible to one which acknowledged that they were in India permanently.

To have a better sense of the numbers and provide relief, the West Bengal government set up the Department of Refugee Relief and Rehabilitation in mid-June 1948.[47] In addition, they commissioned the Indian Statistical Institute[48] and the State Statistical Bureau in West Bengal to conduct surveys from 1948 onwards 'to make a correct assessment of the size of the problem of rehabilitation'.[49]

The government also opened relief camps and transit camps[50] along the new international border and in Calcutta and its adjoining areas. By the mid-1950s, the Government of West Bengal opened 'Interception Centers' that worked in conjunction with the relief camps at the border, where 'migrants on arrival, were questioned and issued with Interception Slips to qualify them as bona fide refugees'.[51] These documents, along with passports and visas, were instrumental in identifying and differentiating economic migrants and political refugees. Once the refugees obtained refugee slips, they were then transported to a transit camp. Here, camp officials collected information about their earlier professions and gave them cards that authorized them to live in regular camps and to draw on maintenance grants.[52] Even those who did not require government help could obtain refugee slips that qualified them as refugees for other benefits, including special quotas for education and jobs.[53]

By 1955, migration by itself was no longer a valid reason to secure relief and rehabilitation. The refugees had to provide documentation to prove not only their migration but also their victimhood. It included migration certificates, refugee slips, and citizenship papers from Pakistan. If the person had none of these documents, then 'their status would be determined on the basis of circumstantial evidence by an officer not below the rank of a subdivisional magistrate'.[54] Ironically, the more the West Bengal state aimed to categorize and identify legitimate refugees or displaced persons, the more difficult it became for those minorities who wanted to cross the border. The institution of migration certificates, which the Indian High Commission at Dacca issued, ostensibly was to sift out the legitimate victims of violence from those who wanted to migrate to India because of economic reasons.[55] It is not clear how the High Commission determined such victimization. Even when the Indian State sought to identify legitimate applicants for the migration certificates, its guidelines were inflected by the state's paternalistic assumptions. Thus, it instructed the Deputy High Commission in Dacca to issue migration certificates to:

1) Orphans with no guardians in East Bengal
2) Unattached women and widows with no means of livelihood in East Bengal
3) Grown up girls coming to India for marriage (the migration certificates in such cases were to be issued only to the girls concerned).
4) Wives joining husbands in India
5) Families living in isolated parts
6) Members of split families a part of which has already settled in India
7) Persons, whose near relatives are in India.[56]

The given list reflects not only the Indian State's paternal concern for unattached women and children, but also followed the general pattern of documented migration that was a unique feature of post-1947 in Bengal. By assuring that priority would be given to such cases, the Indian authorities, in effect, legitimized certain kinds of migration and sought to control movement of specific groups.

In addition to enumeration efforts, the Ministry of Rehabilitation evolved detailed methods of classification for the purposes of claiming refugee status. For example, a family could claim refugee status only if the head of the family fit the above-mentioned definition. Thus, it excluded all those who had followed the traditional path of migration to take advantage of the urban opportunities in Calcutta but now, because of the changed political situation and ensuing turmoil, had had their families migrate to India.[57] A further revision of the definition of a 'refugee' in July 1951 sought to include:

... a person ordinarily resident in the territories now comprising East Bengal or being a Bengalee in the territories now comprising other parts of Pakistan or in an Indian state which is not an acceding state who has since 1st June 1947 arrived from the said territories or state in a place in west Bengal on account of civil disturbances or fear of such disturbances or the Partition of India, and intends to take up his permanent residence in the state of west Bengal in the union of India.[58]

Initially, it appears that this modification encompassed all those migrants who had moved across borders not only during the immediate post-Partition turmoil but also those who had moved after the 'civil disturbances' from 1949 to 1950. The West Bengal government also sought to provide relief and rehabilitation to those who had crossed the border from East Bengal to neighbouring states such as Assam and Tripura before making their way to West Bengal. However, such modifications came with a string of clauses which aimed to exclude those who had moved before June 1947, unless they had been residents of the riot-torn districts of Noakhali and Tipperah, in which case, the beginning date of migration was taken to be 1 October 1946. All government employees who had opted for India would be excluded from rehabilitation benefits.

The status of the head of the family continued to be the primary criteria for any refugee family. Migration in this region often followed the traditional pattern of the eldest able male crossing the border and finding employment, with the crucial difference that, after Partition, he tended to be accompanied by his family. Relief and rehabilitation benefits thus were focused only towards those families who not only crossed the border as a whole but also continued to remain destitute until they sought government aid.

Official policy on rehabilitation on a permanent basis crystallized in the mid-1950s. These rehabilitation schemes were divided into rural assistance programmes, targeting mainly the agriculturalists, and urban resettlement programmes, geared towards providing homestead land in government-sanctioned colonies. In the Calcutta region, the government helped to expand civic amenities to the refugee settlements, and townships such as Ultadanga, Sodepur, Bijoygarh, and Madhyamgram came into existence. The West Bengal government also regularized squatter colonies which had arisen by the end of December 1950.[59] Permanent rehabilitation to the refugees primarily involved the task of finding land for these refugees.[60] The Partition and the consequent demographic changes and boundary adjustments, both in the east and the west, had ensured that West Bengal became the most densely populated state within India. Consequently, the official stand on rehabilitation was that it would be limited since the state lacked financial resources and space to completely rehabilitate the refugees.

In 1955, Renuka Ray, Minister for Relief and Rehabilitation, categorically declared that 'We have reached a saturation point and whereas we must satisfactorily help to settle those who have come earlier, it is beyond the capacity and powers of this state to provide land for cultivators and even for homesteads in urban areas for those who are new comers and will still continue to come.'[61] The solution had to come from incorporating state-level relief and rehabilitation measures with the 'national level' and in urging other states to share the responsibility. Besides requesting states such as Bihar, Orissa, and Assam to assist in rehabilitation, the Indian government also identified areas such as the Andaman and Nicobar Islands and the Dandyakaranya in central India as potential regions for the rehabilitation of East Bengali refugees. Although Bihar and Orissa were initially favourable to the idea of rehabilitating the refugees, inter-state plans were rarely implemented. On its part, Assam was reluctant to resettle East Bengali refugees who might further complicate the concurrent political problems of 'Bengali–Assamese' identities in the region.[62]

To arrange the settlement of refugees in the Andamans, the Government of India undertook explicit campaigns in the media that highlighted the positive features of the islands. Nikunja Behari Maity, the Relief Minister of West Bengal and the leader of the Indian Exploratory Party to the Andaman Islands, submitted a press report extolling the virtues of the islands for immediate settlement. According to the report, not only was 'the climate of the Andamans is [sic] wet and humid', but an agricultural survey conducted by government-appointed experts pointed to 'large possibilities for settlement by those who take to cultivation or fishery as their principal occupation.'[63] Maity's report emphasized all those aspects of livelihood to which the refugees would have been accustomed in their original residence in East Bengal. Moreover, the Bengali refugee would supposedly be free of diseases common to the Bengal delta such as plague, small pox, cholera, and most importantly, malaria. The islands, in official depiction, were idyllic for colonization.

Meagre rehabilitation assistance, coupled with the history of the Andamans as a penal colony, soon elicited a reverse migration from there to West Bengal by those who had earlier decided to accept the government's aid. Instead of acknowledging such problems as barren soil and the lack of agricultural tools in areas that often experienced drought in the successful implementation of rehabilitation, official discourse viewed the return of the refugees from other states as related to the parochial character of the Bengalis.

Convinced that the continuation of the migration was due to economic reasons, the Indian government began to close its relief camps from 1956.[64] By 1958, the West Bengal government followed its lead and shut down most of its relief camps and stopped all financial assistance. The Indian State also declared that anyone crossing the border after 1958 would no longer be legally recognized by the state as a 'refugee'.[65] In effect, there was a clear reorientation of planning and implementation of rehabilitation schemes that occurred from 1958. Subsequently, the Government of India undertook large-scale measures that sought to integrate rehabilitation with the development of the Indian economy.[66]

THE PARADOX OF THE BENGALI REFUGEE

Policy measures towards limiting rehabilitation towards Bengali Hindu refugees were accompanied by the construction of a paradoxical entity: the Bengali refugee, indolent, economically needy, parochial and subversive agent, the focus of rehabilitation policies yet the main reason for their failure. Such a representation, arguably, allowed the state to shift blame from their own failures at rehabilitation to the 'inherent' nature of the Bengali refugees. Any criticism, limitations, or evidence of failure of the rehabilitation schemes did not find place within official publicity.[67]

Perceptions of *psychological* insecurities, that had been invaluable to deny the legitimacy of migration of Bengali Hindus, were now deployed to depict the male Bengali refugee as effeminate who was not only brave enough to remain at home but now preferred the life of an indolent dweller of refugee camps to one of hard work and self-reliance. In U. Bhaskar Rao's account, largely regarded as the official version of the Indian State's rehabilitation efforts, the refugee from *East Bengal* is described as a 'creature apart'. In describing government efforts to shut down relief camps and rehabilitate them in spaces outside of West Bengal, Rao blames the psychological makeup of the East Bengali refugees. 'The more serious difficulty arose out of a certain psychological weakness or deficiency among the fairly large sections of the camp population. Many showed a reluctance to forgo the advantages of gratuitous relief, a disinclination to embrace the rigorous discipline of an independent existence.'[68] Rao argued that although comforts in the camps were meagre, 'one enjoyed the luxury of idleness'.[69] It was this inherent lazy temperament that made the Bengali refugee impervious to 'all inducements' and 'cling precariously to their shelters demanding the impossible—rehabilitation in West Bengal'.[70] The depiction of effeminacy found easy resonance given that it heavily borrowed from nineteenth century colonial tropes which had described the Bengali male as largely lacking vigour, physical strength, and prone to lethargy.[71] To drive the point home, Bengali refugees were often compared with the 'entrepreneurial' Punjab refugees. Thus, Minister of Rehabilitation, A.P. Jain, described the refugees from West Pakistan as full of both 'energy and determination',[72] as compared to those from East Bengal, while Bhaskar Rao depicted the former as symbols of 'toughness ... sturdy sense of self reliance and pride' which never let them 'submit to the indignity of living on doles and charity'.[73]

When Bengali refugees protested against inadequate rehabilitation measures in settling them outside of West Bengal and began returning to West Bengal, the Indian government argued that the Bengali refugees were parochial. Reporting on the government's failure to rehabilitate the Bengali refugees in other parts of the country such as Orissa and Bihar, A.P. Jain noted during his Calcutta tour in January 1951 that 'an important factor that stood in the way of rehabilitation of East Bengal refugees was their disinclination to leave West Bengal and adapt themselves to new environments in other states ...'.[74] Further, the East Bengal refugee, in Jain's opinion, 'was still unsettled in his mind and had not broken all ties with East Bengal' and 'looked back longingly to his paddy field, his cottage and the natural conditions of that province. Many families were also divided half the number having been left behind.'[75] What Jain did not mention in his speech was the fact that the particular region in Orissa where the refugees were settled had experienced famine conditions for the past few years. Instead, psychological insecurities, instead of material conditions, were highlighted as the reason why the rehabilitation of refugees outside of West Bengal had failed.

In contrast to the East Bengal refugees, 'the displaced persons in the west revealed a praiseworthy mobility—they were ready to spread themselves out over the whole country, as it were'.[76] Moreover, the most important thing that differentiated the refugees from the east and west, and determined the failure and success of government efforts respectively towards their rehabilitation, 'was the character of the refugees themselves. In the western region they were tougher, more resilient of spirit and much more adaptable. It was easier for them to turn their hands on any job that came along.'[77] At no point in this comparison did Rao mention that government assistance was skewed towards those migrating in the western zone. Similarly, H.J. Stooks, the Deputy Secretary to the Government of India and attached with the Ministry of Home Affairs, received an official assessment of the phenomenon of return refugees from the Andaman and Nicobar Islands. A.K. Ghosh, the government's man on the spot, reported that although each refugee family had been given more than 5 acres of paddy land, the refugees had only cultivated half the land. His reasons included a shortage of plough animals and also, because the East Bengali refugee lacked the 'pioneering spirit'. Ghosh claimed that:

They come from East Bengal, where the land is flat and soft, and possibly amongst the most fertile in the world; all the cultivator has to do is to scratch the soil, put in his seeds, and then sit back and wait for the harvest. Here they have had to break up virgin soil; and that is one of the reasons why less than half the land has been cultivated this year.[78]

Paradoxically, while official narratives tended to depict the Bengali refugee as shorn of agency, dependent on the state, they tended to view refugee initiatives that were outside the state-sanctioned mechanisms with suspicion and deemed them subversive. For instance, after the riots of 1950, the West Bengal government was unable to quickly provide rehabilitation for the large number of refugees who thronged the city of Calcutta. Instead of waiting for the government aid, some of these refugees decided to undertake self-rehabilitation by taking possession of empty Second World War military barracks and setting up temporary huts in empty land in and around the city.[79] These 'jabardakhal' or squatter colonies became sites of contestation between refugees and the government as the latter viewed such rehabilitation as usurpation rather than entrepreneurship. By December 1950, there were about 149 squatter colonies in the Greater Calcutta metropolitan area. Instead of seeing them as entrepreneurs, the West Bengal government first tried to evict them through police action. When such measures failed, the government sought to 'regularize' these colonies, but not before the protesters had been portrayed as 'troublemakers' in leading newspapers.[80]

As a corroboration of the government's success in relief and rehabilitation, the East Bengali refugee could become hard working and happy in his rehabilitated surroundings. When Maitraye Devi, founder of the Council for the Promotion of Communal Harmony in 1964 and the Vice-President of the All-India Women's Coordinating Council, visited Dandyakaranya in central India to assess the success of government's rehabilitation efforts, one 'settler' reportedly noted, 'It is a Ramrajya.[81] No father can look after his son the way we are looked after by the Government.'[82] In this version, not only was the Bengali settler happy in Dandyakaranya but also regarded the Indian government in paternal terms. Similarly, in a speech in 1955 at a public meeting of representatives of fifty-three squatter colonies in the Dumdum area of Calcutta, Renuka Ray pointed out that:

… most of the refugees who have come at the outset before their numbers have become large, have proved an asset to the state for they struggled and cooperated with the government and are struggling valiantly to settle down. Many of them who are cultivators have helped to solve the food problem and products of other skillful artisans who have come from East Bengal delight the eye and are finding markets.[83]

Underscoring refugee cooperation with governmental rehabilitation efforts as the key formula for success and happiness to the refugees seems deliberate given that she was speaking to representatives of squatter colonies who had earned their political spurs through agitation against the government's rehabilitation efforts.

The Indian State's skewed rehabilitation policies elicited strong responses from the Bengali intelligentsia who critiqued both official policies and countered negative depictions of these refugees. Radha Kamal Mukherjee, a well-known economist and sociologist and a prominent member of Bengal Rehabilitation Organization, described the East Bengali farmers as people with 'the sturdy spirit of individualism, courage and enterprise'[84] that was needed for land colonization. They were the pioneer settlers 'who [had] fought the tiger and the crocodile, and who overcame the hazards of the forest and the flood that created in East Bengal the granary of rice and jute in India'.[85] Mukherjee evoked the historical precedence of Bengali peasants who between the twelfth and the eighteenth centuries had moved eastwards into the Bengal delta and colonized jungles into farmlands.[86]

Others argued against the rehabilitation of refugees outside the borders of West Bengal. Thus, Shyama Prasad Mukherjee, President of the Bengali Rehabilitation Organization, argued that the cultivators amongst the migrants 'were an asset' and that the government would 'do a great disservice to ourselves if we send them to Hyderabad and Mysore without exploiting the rich possibilities of the home state'.[87] Further, he asserted that it was 'moral' duty of the Indian government to ensure that those who crossed the border received adequate relief and rehabilitation. He cautioned that failure to provide such assistance might lead to:

... that inevitable destiny where the abject poverty illiteracy scorn and disdain from all around, and hunger and social disintegration and moral degeneration are sure to lead. The younger boys and girls will become specters of their former selves as they are tending to be; the boys—pickpockets pilferers and thieves and the girls will take to the life of shame and vice beyond redemption.[88]

Mukherjee, a well-known Hindu nationalist who had agitated for a Hindu homeland in Bengal before 1947, now found it easy to urge for rehabilitation for the Bengali refugees who were primarily Hindu.

A number of individuals, both refugees and residents of West Bengal, voiced their protest against the Indian government's policies towards the East Bengali refugees. In an attempt to counter what they considered to be specious hair-splitting on the official definitions and distinctions between a political and economic migrant, their letters to political leaders and to the media provided different justifications towards recognizing the East Bengali Hindu migrant as a 'refugee' and entitled to relief and rehabilitation measures. D.R. Sen, under the pseudonym 'Voice of India', took the argument of moral duty one step further. He wrote a series of letters to Indian leaders and to newspaper editors that were published in a brochure entitled, 'What the Evacuees from *East Bengal* Think'. In these letters, Sen underscored the commonality of culture and religion between the Hindus of East and West Bengal in spite of the Partition. If this connection alone was not enough for the West Bengal government to undertake proper rehabilitation of the refugees, then Sen pointed out that the

'Scheme for rehabilitating the evacuees can well be fitted in with the programmes for constructive works in the rural areas, to which the government is already committed ... The task of rehabilitation involves ... rural constructive schemes, reclamation of wastelands, establishment of schools and hospitals, improvement of sanitation, development of agriculture, cottage industries etc.'[89]

Incorporating such schemes with rehabilitation, Sen argued, would provide 'fresh blood, will have a stimulating bearing on the constructive works in the decadent villages. The conditions recedent [sic] for resuscitating a village is that it must have a virile and sturdy population willing to work.'[90] Sen's depictions of the refugees comprising 'virile and sturdy population willing to work' went counter to the stereotype of the Bengali refugee promoted by the government. Instead of being a drain on the Indian economy, he argued that proper rehabilitation of the refugees would, in fact, infuse the system with much needed 'fresh blood'. Similarly, in September 1948, Jadunath Sarkar urged the government and political leaders to 'engraft this rich racial branch upon its old decaying trunk' for the sake of future prosperity.[91]

Official depictions of East Bengali refugee as an economic migrant was offset also by an editorial in the English daily, *Amrita Bazar Patrika*, that noted, 'We cannot bring ourselves to believe that these multitudes are frivolously leaving their hearths and homes in the prospect of finding ready made comforts and adequate means of living in an unaccustomed surroundings. We believe that the Government of India should accept their share of responsibility for settling emigrants in the best manner possible.'[92] The manner in which government relief and rehabilitation measures were being doled was also under scrutiny. Some sections of the media condemned official action as 'wooden and unimaginative approach to a great challenge.'[93] An editorial in the *Eastern Economist* pointed out, 'There has been ... a pitiful look [sic] of appreciation of the economic issues involved in what is called the "problem of West Bengal". *Charity alone is not what the province needs; charity alone is all the province continues to obtain.'*[94]

Similarly, to counter the negative stereotype of the refugees as economic parasites, A.T. Ganguli noted that the 'East Bengal Hindus are not leaving their ancestral hearths and homes for the mere fun of it. To say that panic is born of the fear of aggression alone is to over-simplify the matter.'[95] Within public discourse, educated refugees underscored the issue that it was the Partition, a decision taken by Indian leaders, which had rendered them homeless. Thus, they were not responsible for the subsequent migration and their demand for rehabilitation. However, given the right amount of relief and rehabilitation, they, too, could become productive citizens of India. In fact, as sufferers of Partition and of violence, they pointed out that they were entitled to receive such humanitarian aid automatically.

Criticism of government efforts towards rehabilitation focused strongly on official efforts to rehabilitate Bengalis outside of West Bengal. The refugees insisted that the Hindu minorities of East Bengal, once they had crossed the border to India, had the right to receive relief and rehabilitation that would lead to their successful incorporation as citizens of India. When the Indian State proposed rehabilitation of Bengali refugees in Assam, Orissa, and Andamans, a widespread public campaign emerged against such plans. Critics argued that 'the government are making full use of this [sic] wandering refugees to strike political bargains with other provinces only to add to their distress by dragging them into none too pleasant controversies of provincialism'.[96] Similarly, a Calcutta resident noted that if the government's plan to resettle refugees outside of the West Bengal was executed, then 'wherever they are resettled they will form a minority community and will undergo the same political social and economic disadvantages that the Bengali Hindus settled at present in Assam, Behar and Orissa have been subjected to'.[97] He feared that in time, 'they will loose their culture, language and customs which are so real to the Bengali Hindus'.[98] A large section of the Bengali intelligentsia argued that West Bengal had the resources of land and money to rehabilitate the refugees within the state. In 1950, the Bengal Rehabilitation Organization presented a plan that claimed that if the rehabilitation process was 'scientifically planned and implemented, [it] may give a new lease of life to the decadent, truncated state'.[99] It suggested that mechanized and cooperative farming through large-scale land colonization would lead to successful rehabilitation.

FROM REFUGEES TO CITIZENS

Even while the Indian State insisted that the refugees return to their homes across the border, the success of their rehabilitation policies depended on the incorporation and transformation of the refugees into productive citizens. The refugees, who had no intention of returning, had a similar end in mind. However, in the absence of clear directives on how these migrants could become citizens of India, it became imperative for some of them to acquire a refugee identity that they hoped would provide them with necessary citizenship documentation in terms of rehabilitation. Becoming a 'refugee' was a conditional stepping stone to acquiring citizenship in India. This is not to say that the East Bengali Hindu migrant preferred the appellative or the circumstances of camp colonies designated for refugees. Rather, adoption of refugee status provided them with the political arsenal in their negotiations with both the government and the general public in West Bengal. Further, their continuing refugee status acted as an indictment of the government's failure to rehabilitate them and transform them into citizens.

According to the enumeration handbook for the Census of 1951 (West Bengal and Sikkim), the 'Determination of Indian Nationality' specified that a person who migrated from Pakistan to India on or after 19 July 1948 but before the 25 July 1949 will be a citizen if he applied for and obtained registration as a citizen and possesses a citizenship certificate (registration as a citizen is different from registration as refugees). But, 'no person who migrates from Pakistan to India on or after the 25th of July 1949 can be an Indian citizen.'[100] Consequently, over 31 lakh East Bengali migrants who had migrated after 25 July 1949, the deadline for refugee registration, signed a petition demanding inclusion within the electoral rolls. Drawn from refugee colonies all over West Bengal, the signatories claimed on behalf of 50 lakh refugees in West Bengal, the right to citizenship and franchise.[101]

The shift in the Indian government's policies towards East Bengali refugees from relief to rehabilitation signified the official acknowledgement that this migration was permanent. The Indian government, however, justified these dilatory attempts towards rehabilitation with the argument that government relief in the form of doles and temporary stays in relief camps had created demoralized and lazy refugees. A 1956 report on relief and rehabilitation of the refugees indicated that, 'In order to counteract the *demoralizing effect* of *prolonged stay* in camps, Government introduced the system of keeping able-bodied men engaged in useful work in places meant for ultimate rehabilitation of the camp people, where they helped in the development of the area.'[102] In fact, these relief camps were 'symbols of continuing dependence'.[103] Government officials feared that the able-bodied males within refugee camps would become accustomed to the meagre relief, which would erode their moral fibre and produce a culture of dependency. They argued that the refugee population 'living on the charity of doles, and in the process of sinking into a state of hopeless demoralization' needed to have 'their self respect and self reliance' restored as soon as was possible.[104] Rehabilitation rather than relief alone was the only way such an end could be achieved.

The Indian State defined rehabilitation 'as a process of reinstating or reestablishing one in the esteem of others'.[105] Thus, rehabilitation would be the 'coping stone' of the Indian State's humanitarian aid and lead to the moral and economic uplift of the refugees. Bhaskar Rao, who was closely connected with the official rehabilitation process, pointed out that providing relief had only been half of the planned efforts at aiding the refugees. The other half consisted of the 'rehabilitation of the hundreds of thousands of people uprooted by the cataclysm', and restoring 'something like their former dignity'.[106] From the 1950s, migrants were taken directly from reception centres to worksite camps, 'where they are provided with work. This helps to check indolence and demoralization.'[107] Rehabilitation measures directed towards *East Bengali* refugees were usually couched within the development rhetoric of the new nation which sought to create new hard-working citizens.[108]

Through the decades of implementing rehabilitation schemes and establishing refugee colonies, the Government of India continued to be concerned about creating ideal citizens instead of idle camp refugees. A publicity booklet, which evaluated the ongoing rehabilitation of the *East Bengali* refugees, noted that:

Idleness is the greatest enemy of the refugee. And because the government is keenly aware of it, endeavor is made to keep the camp population engaged, as far as possible, in useful work connected either with the development of eventual rehabilitation sites, if these are nearby or in the many river valley and industrial projects now in the process of implementation in India.[109]

These development projects were temporary and, at times, seasonal in nature. Moreover, the Indian State had limited its capacity to provide such employment for every male who crossed the border. It strongly believed in the adage of an empty mind being the devil's workshop, and ensured, in areas where it was difficult to find work for the refugee males, that they were 'gainfully' employed.

To make certain that these refugees remained active at all times, the Indian government also provided 'other types of employment such as tent-making, basket making and brick manufacturing in these worksite camps'.[110] Continuing their effort to remake demoralized refugees into 'disciplined, self reliant workers and useful citizens',[111] the Indian government constituted the Rashtriya Vikas Dal Scheme in 1964. Its stated aims were, on the one hand, to 'provide disciplined workers for the execution of development projects' and, on the other hand, to 'provide gainful employment to migrants'.[112] The Indian government argued that membership and participation within this scheme would 'instill the habit of manual work in the migrants and propagate among them the ideal of dignity of labor'.[113] Thus, the state's efforts towards rehabilitation were designed not only towards economic rehabilitation but also aimed to reinstill the moral virtues of hard work that the refugees seemingly had lost by their act of seeking help within relief camps. Although this particular scheme was not specifically targeted towards the refugees from *East Bengal*, in its implementation, it involved significant number of camps where the *East Bengali* refugees had been relocated.[114]

Implicit within the government's efforts towards rehabilitation was the paternalism of a state geared towards enmeshing development with the moral virtues of humanitarianism. In this role, the state sought to define itself as a caregiver and saviour of the refugees. A report assessing the 'success' of the efforts of the Ministry of Rehabilitation, thus concluded, 'throughout the last eighteen and nineteen years, under each rehabilitation programme Government has made efforts to extend to all categories of displaced people a degree of assistance which together with their own enterprise and self help, would enable them to achieve access to a level of livelihood comparable to prevailing standards in India'.[115] The official claim was that the state had been responsible in turning these refugees into 'useful citizens' in their new communities.[116]

Clearly, by 1964, the government no longer asked the refugees to declare loyalty to Pakistan. Rather, in a discursive way, these refugees, by their very presence and continuous migration, gave legitimacy to the stability of India vis-à-vis *East Bengal*. By promoting the creed of 'refugees turned citizens', the Indian State could claim to consolidate its successful benevolent image.

Nowhere was the state's role as the caregiver more apparent than in the case of those they termed as 'permanent liability'. In this group belonged the old and infirm, unattached women, either unmarried or widowed, and orphans.[117] In providing homes for unattached women and their dependents, the Indian State arguably assumed the role of the male provider. Like the men, the state sought to introduce the women to a work ethic 'to keep them busy'. Vocational training for these women concentrated on the traditional women's occupation such as needlework and arts and crafts.

The Indian State instituted a provocatively titled National Discipline Scheme in its eastern and the western borders, 'In order to bring the younger generation under a code of discipline and to infuse in them the ideals of good citizenship and comradeship.'[118] In their efforts to provide physical and spiritual training of displaced children, the government specially trained instructors who were either ex-Indian National Army (INA) members or servicemen. They were to ensure that the children were disciplined in mind and body through physical drills and were 'informed about the country's glorious past, its cultural heritage and the deeds of valour and chivalry of our ancestors'.[119] Nationalism had found ready ground for dissemination. In instituting rehabilitation measures targeting these 'permanent liability' groups, the Indian State recreated the familial traditions of paternalism where the eldest able-bodied male takes care of the women, children, and the old in the national family.

During the 1960s and the 1970s, the official discourse on the Government of India's efforts at rehabilitation described it in terms of heroism and unflinching endeavour in the face of indomitable odds. Bhaskar Rao described the role of the Indian State in rehabilitation as an 'indefatigable effort to bring healing to these bruised masses of humanity, wipe their tears, apply balm to their wounds, assuage their hunger and thirst, clothe their nakedness. And more, to set them on their feet and restore to them the dignity of man.'[120] Such self-congratulatory remarks, at one level, elevated, established, and enhanced the status of the Indian State as the primary donor for all refugees. At another level, it reiterated the portrayal of the refugees as victims of fate, who required the Indian State's help to regain their 'human dignity'. Thus, newspapers and official publicity documents consistently focused on the women and children in their depictions of the refugees from *East Bengal.*

In assessing the 'success' of various schemes that the government had undertaken to integrate the East Bengali refugees into the new nation, a report to the Lahiry Commission in 1964 concluded that the government had, since 1947, recognized the *rehabilitation* of the displaced as a *national* problem. By 1964, the Indian government implicitly acknowledged their paternal role and traced the history of such paternalism to an early response towards rehabilitation from 1947. The government clearly considered the complaints against its meagre relief efforts, limited financial assistance towards East Bengali refugees, and late start on rehabilitation as specious hair-splitting. In providing shelter and 'succor in salvaging remnants of their shattered lives', the report noted that the progress of rehabilitating the refugees from East Bengal had been slow, difficult, and uneven 'by reason of both nature and magnitude'.[121] However, the report continued,

But as all concerned, both inside and outside Government, with rehabilitation work must be aware, the sustained and wide ranging efforts of both the government of India and the government of West Bengal for the resettlement of the lakhs of displaced people who have continued to pour into India at intervals in 1947, have achieved a considerable degree of success in spite of the complexity and massive dimensions of the whole problem.[122]

While acknowledging that rehabilitation efforts had been limited in their ability to help the refugees, this official assessment suggests that such limitations lay in the fact of overwhelming numbers of refugees themselves rather than in faulty mechanisms of the rehabilitation machinery.

The official attempts to represent the Bengali refugees as victims of intangible persecution fears, and later as economic migrants, did not go unchallenged in the realms of public discourse of the time. The refugees themselves used the term 'refugee', and its Bengali variants of *sharanarthi, bastuhara,* and *udvaastu,* to evoke images of victimhood, displacement, and homelessness, and demand automatic citizenship

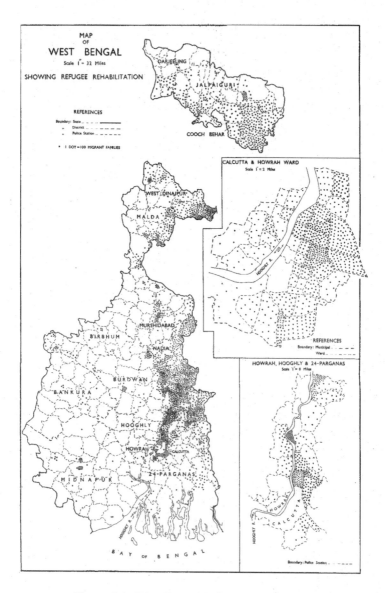

Figure 6.2: West Bengal Refugee Distribution

in this adopted nation. Countering the official perceptions of charity and paternalism associated with their rehabilitation, the refugees organized themselves politically, and appropriated the collective identity of refugees to represent their interests and negotiate for adequate relief and rehabilitation from the Indian State.[123] By 1949, a number of the refugee camps and colonies had their individual bastuhara *samities* or refugee committees to represent their complaints and demands to the local camp superintendent and to the officials within the West Bengal government. In addition, a number of quasi-political organizations took up the cause of refugees' rights in West Bengal. The two main umbrella organizations in this context were the United Central Refugee Council (UCRC) and the Refugee Central Rehabilitation Council (RCRC), both formed in 1950.[124] In later years, these organizations became essential components of political parties, the Communist Party of India (CPI) and the Revolutionary Socialist Party respectively, as articulation of refugee rights became integral to the Left political movement in West Bengal in the late 1960s and the 1970s (Figure 6.2).[125]

NOTES

1. Kanti B. Pakrashi and Indian Statistical Institute, 1971, *The Uprooted: A Sociological Study of the Refugees of West Bengal*, Calcutta: Editions Indian.

2. Prafulla K. Chakrabarty, 1990, *The Marginal Men, the Refugees and the Left Political Syndrome in West Bengal*, Kalyani, West Bengal: Lumière Books.

3. Pranati Chaudhuri, 1983, 'Refugees in West Bengal: A Study of the Growth and Distribution of Refugee Settlements with the CMD', Occasional Paper No. 55, Centre for Studies in Social Sciences, Calcutta, March; Asok Mitra, 1990, 'Parting of Ways: Partition and After in Bengal', *Economic and Political Weekly*, vol. 25, no. 44, 3 November, pp. 2441–6; Jhuma Sanyal, 2003, *Making of a New Space, Refugees in West Bengal*, Kolkata: Ratna Prakashan.

4. Pradip K. Bose (ed.), 2000, *Refugees in West Bengal: Institutional Practices and Contested Identities*, Calcutta: Calcutta Research Group.

5. Joya Chatterji, 2001, 'Right or Charity? The Debate over Relief and Rehabilitation in West Bengal, 1947–50', in Suvir Kaul (ed.), *The Partitions of Memory: The Afterlife of the Division of India*, New Delhi: Permanent Black, pp. 74–110; Gyanesh Kudaisya, 1995, 'The Demographic Upheaval of Partition: Refugees and Agricultural Resettlement in India', *South Asia*, vol. XVIII, Special Issue, pp. 73–94. Also, see an excellent examination of refugee politics in West Bengal by Nilanjana Chatterjee, 1992, 'Midnight's Unwanted Children, East Bengali Refugees and the Politics of Rehabilitation', Unpublished PhD thesis, Brown University.

6. Meghna Guhathakurta, 1997, 'Understanding the Bengal Partition through Reconstructing Family Histories: A Case Study', *Journal of Social Studies*, vol. 76, April, pp. 56–65; Manas Ray, 2002, 'Growing Up Refugee', *History Workshop Journal*, vol. 53, no. 1, Spring, pp. 148–79.

7. Ravinder Kaur, 2008, 'Narrative Absence: The Untouchable Account of Partition Migration', *Contributions to Indian Sociology*, vol. 42, no. 2, pp. 281–306.

8. A recent study explores the fate of Bihari Muslims who left India after 1947 and sought citizenship of Pakistan, and later, after the founding of Bangladesh in 1971, became 'stateless' due to their difference from the Bengali population and their perceived loyalties towards Pakistan. See Papiya Ghosh, 2008, *Community and Nation: Essays on Identity and Politics in Eastern India*, New Delhi: Oxford University Press.

9. That the Indian state, after 1947, had differential policies for the rehabilitation of Punjabi and Bengali refugees is well documented. See, for example, Jasodhara Bagchi and Subhoranjan Dasgupta (eds), 2003, *The Trauma and the Triumph: Gender and Partition in Eastern India*, Kolkata: Stree; Bose (ed.), *Refugees in West Bengal*; and Joya Chatterji, 2007, '"Dispersal" and the Failure of Rehabilitation: Refugee Camp-dwellers and Squatters in West Bengal', *Modern Asian Studies*, vol. 41, no. 5, pp. 995–1032.

10. Sarbani Sen, 2000, 'The Legal Regime for Refugee Relief and Rehabilitation in West Bengal, 1946–1958', in Bose (ed.), *Refugees in West Bengal*, p. 57.

11. Uditi Sen, 2009, 'Refugees and the Politics of Nation Building in India, 1947–71', Unpublished PhD thesis, University of Cambridge.

12. Ravinder Kaur, 2009, 'Distinctive Citizenship: Refugees, Subjects and Post-Colonial State in India's Partition', *Cultural and Social History*, vol. 6, no. 4, pp. 429–46.

13. The total number of migrants from *East Bengal* to India between 1946 and 1950 was around 2 million (20,71,197). This migration was mainly to West Bengal, though other neighbouring states such as Assam, Tripura, Orissa, and Bihar also received refugees. In 1951, the percentage of displaced persons to the total population of each state was 9.24 per cent for West Bengal, 3.13 per cent for Assam, 0.14 per cent for Orissa, and 0.19 per cent for Bihar. See Ministry of Rehabilitation, India, 1971, *Statistical Information Relating to the Influx of Refugees from East Bengal into India till 31st Oct. 1971*, *Vol. 4*, Calcutta: Ministry of Labour and Rehabilitation, Branch Secretariat, Government of India (GoI).

14. In a letter to B.C. Roy, Nehru noted, 'From 1950–52, 9.32 lakhs of Hindus have come to West Bengal and 3.84 lakhs Muslims have gone to *East Bengal*.' See Jawaharlal Nehru, Letter, 2 December 1952, in G. Parthasarathy (ed.), 1985, *Letters to the Chief Ministers 1947–64*, *Vol. III*, New Delhi: Oxford University Press.

15. Another official term to denote refugees which also implied that they had little agency in what was happening to them.

16. At the discussion on a motion on relief and rehabilitation of refugees on 29 November 1947, in the constituent assembly sessions, Nehru declared: 'I should say that any government of India should make itself responsible for the well being of every Indian in this country and not temporarily responsible but permanently responsible ... We as a government and we as a House must realize that it is our responsibility that every India should have food to eat and a house to live in, and education and opportunities of progress. If that is so for everyone in the country, certainly it is so for these unhappy countrymen of ours who have suddenly found themselves lost in the storm that arose. We recognize that responsibility fully.' *Proceedings of the CAI (Legislative) Debates, Vol. II*, 1947, pp. 917–22.

17. Jawaharlal Nehru to B.C. Roy, Letter, 22 March 1948, in Saroj Chakrabarty, 1974, *With Dr. B. C. Roy and Other Chief Ministers: A Record up to 1962*, Calcutta: Benson's, p. 30.

18. *Amrita Bazar Patrika*, 4 July 1948, p. 1.

19. Proceedings of the Inter-Dominion Conference held at Calcutta, 15–18 April 1948, Home Political (Secret) 1948, WBSA.

20. *The Statesman*, 30 January 1951, p. 5.

21. *Hindustan Standard (HS)*, 6 May 1949, p. 6.

22. *The Nation*, 12 February 1949, p. 3.

23. Sarat Bose, 1954, *Selected Speeches and Writings, 1947–1950*, Calcutta: Thacker's Press, p. 72.

24. Hiranmay Bandyopadhya, 1970, *Udvaastu*, Calcutta: Sahitya Sansad, pp. 59–60.

25. Reported in U. Bhaskar Rao, 1967, *The Story of Rehabilitation*, Delhi: Department of Rehabilitation, Ministry of Labour, Employment and Rehabilitation, GoI, p. 146.

26. S.C. Dasgupta, 1948, 'Residential Dharma of East Bengal Hindus', *Amrita Bazar Patrika*, 13 April, p. 4.

27. *Ibid.*

28. S.C. Dasgupta, 'Rehabilitation of East Bengal Evacuees in East Bengal', 29 March 1948, File no. 12-E-1, B Proceedings 59–61, Home Political, July 1948, Bangladesh National Archives (BNA)

29. *Ibid.*

30. *HS*, 16 May 1948, p. 8.

31. *Ibid.*

32. A prominent lawyer and judge, Biswas was also a member of the Bengal Boundary Commission in 1947.

33. *Manchester Guardian*, 18 June 1950, File no. 12 P-26, B Proceedings 41–58, Home Political, September 1951, BNA.

34. Hamidul Haq Chowdhury clearly denied any allegations that minority Hindus were going away because of physical violence, kidnapping, abduction, and forcible conversions. He further added, 'If however a man does not want to reconcile himself to Pakistan and wants to leave the Dominion, he cannot be prevented' (*HS*, 1 November 1948, p. 3).

35. File no. 12C-3 of 1948, B Proceedings 399, Home Political, July 1949, BNA.

36. Nazimuddin's answer given to unstarred question in the East Bengal Legislative Assembly by Jatindra Nath Bhadra, Member of Legislative Assembly (MLA), enquiring about the causes for the evacuation of the minority community from East Bengal. See 2 April 1948 (*ibid.*).

37. Report, 8 April 1948, File no. 12C-9 of 1948, B Proceedings 940, Home Political, April 1953, BNA.

38. *Ibid.*

39. In the press report titled 'No Cause for Exodus from East Bengal', Premier Nurul Amin wrote, 'My Government wish to state in unmistakable terms that there is now no cause whatever for the evacuation or exodus of the minority community from this province ... These special facilities [air lifts] and ... Statements such as that of Dr. Roy are bound to encourage the exodus and retard the return to normal conditions in East and West Bengal.' See *The Statesman*, 24 February 1950, p. 5.

40. See reports published in *The Statesman* between June and December 1950. A government press note to this effect was published in *Ananda Bazar Patrika*, 5 September 1950, p. 1.

41. *Amrita Bazar Patrika*, 14 January 1950, p. 5.

42. *HS*, 25 June 1948, p. 3.

43. *HS*, 26 June 1948, p. 5.

44. *Ananda Bazar Patrika*, 26 June 1948, p. 1.

45. File no. 18R-3/51, B Proceedings 168–71, Home Political, Government of West Bengal (GoWB), 1951, West Bengal State Archives (WBSA).

46. This was in direct contradistinction to the Nehru–Liaquat Pact which urged the displaced to return to their natal villages where their citizenship rights would be guaranteed.

47. It was under the personal purview of B.C. Roy.

48. N.C. Chakravarti, 1949, *Report on the Survey of Refugee Population in West Bengal, 1948*, Calcutta: Government of West Bengal.

49. GoWB, 1956, *Rehabilitation of Refugees: A Statistical Survey*, Calcutta: State Statistical Bureau, p. 2. These surveys were conducted in 1948, 1951, 1955, and 1956.

50. These camps were classified as Temporary and Permanent Liability Camps, Worksite Camps, and Colony Camps. For details on various government measures towards refugees in this period, see Chakrabarty, *The*

Marginal Men; Samir Kumar Das, 2000, 'Refugee Crisis: Responses of the Government of West Bengal', in Bose (ed.), *Refugees in West Bengal*, pp. 7–31; and Sanyal, *Making of a New Space*.

51. Ministry of Rehabilitation, India, 1967, *Statement of the Ministry of Labour, Employment and Rehabilitation (Department of Rehabilitation) to the Lahiri Commission of Inquiry, West Bengal*, New Delhi: GoI, p.1.

52. West Bengal, Refugee Relief and Rehabilitation Department, 1957, *The Great Challenge: 1946 [to] 1957, and and Still the Trek Continues*, Calcutta: Home (Publicity) Department on behalf of the Refugee Relief and Rehabilitation Department, GoWB, p. 15.

53. Ibid. Out of the 13.78 lakh persons displaced by December 1949, only 1.06 lakhs sought admission to these relief camps. In later years, the Indian Statistical Institute conducted several surveys in an attempt to identify the socio-economic origins of the displaced.

54. 'Summary of the Recommendations made by the Conference of the Rehabilitation Ministers from the Eastern State, held at Darjeeling on 20 to 22 October 1955', Ministry of Rehabilitation, India, 1955–6, *Annual Report, 1955–6*, New Delhi: GoI, Appendix A, p. 87. The conference also declared that no person migrating after the 15 October 1952 should be recognized as a displaced person unless he produced a migration certificate.

55. File no.1/1/56-FIII, Ministry of Home Affairs, GoI, 1956, National Archives of India (NAI).

56. Ministry of Rehabilitation, India, 1964–5, *Annual Report*, p. 6.

57. File no. 18R-3/51, B Proceedings 168–71, Home Political, GoWB, 1951, WBSA. In all fairness, authorities also appended a clause that 'If however the RR commissioner or the District officer of the district in which RR facility is sought for is satisfied that even though the head of a family is not a displaced person according to the above definition, the individual status as DP of other members of the family justifies the extension of RR benefits to the family as a whole, he may direct the extension of such benefits in such cases'. However, this left the refugee family at the mercy of the district officer.

58. Note, 10 July 1951, signed by Assistant Secretary, Rehabilitation Branch, RR Department (*ibid.*); emphasis added.

59. A detailed account of the politics of squatter's colonies is provided in Chatterjee, 'Midnight's Unwanted Children', chapters 4 and 5.

60. Most of the later refugees were agriculturalists. Kanti Pakrashi provides a sociological and statistical analysis of the composition of the refugees between 1946 and 1970. See Pakrashi and Indian Statistical Institute, *The Uprooted*, p. 24.

61. Speech given to welcome the Union Minister for Relief and Rehabilitation at a function organized by the Dumdum Rajerghat Rehabilitation and Welfare Board, Calcutta, 7 August 1955, in *Renuka Ray Papers*, File no. 27, Nehru Memorial Museum and Library (NMML).

62. The correspondence between Nehru and Gopinath Bardoloi, the Chief Minister of Assam at the time, clearly outlines Assam's views with regard to the East Bengali refugees. Nehru to Bardoloi, Letter, 29 May 1948, *Jawaharlal Nehru Selected Works, Vol. 6*, p. 118; Nehru to Bardoloi, Letter, 18 May 1949, *JNSW, Vol. 11*, pp. 70–2. Also, see Nehru's note, 21 July 1948, 'Migration from East Bengal to Assam', *JNSW, Vol. 7*, pp. 67–8.

63. 'The Andamans of Today', *Modern Review*, vol. 85, March, 1949, p. 216.

64. At a conference between central (Union Ministers for Finance, Law, and Rehabilitation) and state (Chief Minister and Rehabilitation Minister of West Bengal) ministers held at Calcutta on 3 and 4 July 1958, it was decided that by 31 July 1959, all camps would be closed down. Ministry of Rehabilitation, India, 1958–9, *Annual Report*, p. 9.

65. This changed with the riots of 1964, when the displaced were given permanent refuge in India, through the civil war in Pakistan in 1971, after which *East Bengal* seceded to become the state of Bangladesh.

66. Ministry of Rehabilitation, India, 1958–9, *Annual Report*, pp. 3–4.

67. However, a close reading of the council debates of the West Bengal Legislative Assembly in the years 1952–5 reveals that the government was aware that its efforts towards rehabilitation remained limited and that resources often did not reach their target population. See *Council Debates (Official Report)*, West Bengal Legislative Council, First Session, June–August 1952, Vol. I, 51.

68. Rao, *The Story of Rehabilitation*, p. 155.

69. *Ibid.*

70. Ibid., p. 156.

71. Mrinalini Sinha, 1995, *Colonial Masculinity: The 'Manly Englishman' and the 'Effeminate Bengali' in the Late Nineteenth Century*, New York: Manchester University Press.

72. *The Statesman*, 22 January 1951.

73. Rao, *The Story of Rehabilitation*, p. 38.

74. *The Statesman*, 22 January 1951, p. 5

75. *Ibid.*

76. Rao, *The Story of Rehabilitation*, p. 147.

77. *Ibid.*

78. Letter, 24 September 1949, File no. 53/10/49-AN, Ministry of Home Affairs, GoI, 1949, NAI.

79. For details on squatter's colonies, see Chaudhuri, 'Refugees in West Bengal'.

80. *The Statesman*, 11 November, p. 1; *The Statesman*, 3 December 1950, p. 5.

81. Dandyakaranya is a prominent region depicted in the well-known epic Ramayana. According to mythology, Rama tried to bring agriculture to the wild tracts of Dandyakaranya but did not succeed.

82. Maitraye Devi, 1974, *Exodus*, Calcutta: S. Das, p. 12.

83. *Renuka Ray Papers*, File no. 27, NMML.

84. *Ibid.*

85. *Ibid.*

86. See Richard Eaton, 1993, *Rise of Islam in the Bengal Frontier, 1204–1760*, Berkeley: University of California Press, where he outlines the different political, ecological, and social reasons that facilitated such settlements and helped to establish specific strains of Islam in the Bengal delta.

87. 'The Problem of Refugees from East Bengal', in *Shyama Prasad Mukherjee* (*SPM*) *Papers*, File no. 34, Index 1, 1949–51, NMML.

88. *Ibid.*

89. Voice of India, 1966, *A Tale of Woes of East Bengal Minorities*, 1st edition, Calcutta: D.R. Sen, p. 2.

90. *Ibid.*, p. 3.

91. Jadunath Sarkar, 1948, 'Brothers from Over the River: The Refugee Problem in India', *Modern Review*, vol. 84, September, p. 236.

92. *Amrita Bazar Patrika*, 14 March 1948, p. 4.

93. *Ibid.*

94. 'Piercing the Pact', *Eastern Economist*, vol. XV, no. 6, 11 August 1950, in *SPM Papers*, File no. 39, Index 1, NMML; emphasis added.

95. *Amrita Bazar Patrika*, 17 April 1948, p. 4.

96. Letter, 3 September 1949, 'Rehabilitation of East Bengal Refugees', in Voice of India, *A Tale of Woes*, p. 21.

97. *Ibid.*

98. *HS*, 16 November 1948, p. 4.

99. Bengal Rehabilitation Organization, 'Summary of Refugee Rehabilitation Plan', in *SPM Papers*, File no. 38, Index 4, NMML.

100. *Ibid.*

101. *SPM Papers*, Refugees and Minorities, 1950–1951, File no. 39, Index vol. 1, NMML.

102. West Bengal, Refugee Relief and Rehabilitation Department, 1956, *Relief and Rehabilitation of Displaced Persons in West Bengal*, Calcutta: Home (Publicity) Department, on behalf of the Refugee Relief and Rehabilitation Department, GoWB, p. 2; emphasis added.

103. *Ibid.*

104. Rao, *The Story of Rehabilitation*, p. 160.

105. *Ibid.*, p. 48.

106. *Ibid.*

107. Ministry of Rehabilitation, India, 1955–6, *Annual Report*, p. 4.

108. Joya Chatterji argues that the Indian state constructed the relief and rehabilitation measures as charity rather than under any obligation towards the refugees. Chatterji, 'Right or Charity?', p. 84.

109. West Bengal, Refugee Relief and Rehabilitation Department, *The Great Challenge*, p. 16.

110. West Bengal, Refugee Relief and Rehabilitation Department, *Relief and Rehabilitation of Displaced Persons in West Bengal*, p. 2.

111. Ministry of Rehabilitation, India, 1966–7, *Annual Report*, p. 50.

112. *Ibid.*

113. *Ibid.*

114. For example, out of the 1,790 *sahakaris* (as these workers were called) deployed for rehabilitation, 187 were from Dandyakaranya projects, 495 from the Andamans, and 314 from the Chanda project in Maharashtra, where the main inhabitants were the 'new migrants' from *East Bengal*. Ibid., pp. 50–1.

115. Ministry of Rehabilitation, India, *Statement of the Ministry of Labour, Employment and Rehabilitation (Department of Rehabilitation) to the Lahiri Commission of Inquiry*, p. 22.

116. *Ibid.*

117. According to official estimates, around 53,232 persons fell within this category by 1956 and were in various government-instituted homes. West Bengal, Refugee Relief and Rehabilitation Department, *The Great Challenge*, p. 16.

118. This scheme was the brainchild of J.K. Bhonsle who was the Deputy Minister of Rehabilitation in 1955. Around 7,000 children participated in this programme in West Bengal out of 40,000. Ministry of Rehabilitation, India, 1955–6, *Annual Report*, pp. 12–13.

119. *Ibid.*

120. Rao, *The Story of Rehabilitation*, pp. 1–2.

121. Ministry of Rehabilitation, India, *Statement of the Ministry of Labour, Employment and Rehabilitation (Department of Rehabilitation) to the Lahiri Commission of Inquiry*, p. 22

122. *Ibid.*

123. For more on this perception of right to charity, see Chatterji, 'Right or Charity?'.

124. The UCRC central council included members with affiliations with the Communist Party of India (CPI), Forward Bloc, the Socialist Unity Centre of India, the Revolutionary Communist Party of India (RCPI), the Democratic Vanguard, the Bolshevik Party, the Socialist Republican Party, and the Hindu Mahasabha. The RCRC also consisted of card-carrying members of such Left parties as the Revolutionary Socialist Party, RCPI, and the Socialist Party. A meeting held at the Calcutta Maidan to protest against government apathy, organized by the UCRC, was attended by 50,000 refugees. For more details on these organizations and their activities with regard to refugee mobilization, see Chakrabarty, *The Marginal Men*, pp. 76–88.

125. Prafulla Chakrabarty has argued that the refugees provided the fodder or the stepping stone for the Left parties to come power in West Bengal from the late 1970s. Joya Chatterji has disputed such claims by arguing that the refugee movement in its quasi-political form had began to demand rehabilitation rights much before the Left politics managed to organize the refugees and their political demands. Chatterji, 'Right or Charity', pp. 83–5.

Epilogue
Memories and Realities

While 1947 is a momentuous year in the history of modern South Asia, its significance is disparate depending on the regional and national context. The year witnessed three Partitions, two Independences and one messy decolonization processes. Nationalist official histories in India seek to confine the Partition narrative as an inevitable, albeit unfortunate hypertext to the grand narrative of anti-colonial struggle. It is evoked periodically as an explanation of decolonization, of political accommodation and the achievement of the most important political prize of all, nationhood. In Pakistan, 1947 marks the year of triumph, not only from British colonialism but also of decades long demands for self representation. Whether tragedy or triumph, both narratives see 1947 as starting point for their respective nation-states.

Such official recollections of the Partition have led to a problematic erasure of any memory of the process of the framing and establishment of two new nations. One is led to imagine that in August 1947, the Partition generated automatically and fully formed nation-states, albeit under short-term chaos and violence. Reflexive and oppositional nationalisms in India, Pakistan which are a constant feature of contemporary South Asian life, are then imagined to have come about at the moment of origin, at Partition.

Popular and personal memories of the event contradict nationalist narratives. Memories of migrants, refugees and new citizens of India and Pakistan highlight their uncertainties, the contingent, messy, and protracted nature of the event which continued to impact their lives and of their families for decades to come. In such narratives, Partition is significant in generating large-scale uprooting, exile, violence and victimhood and the search for security and belonging in a *foreign* land. It is not the self-contained neat story found in history text books but one that is chaotic, erratic and incomplete.

In Bangladesh, which emerged as a new nation state in 1971 from the erstwhile East Pakistan, political memory has been subverted to pay lip service to the nationalist impulses which have sought to redefine region and religion and erase the history of 1947 to accommodate a seamless history of Bengali Muslim nationalism. 1971 rather than 1947 is seen as the crucial 'watershed' for East Pakistani/Bangladeshi national identity. The period under Pakistani authority finds little space within the official history of Bangladesh or the memories of Bangladeshis. The renewed interest in the 1971 this year which marks the 40th anniversary of the Liberation War make little mention of the erstwhile linkages to Pakistani identity other than to serve the purpose of showing causality, albeit a complicated one, towards freedom.[1] The impact of the Bengal Partition on the emergence and rise of Bengali nationalism in East Pakistan is a topic that has yet to be researched to its fullest.

One of the aims of this book has been to contest such erasures in Bangladesh and challenge the privileging of a particular paradigm of Partition in India in which both official and popular memories of the event invoke the Punjab experience as standard. The experiences of the Bengal Partition, if they at all make an appearance are cast as an exception to the rule, a side story to the *main* event. But in reality the Bengal Partition, which witnessed low scale violence, protracted migration over two decades, Bengali Hindu refugee initiatives which brought in political change in West Bengal, the Bengali language movement in East Pakistan, was not a regional anomaly but is a distinct and alternative template to understand the process and impact of such divisions. It was in divided Bengal that one can witness clearly the interactions between the new states and their citizens as ordinary Hindus and Muslims, along with their extended families, lived through extraordinary times, moved back and forth across a new border, facing bureaucratic hurdles and small scale violence, and attempted to answer or deflect impertinent questions about their citizenship and belonging.

It was also in divided Bengal that one finds the easy co-relation between territorial boundary and citizenship put to test. After Partition, one is led to imagine and sometimes argue that citizenship was determined by the demarcation of the new borders. Those who were included became *citizens* and those who lived outside became *foreigners*. However such assumptions fail when one shifts focus to one of the quintessential features of the Bengal Partition, the one hundred and sixty-two Indo-Bangladesh enclaves and their inhabitants. Denied the markers of citizenship such as the right to vote, a ration card or Passport by both India and Bangladesh, their legal and constitutional existence continues to be in question sixty years after the Partition. Recent bilateral talks between India and Bangladesh have elicited a preliminary agreement to 'exchange' enclaves situated in each other's territory.[2] India will relinquish claims on the one hundred and eleven enclaves situated in Bangladesh territory while Bangladesh will let go of the fifty-one in Indian territory. The inhabitants would have the right to choose their nations with the expectation that they would choose the nation within which their enclave is located. However, until the logistics of such transfers are worked out by the two governments, the residents in these enclaves will continue to remain 'stateless', denied of basic public amenities and documentary identities.

Citizenship in partitioned Bengal remained complicated even when one moved beyond the enclaves to the literal 'mainland', Although the new border defined national jurisdiction, it was unable to determine the citizenship of migrants who moved across it. India and East Pakistan promulgated various piecemeal policies which aimed at controlling movement of people and decide one way or the other the nationality of these migrants. However, they were unable to resolve the question of citizenship. In fact, citizenship has acquired new political urgency in recent years in states such as Assam which also has a border with Bangladesh. After the 1971 Bangladesh War which witnessed large-scale migration from the erstwhile East Pakistan into the Indian states of Assam, Tripura and West Bengal, sub-nationalist movements in Assam have begun to question the citizenship rights of nearly thirty five percent of its population.[3] The response of the Indian state in most instances has been legislative which allow migrants the rights of citizenship through the proclamation of specific key dates by which migrants need to be on the *right* side of the border. Such efforts, in conjunction with periodic bilateral talks and attempts to fence the border, aim to contain rather than stop the migration. While Indian law cannot make a distinction between Hindu and Muslim migrants from Bangladesh, implicit within some of these measures have been an understanding that Hindu migrants from East Pakistan have a 'right to return' while Muslim migrants are either economic migrants or 'infiltrators.' These have been further complicated by pre-Partition anxieties about the dilution of Assamese identity and of the threat of becoming (linguistic) minorities in their 'own state'.

Similarly, the citizenship of 'illegal migrants', most of who come from Bangladesh, have become extremely politicized and linked to Hindu right wing movements in places such as Maharashtra and Delhi.[4] Although the xenophobia towards illegal Bangladeshi migrant is of recent vintage, they find their roots within post-Partition politics surrounding the citizenship of migrants and the porosity of the Bengal border.

Although both India and East Pakistan claimed secular credentials after Partition, both failed to live up to it effectively in their public life. Bangladesh too claimed secular credentials but its political and national life has increasingly taken a turn towards Islamacization[5] culminating in the constitutional adoption of Islam as the State religion in 1988. Subsequent politics of Bangladeshi vs Bengali national identity have covertly and overtly privileged a Muslim citizenship in Bangladesh. In such discourses, Bangladeshi Hindus, tribal groups who live in the Chittagong Hill tracts and are mostly non-Muslim find limited space.

How does one determine citizenship of people who are linguistically and ethnically similar and bear little or no marks of their religious denominations? This question had plagued policy makers in the 1950s, especially for Bengal, and has continued to plague Indian policy makers today. While the Passport and Visa regime of the 1950s sought to impose a documentary identity on legal border-crossers, the most recent answer has been the fascination with biometric identity cards. In mid 2009, India declared that that it aims to ascribe a unique number to each of its citizens ostensibly to help within its disbursement of welfare to underprivileged groups.[6] While some have pointed both to the technical and financial difficulties of implementing such a project, and the potential for misuse, others have indicated that rather than empowering the poor, such a system would lead to greater surveillance by the Indian state. In a country where most people still don't have birth certificates, Indians now have a large plethora of cards to choose from – pan card, ration card, voter card, passport, rent or property ownership papers – to prove residence and citizenship. Most illegal immigrants have also become 'paper citizens' acquiring access to one or more these documents to have uninterrupted access to work.[7] Significantly, access to such documents continues to be controlled by the whims and contextual interpretation of low level officials at passport and revenue offices. Even so, biometric cards, unlike other identification documents, have the potential for becoming the single test, which determines identity rather than citizenship and residency, and be linked to border 'security' policies.[8]

Partition continues to cast a long shadow in the making of modern South Asia. A mosaic of national, regional and personal memories surround it as it acquires new depth with each passing decade and new research and scholarship. The frequent occurance of large-scale communal riots, shaky or failed diplomacy between India, Pakistan and Bangladesh, the continuation of border disputes and harassments of travellers between these countries ensures that Partition remains an 'active category.'[9] It is ironic then, that post-Partition experience in Bengal which remains largely forgotten, should continue to influence both foreign and domestic policies of India and Bangladesh today.

NOTES

1. Several scholarly and popular books have been published in 2011 which marks the fortieth anniversary of the Liberation War. See, Yasmin Saikia, 2011, *Women War and the Making of Bangladesh: Remembering 1971*, Duke University Press; Sharmila Bose, 2011, *Dead Reckoning: Memories of the 1971 Bangladesh War*, Columbia University Press.

2. Ipsita Chakrabary, 2011, 'Living with a border in the Backyard' *The Telegraph*, 1 September.

3. Citizenship in Assam has for long been a contentious issue predating 1947, based primarily along ethnic, cultural and linguistic lines. For more details see Sanjib Baruah, *India Against Itself*.

4. Willem Van Schendel, *The Bengal Borderland*, p. 198. For the propaganda on 'illegal migrants' For details, see Michael Gillan, 2002, 'Refugees or infiltrators? The Bharatiya Janata Party and illegal migration from Bangladesh', *Asian Studies Review*. Vol. 26, No. 1,pp. 73–95; Satadru Sen, 2003, 'Border of Insanity: Deporting Bangladeshi Migrants', *Economic and Political Weekly*, vol. 38, no. 7, pp. 611–12.

5. Amena Mohsin argues that General Irshad and the ruling elite has tried to make Bangladesh into a 'mosque-centered' society. Amena Mohsin, 2001, *The State of 'Minority' Rights in Bangladesh*, Colombo: International Centre for Ethnic Studies.

6. For specific criticisms of the UID scheme, see Ravi S. Shukla,2010, 'Reimagining Citizenship: Debating India's Unique Identification Scheme', *Economic and Political Weekly*, vol. XLV, no. 2, pp. 31–6; Usha Ramanathan, 2010, 'The Personal is the Personal' *Indian Express*, 6 January. Available at http://www.indianexpress.com/news/the-personal-is-the-personal/563920/ (last accessed on 11 September 2011).

7. Kamal Sadiq, 2001, *Paper Citizens: How Illegal Immigrants Acquire Citizenship in Developing Countries*, Oxford: Oxford University Press.

8. A recent Parliamentary Committee has raised doubts about the implementation of the ID scheme citing the possibility of illegal immigrants getting access to such IDs. Soutik Basu, 2011, 'Is India's Identity Number Scheme Unravelling?' *BBC News*, 14 December. Available at http://www.bbc.co.uk/news/world-asia-india-16177163 (last accessed on 5 January, 2012).

9. Ranabir Samaddar, 2003, 'The Last Hurrah That Continues', in Ghislaine Glasson Deschaumes and Rada Ivekovic (eds), *Divided Countries, Separated Cities, The Modern Legacy of Partition*, New Delhi: Oxford University Press, pp. 21–35.

Select Bibliography

MANUSCRIPT RECORDS

India

National Archives of India (NAI) (New Delhi)

Proceedings of Ministry of Home (Political) Affairs, Government of India (GoI)

Proceedings of Ministry of External Affairs and Commonwealth Relations, GoI

Nehru Memorial Museum and Library (NMML) (New Delhi)

Institutional and Individual Collections

All India Congress Committee Papers (AICC)
All India Hindu Mahasabha Papers
Ashutosh Lahiry Papers
Mohanlal Saxena Papers
Mridula Sarabhai Papers
Nalini Ranjan Sarkar Papers
Renuka Ray Papers
Shyama Prasad Mukherjee Papers

Oral History Transcripts

Interview with Aurobindo Bose
Interview with Kamala Dasgupta
Interview with S.C. Dasgupta
Interview with Ashalata Sen

Interview with Prafulla Chandra Sen
Interview with Nellie Sengupta

West Bengal State Archives (WBSA) (Calcutta)

Home Political (Secret) Records, Government of West Bengal (GoWB)
Home Police (Confidential) Records, GoWB

West Bengal Police (Special Branch) Archives (Calcutta)

Special Branch 'PM' series, GoWB

West Bengal Police (Intelligence Branch) Archives (Calcutta)

Intelligence Branch, Passport Section II and III series, GoWB

Bangladesh

Bangladesh National Archives (BNA) (Dhaka)

Finance and Revenue Department, Branch Requisition, B Proceedings, Government of East Bengal (GoEB)
Home (Political), Branch Political, B Proceedings, GoEB
Legislative and Judicial Department, Branch Legislative, B Proceedings, GoEB
Public Relations Department, Branch P & D, B Proceedings, GoEB

University of Dhaka Library (Dhaka)

Constituent Assembly of Pakistan Debates, Government of Pakistan (GoP)
East Bengal Legislative Assembly Debates, GoEB

Britain

India Office Library and Records (London)

India Office Records

L/Public and Judicial (P&J)/7
L/P& J/8
L/PJ/7-12, Part III

Private Papers

Margaret Stavridi Papers, Mss. Eur. (European Manuscript) C.808.
Great Britain. 2011, *Foreign Office Files for India, Pakistan and Afghanistan. Section I, Independence, Partition and the Nehru Era, 1947–1964*, Marlborough, England: Adam Matthew Digital, available at <https://login.proxy.bib.uottawa.ca/login?url=http://www.archivesdirect.amdigital.co.uk/Introduction/FO_India/default.aspx> (accessed between April and June 2011).

PRINTED OFFICIAL PUBLICATIONS

Allahabad, India (State). 1951, *The All India Reporter,* Allahabad Section. Nagpur: The All India Reporter.

Bhopal, India (State). 1954, *The All India Reporter,* Bhopal Section. Nagpur: The All India Reporter.

Calcutta, India (State). 1952, *The All India Reporter,* Calcutta Section. Nagpur: The All India Reporter.

Hyderabad, India (State). 1954, *The All India Reporter,* Hyderabad Section. Nagpur: The All India Reporter.

Census of India. 1951–71, General Reports and Reports and Tables for West Bengal,. New Delhi: GoI.

Census of Pakistan. 1951–61, General Reports and Reports and Tables for East Bengal and East Pakistan. Karachi: GOP.

Constituent Assembly (Legislature) of Pakistan Debates. 1953, Vol. 1. No. 14, Karachi: Manager of Publications.

De, Satyendralal and A.K. Bhattacharjee. 1973, *Social Consciousness and Fertility Patterns of the Refugee Settlers in the Sunderbans, West Bengal,* Calcutta: Indian Statistical Institute.

_____. 1973, *The Refugee Settlement in the Sunderbans, West Bengal: A Socio-Economic Study,* Calcutta: Indian Statistical Institute.

East Bengal Home Department. 1950, *Note on the Genesis of Communal Disturbances in West Bengal,* Dacca: East Bengal Government Press.

East Bengal, Pakistan. 1948–58, *Legislative Assembly Proceedings: Official Report,* Dacca: East Bengal Government Press.

Government of India (GoI). 1975, *Study of the Problem of Unemployment in Some Selected Urban and Rural areas of West Bengal.* New Delhi: Committee on Unemployment, Ministry of Labour and Rehabilitation, Department of Labour and Employment, GoI.

_____. 1958, *Parliamentary Debates Official Report (Questions and Answers),* Vol. 1, Delhi: Manager of Publications.

Government of West Bengal(GoWB),1949, *Two Years Since Independence: A Resume of the Activities of the Government of West Bengal, August 15, 1947–49.* Calcutta: Publicity Department.

_____. 1951, *Report on the Complete Enumeration of Displaced Persons Migrating from Eastern Pakistan to the State of West Bengal.* West Bengal: GoWB, Refugee Rehabilitation Department.

_____. 1952, *Bengal: Five Years Since Independence, 1947-52,* Calcutta: Publicity Department.

_____. 1954, *Report of the Committee of Ministers for the Rehabilitation of Displaced Persons in West Bengal,* Calcutta: Manager, GoI Press.

GoWB. 1956, *Rehabilitation of Refugees: A Statistical Survey*, Calcutta: State Statistical Bureau.

_____.1956, West Bengal, Refugee Relief and Rehabilitation Department, *Relief and Rehabilitation of Displaced Persons in West Bengal*, Calcutta: Home (Publicity) Department on behalf of the Refugee Relief and Rehabilitation Department.

_____. 1957, *The Great Challenge: 1946 [to] 1957, and Still the Trek Continues*, Calcutta: Home (Publicity) Department on behalf of the Refugee Relief and Rehabilitation Department.

India (Dominion) Ministry of Information and Broadcasting. 1948, *After Partition*, Delhi: Publications Division, GoI.

_____. 1949, *Millions on the Move the Aftermath of Partition*, Delhi: Publications Division, GoI.

Imperial Gazetteer of India. 1984, Provincial Series, Bengal Vol. 2, Calcutta: Usha Publishers.

Committee of Review of Rehabilitation Work in West Bengal. 1969, *Report on Educational Facilities for New Migrants from East Pakistan in West Bengal*.

Ministry of Rehabilitation, India. 1952–69, *Annual Reports*, New Delhi: GoI.

_____. *Nine Year's Report, 1947-58*. New Delhi: GoI.

_____. 1967, *Statement of the Ministry of Labour, Employment and Rehabilitation (Department of Rehabilitation) to the Lahiri Commission of Inquiry, West Bengal*, Delhi: GoI.

_____. 1971, *Statistical Information relating to the Influx of Refugees from East Bengal to India till 31st Oct. 1971, Vol. 4*, Calcutta: Ministry of Labour and Rehabilitation, Branch Secretariat, GoI.

Luthra, P. N. 1972, *Rehabilitation*, New Delhi: GoI, Publications Division Ministry of Information and Broadcasting.

Mohammad, Ashraf. 1957, *Evacuee & Rehabilitation Laws, Containing up to date Central & Provincial.*

Acts and Ordinances…: With Rehabilitation Resettlement Scheme Punjab…& Inter-domain Agreements Regarding Evacuees (India & Pakistan), Lahore: All Pakistan Legal Publications.

Ministry of Refugees and Rehabilitation, Pakistan.1951, *The Evacuee Property Problem in India and Pakistan: Pakistan's Case*, Karachi: Department of Advertising, Films and Publication, GOP.

Rao, U. Bhaskar. 1967, *The Story of Rehabilitation*, Delhi: Department of Rehabilitation, Ministry of Labour, Employment and Rehabilitation, GoI.

West Bengal Legislative Assembly. 1950–55, *Assembly Proceedings, Official Report*, Alipore: West Bengal Government Press.

NEWSPAPERS AND JOURNALS

Amrita Bazar Patrika (Calcutta)
Ananda Bazar Patrika (Calcutta)
Azad (Calcutta, Dhaka)
Bharatvarsha (Calcutta)
Dainik Basumati (Calcutta)
Dawn (Calcutta, Karachi)
Hindustan Standard (Calcutta)
Hindustan Times
Indian Express
Jai Hind
Jugantar
Modern Review (Calcutta)
Morning News (Dhaka)
Pakistan Observer
Sonar Bangla (Dhaka)
Star of India (Calcutta)
The Hindu
The Nation (Calcutta)
The Statesman (Calcutta)
The Telegraph
The Times (London)

CONTEMPORARY DOCUMENTS, SPEECHES, AND MEMOIRS

Acarya, Durgadas.1978, *Udvastu, Dandyakaranya o Andamana*, Calcutta: Indian Progressive Publishing Company.

Alexander, H. 1951, *New Citizens of India*, London: Oxford University Press.

Ali, S. Wajid. 1945, *Bengalees of Tomorrow*, Calcutta: K.C. Dasgupta.

All India Convention on East Pakistan Minorities.1964, *Report*, Delhi.

Azad, Maulana Abul Kalam. 1960, *India Wins Freedom*, New York: Longmans, Green and Co.

Bandyopadhya, Hiranmay. 1970, *Udvaastu*, Calcutta: Sahitya Sansad.

Bengal Anti-Communal Award, A Report. 1939, Calcutta: The Secretaries Bengal Anti-Communal Award Committee.

Bose, Sarat. 1954, *Selected Speeches and Writings, 1947–1950*, Calcutta: Thackers Press.

Bose, Sharmila. 2011, *Dead Reckoning: Memories of the 1971 Bangladesh War*, New York: Columbia University Press.

Campbell–Johnson, Alan. 1953, *Mission with Mountbatten*, New York: Dutton.

Chakrabarty, Saroj. 1974, *With Dr. B. C. Roy and Other Chief Ministers: A Record up to 1962*, Calcutta: Benson's.

Chakravarti, N.C. 1949, *Report on the Survey of Refugee Population in West Bengal, 1948*, Calcutta

Chatterjee, S. P and Geographical Society of India. 1947, *The Partition of Bengal a Geographical Study*, Calcutta: D.R. Mitra.

Chaudhuri, Manoranjan. 1964, *Partition and the Curse of Rehabilitation*, Calcutta: Bengal Rehabilitation Organization.

Chaudhuri, Nirad C. 1951, *The Autobiography of an Unknown Indian*, London: Chatto and Windus.

Collected Works of Mahatma Gandhi, 1958–73, New Delhi: Publications Division, Government of India.

Darling, M.L. 1949, *At Freedom's Door*, London: Oxford University Press.

Das, Durga (ed.). 1972, *Sardar Patel's Correspondence, 1945–50*, Vols 1–8, Ahmedabad: Navajivan Publishing House.

Devi, Maitraye. 1974, *Exodus*, Calcutta: S. Das.

East Pakistan Geographical Society. 1962, *District Boundary Changes and Population Growth for Pakistan*. Dacca: East Pakistan Geographical Society and Geography Department, Dacca University.

Ebright, D.F. 1954, *Free India: The First Five Years*, Nashville: Parthenon Press.

Gokhle, S.M. 1948, *India's Refugee Problem, Causes and Cures*. Baroda: Prakash Publications.

Gopal, S. (ed.). 1972, *The Selected Works of Jawaharlal Nehru, Second Series*, Vols 1–6, New Delhi: Orient Longman.

Guha, Samar. 1951, *Non-Muslims behind the Curtain of East Pakistan*, Dacca: East Bengal Minorities Association.

_____. 1965, *Wither Minorities of Eastern Pakistan?* Calcutta: Guha.

Government of India (GoI). 1958, *Decisions of the Indo Pakistan Boundary Disputes Tribunal, 1949*.

_____. 1950, *The Constitution of India*, available at http://www.constitution.org/cons/india/const.html (last accessed on 14 March 2009).

Government of West Bengal (GoWB). 1980, *Report of the Refugee Rehabilitation Committee*, Calcutta: Saraswati Press.

Indian Commission of Jurists. 1965, *Recurrent Exodus of Minorities from East Pakistan and Disturbances in India*, New Delhi: Indian Commission of Jurists.

Khosla, G.D. 1949, *Stern Reckoning: A Survey of Events Leading up to and Following the Partition of India*, Oxford: Oxford University Press.

Lahiri, Bhupendra Chandra. 1947, *Bange Hindu Rashtra Chai*, Calcutta.

Lahiry, Pravash Chandra. 1968, *Pak Bharater Ruparekha* (An Outline of India and Pakistan), Chakdah, Nadia: Shyama Prakashani.

Majumdar, R.C. 1945, *Bangladesher Itihasa*, Calcutta: S.C Das.

Mansergh, N. and E.W.R. Lumby (eds). 1970, *Constitutional Relations Between Britain and India: The Transfer of Power, 1942–7*. Vol. 1–12, London: Her Majesty's Stationary Office.

Memorandum Presented by the Muslim Members of the West Bengal Legislative Assembly to the Prime Minister of Bharat. 1950, *Tragedy of Calcutta, January–March 1950*, 7 March, Dacca: West Bengal Refugees Association.

Menon, V.P. 1957, *The Transfer of Power in India*, Bombay: Orient Longman.

Moon, P. 1961, *Divide and Quit: An Eyewitness Account of the Partition of India*, New Delhi: Oxford University Press

Mukherji, Santosh Kumar. 1947, *Boundary Problem of New Bengal*, Calcutta: Hindustan Socialist Party.

Nehru, Jawaharlal. 1984, *Selected Works of Jawaharlal Nehru. Second Series*, New Delhi: Jawaharlal Nehru Memorial Fund.

Pal, Bipin Chandra. 1916, *Nationality and Empire, A Running Study of Some Current Indian Problems*, Calcutta: Thacker, Spink & Co.

Parthasarathy, G. (ed.). 1985, *Letters to the Chief Ministers 1947–64, Vol. III*, New Delhi: Oxford University Press.

Poplai, S.L. (ed.). 1970, *India 1947–50, Select Documents on Asian Affairs*, Vol. II, New York: Oxford University Press.

Rehabilitating the Uprooted. 1951, Pamphlet.

Rehabilitation of Displaced Persons. 1948, Pamphlet.

Stock, A.G. 1973, *Memoirs of Dacca University, 1947–51*, Dacca: Green Book House Ltd.

Tuker, Francis. 1950, *While Memory Serves*, London: Cassell and Co. Ltd.

Voice of India. 1966, *A Tale of Woes of East Pakistan Minorities*, 1st edition, Calcutta: D.R. Sen.

Zinkin, Taya.1962, *Reporting India*, London: Chatto & Windus.

UNPUBLISHED PhD THESES

Chatterjee, Nilanjana. 1992, 'Midnight's Unwanted Children: East Bengali Refugees and the Politics of Rehabilitation', Unpublished PhD thesis, Brown University.

Anjan Ghosh. 1998, 'Partial Truths: Rumor and Communal Violence in South Asia, 1946–1992, Bangladesh, India. PhD thesis, University of Michigan.

Ghosh Semanti.2000, 'Nationalism and the Problem of 'Difference', Bengal, 1905–47. PhD thesis, Tufts University.

Sen, Uditi. 2009, 'Refugees and the Politics of Nation Building in India, 1947–71', Unpublished PhD thesis, Cambridge University.

SECONDARY SOURCES

Ahmed, Abul Mansoor. 1975, *Aamar Dekha Rajnitir Panchash Bachchar*, Dhaka: Naoroze Kitabistan.

_____. 1978, *Atmakatha*, Dhaka: Mohinuddin Ahmed.

Ahmad, Aijaz.2000, *Lineages of the Present*. London: Verso.

Ahmad, Kamruddin. 1967, *The Social History of East Pakistan*, Dacca: Raushan Ara Ahmed.

Ahmed, Rafiuddin. 1981, *The Bengal Muslims, 1871–1906, A Quest for Identity*, Delhi, New York: Oxford University Press.

_____. 2001, *Understanding the Bengal Muslims Interpretative Essays*, New Delhi: Oxford University Press.

Ahmed, Sufia. 1996, *Muslim Community in Bengal, 1884–1912*, Dhaka: University Press Limited.

Aiyar, Swarna.1998, '"August Anarchy": The Partition Massacres in Punjab, 1947', in D.A. Low and Howard Brasted (eds), *Freedom Trauma Continuities: Northern India and Independence*, New Delhi: Sage, pp. 15–38.

Amin, Sonia N. 1996, *The World of Muslim Women in Colonial Bengal, 1876–1939*, Leiden: EJ Brill.

Anisuzzaman, M. 1993, *Creativity, Reality, and Identity*, Dhaka: International Centre for Bengal Studies, University Press Limited.

Anderson, Benedict. 1983, *Imagined Communities, Reflections on the Origins and Spread of Nationalism*, London: Verso.

Ansari, Nasim. 1991, *Choosing to Stay: Memoirs of an Indian Muslim*, Karachi: City Press.

Ansari, Sarah. 1998, 'Partition, Migration and Refugees: Responses to the Arrival of Muhajirs in Sind During 1947–48', in D.A. Low and Howard Brasted (eds), *Freedom Trauma Continuities: Northern India and Independence*, New Delhi: Sage, pp. 91–104.

_____. 2005, *Life after Partition: Migration, Community and Strife in Sindh, 1947–1962*, Karachi: Oxford University Press.

Bagchi, Jasodhara and Subhoranjan Dasgupta (eds). 2003, *The Trauma and the Triumph: Gender and Partition in Eastern India*, Kolkata: Stree.

Bandyopadhyaya, Sandipa.1994, *Deshabhaga-Deshatyaga*, Calcutta: Anushtupa.

_____. 1993, *Itihasera Dike Phire,Checallishera Danga*, Calcutta: Utsa Manusha Samkalana.

Bandyopadhyay, Sekhar. 2004, *Caste, Culture, and Hegemony Social Domination in Colonial Bengal*, New Delhi, Thousand Oaks: Sage Publications.

_____(ed.). 2001, *Bengal: Rethinking History, Essays in Historiography*, New Delhi: Manohar.

Bandyopadhyay, Sekhar. 1994, 'Development, Differentiation and Caste: The Namasudra Movement in Bengal, 1872–1947', in Sekhar Bandyopadhya, Abhijit Dasgupta, and Willem Van Schendel (eds), *Bengal: Communities, Development and States*, New Delhi: Manohar, pp. 90–119.

_____. 1997, *Caste, Protest and Identity in Colonial India: The Namasudras of Bengal, 1872–1947*, Richmond, Surrey: Curzon Press.

Banerjee, Bireswar and Neal M Bowers. 1965, *The Changing Cultural Landscape of Nadia: A Border District of West Bengal, India*, Calcutta: Indian Publications.

Barkat, Abul (ed.). 2000, *An Inquiry into Causes and Consequences of Deprivation of Hindu Minorities in Bangladesh through the Vested Property Act: Framework for a Realistic Solution*, Dhaka: PRIP Trust.

Baruah, Sanjib. 1999, *India against Itself: Assam and the Politics of Nationality*, Philadelphia: University of Pennsylvania Press.

Basu, Tapan, Pradip Datta, Sumit Sarkar, Tanika Sarkar, and Sambuddha Sen. 1993, *Khaki Shorts and Saffron Flags: A Critique of the Hindu Right*, New Delhi: Orient Longman.

Baud, Michiel and Willem Van Schendel. 1997, 'Toward a Comparative History of Borderlands', *Journal of World History*, 8(2): 211–42.

Bayly, C. A. 2005, *Origins of Nationality in South Asia: Patriotism and Ethical Government in the Making of Modern India*, New Delhi: Oxford University Press.

Bhalla, Alok. 1994, *Stories About the Partition of India*. Vol. 1–3, New Delhi: Indus.

Bhattacharjea, Ajit. 1997, *Countdown to Partition: The Final Days*, New Delhi: HarperCollins.

Biswas, Sukumar and Hiroshi Sato. 1993, *Religion and Politics in Bangladesh and West Bengal*, Tokyo, Japan: Institute of Developing Economies.

Bose, Pradip K. (ed.). 2000, *Refugees of West Bengal: Institutional Practices and Contested Identities*, Calcutta: Calcutta Research Group.

Bose, Sugata. 1986, *Agrarian Bengal Economy, Social Structure, and Politics, 1919–1947*, Cambridge South Asian Studies, Cambridge: Cambridge University Press.

_____. 1993, *The New Cambridge History of India: Peasant Labour and Colonial Capital*, Cambridge: Cambridge University Press.

_____. 2001, 'Between Monolith and Fragment: A Note on Historiography of Nationalism in Bengal', in Sekhar Bandyopadhyay (ed.), *Bengal: Rethinking History, Essays in Historiography*, New Delhi: Manohar, p. 288.

Bose, Sugata and Ayesha Jalal. 2004, *Modern South Asia History, Culture, Political Economy*, New York: Routledge.

_____ (eds). 1997, *Nationalism, Democracy, and Development: State and Politics in India*, New Delhi: Oxford University Press.

Brubaker, Rogers. 1992, *Citizenship and Nationhood in France and Germany*, Cambridge, MA: Harvard University Press.

Butalia, Urvashi. 2000, *The Other Side of Silence: Voices from the Partition of India*, Durham, NC: Duke University Press.

———. 2000, 'Community, State and Gender: Some Reflections on the Partition of India', in Mushirul Hasan (ed.), *Inventing Boundaries: Gender, Politics and the Partition of India*. New Delhi: Oxford University Press, pp. 178–207.

———. 1995, 'Muslims and Hindus, Men and Women: Communal Stereotypes and the Partition of India', in Tanika Sarkar and Urvashi Butalia (eds), *Women and Right Wing Movements: Indian Experiences*, London: Zed Books, pp. 58–81.

Chakrabarty, Prafulla K. 1990, *The Marginal Men, the Refugees and the Left Political Syndrome in West Bengal*, Kalyani, West Bengal: Lumière Books.

Chakrabarty, Bidyut. 2004, *The Partition of Bengal and Assam, 1932–1947 Contour of Freedom*, London: Routledge Curzon.

———. 1993, 'The 1947 United Bengal Movement: A Thesis without Synthesis', *The Indian Economic and Social History Review*, XXX(4): 467.

Chakrabarty, Dipesh. 1998, 'Remembered Villages: Representations of Hindu-Bengali Memories in the Aftermath of the Partition', in D.A. Low and Howard Brasted (eds), *Freedom Trauma Continuities: Northern India and Independence*, New Delhi: Sage, pp. 133–52.

Chakrabarty, Janardan. 1965, *Smritibharey*, Calcutta: General Printers and Publishers Private Limited.

Chandra, Bipan. 2000, *India After Independence, 1947–2000*, New Delhi: Penguin.

———. 1988, *India's Struggle for Independence, 1857–1947*, New Delhi, India: Viking.

———. 1993, *Essays on Indian Nationalism*, New Delhi: Har-Anand Publications.

Chatterjee, Partha 2002, *A Princely Impostor? The Strange and Universal History of the Kumar of Bhawal*, Princeton, NJ: Princeton University Press.

———. 1998, *Wages of Freedom Fifty Years of the Indian Nation-State*, Delhi, New York: Oxford University Press.

———. 1997, *The Present History of West Bengal Essays in Political Criticism*, New Delhi: Oxford University Press.

———. 1993, *The Nation and Its Fragments Colonial and Postcolonial Histories*, Princeton, N.J.: Princeton University Press.

———. 1991, *Nationalist Thought and the Colonial World: A Derivative Discourse?*, Minneapolis: University of Minnesota Press.

Chatterjee, Partha and Anjan Ghosh. 2002, *History and the Present*, Delhi, Bangalore: Permanent Black. Distributed by Orient Longman.

Chatterji, Joya. 1994, *Bengal Divided: Hindu Communalism and Partition, 1932–1947*, Cambridge: Cambridge University Press.

_____. 1999, 'The Fashioning of a Frontier: The Radcliffe Line and Bengal's Border Landscape, 1947–52', *Modern Asian Studies*, 33(1): 185–242.

_____. 2001, 'Right or Charity? The Debate over Relief and Rehabilitation in West Bengal, 1947–50', in Suvir Kaul (ed.), *The Partitions of Memory: The Afterlife of the Division of India*, New Delhi: Permanent Black, pp. 74–110.

_____. 2005, 'Of Graveyards and Ghettos: Muslims in Partitioned West Bengal 1947–67', in Mushirul Hasan and Asim Roy (eds), *Living Together Separately: Cultural India in History and Politics*, New Delhi: Oxford University Press, pp. 222–49.

_____. 2007, *The Spoils of Partition: Bengal and India, 1947–1967*, Cambridge: Cambridge University Press.

_____. 1999, 'The Making of a Borderline: The Radcliffe Award for Bengal', in Ian Talbot and Gurharpal Singh (ed.), *Region and Partition: Bengal, Punjab and the Partition of the Subcontinent*, Oxford: Oxford University Press.

_____. 2007, '"Dispersal" and the Failure of Rehabilitation: Refugee Camp-dwellers and Squatters in West Bengal', *Modern Asian Studies*, 41(5): 995–1032.

Chaudhuri, Ahindra. 1971, *Nijerey Haraye Khunji*, Vol. 1–2, Calcutta: Indian Associated Publishing Company Private Limited.

Chaudhuri, Pranati. 1983, 'Refugees in West Bengal: A Study of the Growth and Distribution of Refugee Settlements with the CMD', Occasional Paper No. 55, Centre for Studies in Social Sciences, Calcutta, March.

Chaudhuri, S. (ed.), 1990, *Calcutta: The Living City, The Present and the Future. Vol. 2*, Calcutta: Oxford University Press.

Chester, Lucy. 2009, *Borders and Conflict in South Asia: The Radcliffe Boundary Commission and the Partition of Punjab*, Manchester: Manchester University Press.

Das, Samir Kumar. 2000, 'Refugee Crisis: Responses of the Government of West Bengal', in Pradip Kumar Bose (ed.), *Refugees in West Bengal: Institutional Practices and Contested Identities*, Calcutta: Calcutta Research Group, pp. 7–31.

Das, Suranjan. 1991, *Communal Riots in Bengal, 1905–1947*, New Delhi: Oxford University Press.

Das, Veena. 1990, *Mirrors of Violence: Communities, Riots and Survivors in South Asia*, New Delhi: Oxford University Press.

_____. 1996, *Critical Events: An Anthropological Perspective on Contemporary India*, Delhi: Oxford University Press.

Datta, Pradip K. 1999, *Carving Blocs: Communal Ideology in Early Twentieth Century Bengal*, New Delhi: Oxford University Press.

De, Soumitra. 1992, *Nationalism and Separatism in Bengal a Study of India's Partition*, New Delhi: Har-Anand Publications.

Devi, Jyotirmayee. 1995, *Epar Ganga–Opar Ganga* (The River Churning), trans. by Enakshi Chatterjee, New Delhi: Kali.

Eaton, Richard. 1993, *The Rise of Islam in the Bengal Frontier, 1204–1760*, Berkeley: University of California Press.

_____. 2003, *India's Islamic Traditions, 711–1750*, New Delhi: Oxford University Press.

Edney, Mathew. 1997, *Mapping an Empire: The Geographical Construction of British India 1765–1843*, Chicago: University of Chicago Press.

Feldman, Shelly. 1999, 'Feminist Interruptions: The Silence of East Bengal in the Story of Partition', *Interventions*, 1(2): 167–82.

Ghosh, Amitav. 1995, *Shadowlines*, Delhi: Oxford University Press.

Ghosh, Binay Bhushan. 1979, *Dvijatitattva o Banali*, Calcutta: Riphlekta.

Ghosh, Gautam. 1998, '"God is a Refugee": Nationality, Morality and History in the 1947 Partition of India', *Social Analysis*, 42(1): 33–62.

Ghosh, Suniti Kumar and Indian Academy of Social Sciences. 2002, *The Tragic Partition of Bengal*. 1st ed, Allahabad: Indian Academy of Social Sciences.

Ghosh, Papiya. 2008, *Community and Nation: Essays on Identity and Politics in Eastern India*, New Delhi: Oxford University Press.

Gillan, Michael. 2002, 'Refugees or Infiltrators? The Bharatiya Janata Party and Illegal Migration from Bangladesh', *Asian Studies Review*, 26(1): 73–95.

Glasson Deschaumes, Ghislaine and Rada Ivekovic. 2003, *Divided Countries, Separated Cities the Modern Legacy of Partition*, New Delhi, New York: Oxford University Press.

Gopal, Sarvepalli. 1975, *Jawaharlal Nehru: A Biography*. London: J. Cape.

Gossman, Patricia. 1999, *Riots and Victims Violence and the Construction of Communal Identity among Bengali Muslims, 1905–1947*, Boulder, CO: Westview Press.

Guha, Ramachandra. 2007, *India After Gandhi:The History of the World's Largest Democracy*, London.

Guhathakurta, Meghna. 1997, 'Understanding the Bengal Partition through Reconstructing Family Histories: A Case Study', *Journal of Social Studies*, 76(April): 56–65.

Haldar, N. 1979, *Maricajhampi*, Calcutta: Sitijenasa Phara Demokretika Raitasa.

Hasan, Mushirul. 1993, *India's Partition: Process, Strategy and Mobilization*, New Delhi: Oxford University Press.

_____. 1995, *India Partitioned the Other Face of Freedom*, New Delhi: Lotus Collection.

Hasan, Mushirul. 1998, 'Memories of a Fragmented Nation: Rewriting the Histories of India's Partition', *Economic and Political Weekly*, 33(41): 2662–8.

Hasan, Mushirul. 2002, *Inventing Boundaries Gender, Politics, and the Partition of India*, New Delhi, New York: Oxford University Press.

_____. 1997, *Legacy of a Divided Nation India's Muslims since Independence*, Boulder, Colorado: Westview Press.

Hasan, Mushirul and Nariaki Nakazato. 2001, *The Unfinished Agenda Nation Building in South Asia*, New Delhi: Manohar Publishers.

Hashmi, Taj ul-Islam. 1992, *Pakistan as a Peasant Utopia: The Communalization of Class Politics in East Bengal, 1920–1947*, Boulder: Westview Press.

Islam, Sirajul. 1992, *History of Bangladesh, 1704–1971, Vols 1–3*, Dhaka: Asiatic Society of Bangladesh.

Jalal, Ayesha. 1985, *The Sole Spokesman: Jinnah, the Muslim League and the Demand for Pakistan*, Cambridge: Cambridge University Press.

_____. 1990, *The State of Martial Rule: The Origins of Pakistan's Political Economy of Defence*, Cambridge: Cambridge University Press.

_____. 1996, 'Secularists, Subalterns and the Stigma of "Communalism": Partition Historiography Revisited', *Modern Asian Studies*, 30(3): 681–737.

Jasimuddin. 1971, *Jiban Katha*, Calcutta: Grantha Prakash.

Jayawardena, K. and M. de Alwis (eds).1996, *Embodied Violence: Communalizing Women's Sexuality in South Asia*, London: Zed Books.

Jones, Stephen B. 1945, *Boundary Making: A Handbook for Statesmen, Treaty Editors and Boundary Commissioners*, Washington: Carnegie Endowment for International Peace.

Kabir, Muhammad Ghulam. 1980, *Minority Politics in Bangladesh*, New Delhi: Vikas.

Ahmed, Kamal. 1992, 'East Bengal at Independence', Sirajul Islam (ed.), *History of Bangladesh, 1704–1971, Vols 1–3*, Dhaka: Asiatic Society of Bangladesh, pp. 407–35.

Kamal, Mesbah and Eshani Chakraborty. 2001, *Nacholer Krishak Bidroho: Shamokalin Rajniti O Ila Mitra*, Dhaka: Institute of Liberation Bangabandhu and Bangladesh Studies, National University.

Kaul, Suvir (ed.). 2001, *Partitions of Memory: The Afterlife of the Division of India*, New Delhi: Permanent Black.

Kaur, Ravinder. 2008, 'Narrative Absence: The Untouchable Account of Partition Migration', *Contributions to Indian Sociology*, 42(2): 281–306.

_____. 2009, 'Distinctive Citizenship: Refugees, Subjects and Post-Colonial State in India's Partition', *Cultural and Social History*, 6(4): 429–46.

Keller, S. L. 1975, *Uprooting and Social Change: The Role of Refugees in Development*, Delhi: Manohar Book Service.

Khan, Tamizuddin. 1989, *The Test of Time My Life and Days*, Dhaka: University Press.

Khan, Yasmin. 2007, *The Great Partition: The Making of India and Pakistan*, New Haven, Conn.: Yale University Press.

Kudaisya, Gyanesh. 1995, 'The Demographic Upheaval of Partition: Refugees and Agricultural Resettlement in India', *South Asia*, XVIII, Special Issue, pp. 73–94.

_____. 1998, 'Divided Landscapes, Fragmented Identities: East Bengal Refugees and their Rehabilitation in India, 1947–79', in D.A. Low and Howard Brasted (eds), *Freedom, Trauma, Continuities: Northern India and Independence*, New Delhi: Sage, pp. 105–32.

Kumar, Priya. 1999, 'Testimonies of Loss and Memory: Partition and the Haunting of a Nation', *Interventions*, 1(2): 200–215.

Malkki, Liisa H.1995, 'Refugees and Exile: From "Refugee Studies" to the National Order of Things', *Annual Review of Anthropology*, Vol. 24, pp. 495–523.

Mandal, Jagadishchandra. 1977, *Banga Bhanga*, Calcutta: Mahapran Publishing Society.

Manto, Saadat Hasan. 1991, *Partition Sketches and Stories*, New Delhi: Viking.

Mazumdar, Ramesh C. 1957, *Bangla Desher Itihash*, Calcutta: General Printers and Publishers.

Menon, Ritu. 2004, *No Woman's Land Women From Pakistan, India & Bangladesh Write on the Partition of India*, New Delhi: Women Unlimited.

Menon, Ritu and Kamla Bhasin. 1998, *Borders and Boundaries: Women in India's Partition*, New Delhi: Kali.

Migdal, Joel S. 1988, *Strong Societies and Weak States: State–Society Relations and State Capabilities in the Third World*, Princeton: Princeton University Press.

_____. 2004, *Boundaries and Belonging: States and Societies in the Struggle to Shape Identities and Local Practices*, Cambridge: Cambridge University Press.

Mitra, Asok. 1990, 'Parting of Ways: Partition and After in Bengal', *Economic and Political Weekly*, 25(44): 2441–6.

Mohsin, Amena. 2001, *The State of 'Minority' Rights in Bangladesh*, Colombo: International Centre for Ethnic Studies.

Moore, Robin. 1983, *Escape from Empire: The Attlee Government and the Indian Problem*, New Delhi: Oxford University Press.

Mukhopadhyaya, Bamanacandra. 1984, *Smrti-Parikrama*, Kalikata: Barisala Sebasamiti.

Murshid, Tazeen M. 1995, *The Sacred and the Secular Bengal Muslim Discourses, 1871–1977*, Calcutta: Oxford University Press.

Nanda, B.R. 1958, *Mahatma Gandhi: A Biography*, New Delhi.

Page, David. 1982, *Prelude to Partition: The Indian Muslims and the Imperial System of Control, 1920–1932*, New Delhi and New York: Oxford University Press.

Pakrashi, Kanti B. and Indian Statistical Institute. 1971, *The Uprooted: A Sociological Study of the Refugees of West Bengal, India,* Calcutta: Editions Indian.

Pandey, Gyanendra. 1990, *The Construction of Communalism in Colonial North India,* Delhi: Oxford University Press.

_____. 1994, 'The Prose of Otherness', in David Hardiman and David Arnold (eds), *Subaltern Studies, Vol. VIII,* New Delhi: Oxford University Press, pp. 188–221.

_____. 2001, *Remembering Partition: Violence, Nationalism, and History in India,* New York: Cambridge University Press.

_____. 2006, *Routine Violence: Nations, Fragments, Histories,* Stanford, California: Stanford University Press.

Pandey, Gyanendra and Centre for Studies in Social Sciences. 1999, *Memory, History, and the Question of Violence Reflections on the Reconstruction of Partition,* Calcutta: Centre for Studies in Social Sciences, K.P. Bagchi & Co.

Philips, C. H and Mary Doreen Wainwright. 1970, *The Partition of India Policies and Perspectives, 1935–1947.* Cambridge: MIT Press.

Rahman, Md. Mahabubar and Willem Van Schendel, 2003, '"I am not a Refugee": Rethinking Partition Migration', *Modern Asian Studies,* 37(3): 551–84.

Rashid, Harun-or-. 2003, *The Foreshadowing of Bangladesh: Bengal Muslim League and Muslim Politics, 1906–47,* Dhaka: Dhaka University Press.

_____. 2003, *Inside Bengal Politics, 1936–1947 Unpublished Correspondence of Partition Leaders,* Dhaka: University Press.

Ray, Manas. 2001, 'Growing Up Refugee', *History Workshop Journal,* 53(1): 148–79.

Ray, Rajat Kanta. 2003, *The Felt Community Commonalty and Mentality Before the Emergence of Indian Nationalism,* New Delhi: Oxford University Press.

Raychaudhuri, Tapan. 1993, *Romanthan Athaba Bhimratipraptar Paracharitcharcha,* Calcutta: Ananda Publishers.

Read, Anthony and David Fisher. 1998, *The Proudest Day: India's Long Road to Independence,* New York: W.W. Norton & Company.

Sadiq, Kamal. 2009, *Paper Citizens: How Illegal Immigrants Acquire Citizenship in Developing Countries,* Oxford: Oxford University Press.

Saikia, Yasmin, 2011, *Women War and the Making of Bangladesh: Remembering 1971,* Duke University Press.

Samaddar, Ranabir. 2001, *A Biography of the Indian Nation, 1947–1997,* New Delhi: Sage.

_____. 1999, *The Marginal Nation: Trans-border Migration from Bangladesh to West Bengal,* New Delhi: Sage.

Samaddar, Ranabir and Calcutta Research Group. 1997, *Reflections on Partition in the East,* Calcutta: Calcutta Research Group.

Sanyal, Jhuma. 2003, *Making of a New Space, Refugees in West Bengal*, Kolkata: Ratna Prakashan.

Sen, Asok.1992, *Life and Labour in a Squatter's Colony*, Calcutta: Center for Studies in Social Sciences.

Sen, Manikuntala.2001, *In Search of Freedom: An Unfinished Journey*, Calcutta: Stree.

Sen, Satadru. 2003, 'Border of Insanity: Deporting Bangladeshi Migrants', *Economic and Political Weekly*, 38(7): 611–12.

Sen, Shila. 1976, *Muslim Politics in Bengal, 1937–1947*, New Delhi: Impex India.

Sen, Sukumar. 1999, *Bharata-Bibhaga, Itihasera Svapnabhanga*, Kalikata: Bhasha o Sahitya.

Sengupta, Jyoti. 1963, *Eclipse of East Pakistan:Chronicles of Events Since Birth of East Pakistan till October 1963*, Calcutta: Renco.

Shukla, Ravi S. 2010, 'Reimagining Citizenship: Debating India's Unique Identification Scheme', *Economic and Political Weekly*, 45(2): 31–6.

Singh, Anita Inder. 1987, *The Origins of the Partition of India, 1936–1947*, New Delhi and New York: Oxford University Press.

Singh, Khushwant. 1956, *Train to Pakistan*, London: Chatto & Windus.

Sinha, Mrinalini. 1995, *Colonial Masculinity: The 'Manly Englishman' and the 'Effeminate Bengali' in the Late Nineteenth Century*, New York: Manchester University Press.

Talbot, Ian and Gurharpal Singh. 1999, *Region and Partition: Bengal, Punjab and the Partition of the Subcontinent*, Oxford, NY: Oxford University Press.

Tan, Tai Yong and Gyanesh Kudaisya. 2000, *The Aftermath of Partition in South Asia*, New York: Routledge.

Tarlo, Emma. 1996, *Clothing Matters: Dress and Identity in India*, Chicago: University of Chicago Press.

Taylor, Charles. 1995, 'Liberal Politics and the Public Sphere', in *Philosophical Arguments*, Cambridge, MA: Harvard University Press.

Thompson, E.P. 1995, *The Poverty of Theory or an Orrey of Errors*, London: Merlin Press.

Torpey, John C. 2000, *The Invention of the Passport, Surveillance, Citizenship and the State*, Cambridge: Cambridge University Press.

Umar, Badruddin. 1987, *Bangabhanga o Sampradayika Rajaniti*, Calcutta: Cirayata Prakasana.

————. 1974, *Politics and Society in East Pakistan and Bangladesh*, Dhaka: Mowla Bros.

————. 1970, *Pūrbabā alāra Bhāshā Āndolana o Ta kālīna Rājanīti* (The Language Movement in East Bengal and Contemporary Politics), Dhaka: Moula Brothers.

Van Schendel, Willem. 2001, 'Working through Partition: Making a Living in the Bengal Borderlands', *International Review of Social History*, 46(3): 393–421.

_____. 2002, 'Stateless in South Asia: The Making of the India–Bangladesh Enclaves', *The Journal of Asian Studies*, 61(1): 115–47.

_____. 2005, *The Bengal Borderlands: Beyond State and Nation in South Asia*, London: Anthem.

_____. 2009, *A History of Bangladesh*, Cambridge: Cambridge University Press.

Schendel, Willem van and Itty Abraham. 2005, *Illicit Flows and Criminal Things: States, Borders, and the Other Side of Globalization*, Bloomington: Indiana University Press.

Winichakul, Thongchai. 1994, *Siam Mapped: A History of the Geo-Body of a Nation*, Honolulu: University of Hawaii Press.

Zamindar, Vazira Fazila-Yacoobali. 2007, *The Long Partition and the Making of Modern South Asia: Refugees, Boundaries, Histories*, New York: Columbia University Press.

Index